iPhone® 4

PORTABLE GENIUS

iPhone® 4

PORTABLE GENIUS

by Paul McFedries

WILEY

Wiley Publishing, Inc.

iPhone® 4 Portable Genius

Published by
Wiley Publishing, Inc.
10475 Crosspoint Blvd.
Indianapolis, IN 46256
www.wiley.com

ISBN: 978-0-470-64205-4

Manufactured in the United States of America

10   9   8   7   6   5   4   3   2

For general information on our other products and services or to obtain technical support, please contact our Customer Care Department within the U.S. at (877) 762-2974, outside the U.S. at (317) 572-3993 or fax (317) 572-4002.

Wiley also publishes its books in a variety of electronic formats. Some content that appears in print may not be available in electronic books.

Library of Congress Control Number: 2010931800

WILEY

About the Author

Paul McFedries is a Mac expert and full-time technical writer. Paul has been authoring computer books since 1991 and has more than 70 books to his credit. Paul's books have sold more than three million copies worldwide. These books include the Wiley titles *iPad Portable Genius*, *Macs Portable Genius*, *MacBook Air Portable Genius*, *Switching to a Mac Portable Genius*, *Teach Yourself VISUALLY Macs*, and *Teach Yourself VISUALLY Microsoft Office 2008 for Mac*. Paul is also the proprietor of Word Spy (www.wordspy.com), a Web site that tracks new words and phrases as they enter the language. Paul invites you to drop by his Web site at www.mcfedries.com and follow his tweets at www.twitter.com/paulmcf.

Credits

This book is dedicated to the loving memory of Gypsy, the Best Dog Ever.

Acknowledgments

If you think using the iPhone is a blast, you should try *writing* about it! I had so much fun poking and prodding the iPhone 4 to see just what it's capable of, that I'm worried my publisher won't pay me next time. (Kidding!) Adding to the fun were the great people at Wiley that I got to work with. They included Senior Acquisitions Editor Stephanie McComb, who was kind enough (or was it brave enough?) to ask me to write the book; Project Editor Cricket Krengel, whose unflappable calm under intense pressure is beyond admirable; and Technical Editor Thomas Myer, who made sure my instructions didn't zig when they were supposed to zag. Many heartfelt thanks to all of you for outstanding work on this project.

Contents

How Do I Connect My iPhone to a Network?   40

chapter 7

How Can I Get More Out of My
iPhone's Audio Features?   152

chapter 8

How Do I Max Out My iPhone's
Photo and Video Features?   174

chapter 9

Can I Use My iPhone to Manage
Contacts and Appointments?

How Do I Use My iPhone to
Navigate My World? 232

chapter 13

How Do I Fix My iPhone?   278

Introduction

The iPhone is a success not because tens of millions of them have been sold (or, I should say, not *only* because tens of millions of them have been sold; that's a lot of phones!), but because the iPhone in just a couple of years has reached the status of a cultural icon. Even people who don't care much for gadgets in general and cell phones in particular know about the iPhone. And for those of us who *do* care about gadgets, the iPhone elicits a kind of technological longing that can only be satisfied in one way: by *buying* one. (Or, in my case, by buying four of them!)

Part of the iPhone's iconic status comes from its gorgeous design and from its remarkable interface which makes all the standard tasks — surfing, e-mailing, texting, scheduling, playing — easy and intuitive. But just as an attractive face or an easygoing manner can hide a personality of complexity and depth, so too does the iPhone hide many of its most useful and interesting features.

When you want to get beyond the iPhone's basics and solve some of its riddles, you might consider making an appointment with your local Apple Store's Genius Bar, and more often than not the on-duty genius gives you good advice on how to get your iPhone to do what you want it to do. The Genius Bar is a great thing, but it isn't always a convenient thing, and in some cases, you may need to leave your iPhone for a while (No!) to get the problem checked out and hopefully resolved.

What you really need is a version of the Genius Bar that's easier to access, more convenient, and doesn't require tons of time or leaving your iPhone in the hands of a stranger. What you really need is a "portable" genius that enables you to be more productive and solve problems wherever you and your iPhone happen to be.

Welcome, therefore, to *iPhone 4 Portable Genius*. This book is like a mini Genius Bar all wrapped up in an easy-to-use, easy-to-access, and eminently portable format. In this book, you learn how to get more out of your iPhone 4 (and your iPhone 3GS, too) by learning how to access all the really powerful and timesaving features that aren't obvious at a casual glance. In this book, you learn about all of the amazing new features found in the iPhone 4 and in iOS 4.0, including FaceTime video calling; HD video recording; advanced video editing with iMovie for the iPhone; managing your eBooks collection with the iBooks app; Mail's universal Inbox; and much more. In this book, you learn how to prevent iPhone problems from occurring, and just in case your preventative measures are for naught, you learn how to fix many common problems yourself.

This book is for iPhone users who know the basics but want to take their iPhone education to a higher level. It's a book for people who want to be more productive, more efficient, more creative, and more self-sufficient (at least as far as the iPhone goes). It's a book for people who use their iPhone every day, but would like to incorporate it into more of their day-to-day activities. It's a book I had a blast writing, so I think it's a book you'll enjoy reading.

The iPhone is justly famous for its stylish, curvaceous design and for its slick, effortless touchscreen. However, although good looks and ease of use are important for any smartphone, it's what you do with that phone that's important. The iPhone helps by offering lots of features, but chances are those features aren't set up to suit the way you work. Maybe your most-used Home screen icons aren't at the top of the screen where they should be, or perhaps your iPhone goes to sleep too soon. This chapter shows you how to configure your iPhone to solve these and many other annoyances so the phone works the way you do.

Customizing the Home Screen to Suit Your Style

The Home screen is your starting point for all things iPhone, and what could be simpler? Just tap the icon you want and the app loads lickety-split. Ah, but things are never so simple, are they? In fact, there are a couple of hairs in the Home screen soup:

- The icons in the top row are a bit easier to find and a bit easier to tap.

- If you have more than 16 icons, they extend onto a second (or third or fourth) Home screen. If the app you want isn't on the main Home screen, you must first flick to the screen that has the app's icon (or tap its dot) and then tap the icon.

Note How do you end up with more than 16 icons? Easy: the App Store. This is an online retailer solely devoted to apps designed to work with the iPhone's technologies: multi-touch, GPS, the accelerometer, wireless, and more. You can download apps via your cellular network or your Wi-Fi connection, so you can always get apps when you need them. I discuss the App Store a bit later in this chapter.

All this means that you can make the Home screen more efficient by moving your four most-used icons to the top row of the main Home screen, and make sure that any icon you tap frequently appears somewhere on the main Home screen. You can do all this by rearranging the Home screen icons as follows:

1. **Display the Home screen.**
2. **Tap and hold any Home screen icon.** When you see the icons wiggling, release your finger.
3. **Tap and drag the icons into the positions you prefer.**
4. **Press the Home button.** Your iPhone saves the new icon arrangement.

Genius The icons in the Home screen's menu bar are also fair game. That is, you can drag them left and right to change the order, and you can replace the menu bar icons with any other Home screen icons. For the latter, set the icons jiggling, and then tap and drag an icon off the menu bar to create some space. Now tap and drag any Home screen icon into the menu bar.

iOS 4.0

Creating an app folder

The best way to make the main Home screen more manageable is to reduce the total number of icons you have to work with. This isn't a problem when you're just starting out with your iPhone, since out of the box it comes with only a limited number of apps. However, the addictive nature of the App Store almost always means that you end up with screen after screen of apps. In fact, the iPhone lets you use a maximum of 11 screens, and if you fill each screen to the brim — that's 16 apps per screen — you end up with 180 total icons (including the four Dock icons). That's a lot of icons.

Now, when I tell you to reduce the number of icons on the Home screens, I don't mean that you should delete apps. Too drastic! Instead, you can take advantage of a great new feature in iOS 4.0: app folders. Just like a folder on your hard drive, which can store multiple files, an app folder can store multiple app icons — up to 16, in fact. This enables you to group related apps together under a single icon, which not only reduces your overall Home screen clutter, but it can also make individual apps easier to find.

Here are the steps to follow to create and populate an app folder:

1. **Navigate to the Home screen that contains at least one of the apps you want to include in your folder.**

2. **Tap and hold any icon until you see all the icons wiggling.**

3. **Tap and drag an icon that you want to include in the folder, and drop it on another icon that you want to include in the same folder.** Your iPhone creates the folder and displays a text box so that you can name the folder. The default name is the underlying category used by the apps, as shown in Figure 1.1. (If the apps are in different categories, your iPhone uses the category of the app you dragged-and-dropped.)

1.1 Drop one app icon on another to create an app folder.

5

4. **Tap inside the text box to edit the name, if you feel like it, and tap Done when you're finished.**

5. **Press the Home button.** Your iPhone saves your new icon arrangement.

Use the following techniques to work with your app folders:

- To add another app to the folder, tap and drag the app icon and drop it on the folder.

- To launch an app, tap the folder to open it (see Figure 1.2) and tap the app.

- To rename a folder or rearrange the apps within a folder, tap the folder to open it, then tap and hold any app icon within the folder. You can then edit the folder name and drag and drop the apps within the folder.

1.2 Tap an app folder to reveal its icons.

- To remove an app from a folder, tap the folder to open it, tap and hold any app icon within the folder, then drag the app out of the folder.

Adding a Safari Web Clip to the Home screen

Do you have a Web page that you visit all the time? You can set up that page as a bookmark in iPhone's Safari browser, but there's an even faster way to access the page: add it to the Home screen as a Web Clip icon. A *Web Clip* is a link to a page that preserves the page's scroll position and zoom level. For example, suppose a page has a form at the bottom. To use that form, you have to navigate to the page, scroll to the bottom, and then zoom in to the form to see it better. However, you can perform all three actions — navigate, scroll, and zoom — automatically with a Web Clip.

Follow these steps to save a page as a Web Clip icon on the Home screen:

1. **Use your iPhone's Safari browser to navigate to the page you want to save.**

2. **Scroll to the portion of the page you want to see.**

3. **Pinch and spread your fingers over the area you want to zoom in on until you can comfortably read the text.**

4. **Press + at the bottom of the screen.** iPhone displays a list of options.

5. **Tap Add to Home Screen.** iPhone prompts you to edit the Web Clip name, as shown in Figure 1.3.

6. **Edit the name as needed.** Names up to about 10-14 characters can display on the Home screen without being broken. (The fewer uppercase letters you use, the longer the name can be.) For longer names, iPhone displays the first few and last few characters (depending on the locations of spaces in the name), separated by an ellipsis (...). For example, if the name is My Home Page, it appears in the Home screen as My Ho...Page

7. **Tap Add.** iPhone adds the Web Clip to the Home screen and displays the Home screen. (If your main Home screen is already full to the brim with icons, iPhone adds the Web Clip to the first screen that has space available.) Figure 1.4 shows a Home screen with a Web Clip added.

1.3 You can edit the Web Clip name before adding the icon to the Home Screen.

1.4 The Google Web Clip has been added to the Home Screen.

Genius

To delete a Web Clip from the Home screen, tap and hold any Home screen icon until the icon dance begins. Each Web Clip icon displays an X in the upper-left corner. Tap the X of the Web Clip you want to remove. When iPhone asks you to confirm, tap Delete, and then press the Home button to save the configuration.

Resetting the default Home screen layout

If you make a bit of a mess of your Home screen, or if someone else is going to be using your iPhone, you can reset the Home screen icons to their default layout. Follow these steps:

1. **On the Home screen, tap Settings.** The Settings app appears.

2. **Tap General.** The General screen appears.

3. **Scroll down and tap Reset.** The Reset screen appears.

4. **Tap Reset Home Screen Layout.** iPhone warns you that the Home screen will be reset to the factory default layout.

5. **Tap Reset Home Screen.** iPhone resets the home screen to the default layout, but it doesn't delete the icons for any apps you've added.

Setting the iPhone Wallpaper

iOS 4.0

The iPhone wallpaper is a background image that appears on two different screens:

- **Lock Screen.** This is the background image you see when you unlock the phone. That is, it's the image you see when the Slide to Unlock screen appears, and also when the Enter Passcode screen appears if you're protecting your iPhone with a passcode (as described later in this chapter).

- **Home Screen.** In iOS 4.0, this is the background image you see on the Home screen (or screens). If you're getting a bit tired of looking at the default wallpapers, no worries! Your iPhone comes with 26 other wallpapers you can choose, and you can even use one of your own photos as the wallpaper.

Using a predefined wallpaper

Here are the steps to follow to use one of iPhone's predefined wallpapers:

1. **On the Home screen, tap Settings.** The Settings app appears.

2. **Tap Wallpaper.** The Wallpaper screen appears.

3. **(iPhone 3GS or 4 only) Tap your current wallpaper images.** The Wallpaper screen appears.

4. **Tap Wallpaper.** Your iPhone displays its collection of wallpaper images, as shown in Figure 1.5.

5. **Tap the image you want to use.** The Wallpaper Preview screen appears.

6. **Tap Set.**

7. **(iPhone 3GS or 4 only) Tap where you want the wallpaper applied: Set Lock Screen, Set Home Screen, or Set Both.** Your iPhone sets the image as the wallpaper.

1.5 Your iPhone comes with a number of predefined wallpaper images.

Using an existing photo as the wallpaper

If you have images in your iPhone's Camera Roll or in a photo album synced from your computer, you can use one of those images as your wallpaper by following these steps:

1. **On the Home screen, tap Settings.** The Settings app appears.

2. **Tap Wallpaper.** The Wallpaper screen appears.

3. **(iPhone 3GS or 4 only) Tap your current wallpaper images.** The Wallpaper screen appears.

4. **Tap either Camera Roll or the photo album that contains the image you want to use.** iPhone displays the images in the album you choose.

5. **Tap the image you want to use.** The Move and Scale screen appears, as shown in Figure 1.6.

6. **Tap and drag the image so that it's positioned on the screen the way you want.**

7. **Pinch and spread your fingers over the image to set the zoom level you want.**

8. **Tap Set.**

9. **(iPhone 3GS or 4 only) Tap where you want the wallpaper applied: Set Lock Screen, Set Home Screen, or Set Both.** Your iPhone sets the image as the wallpaper.

Taking a wallpaper photo with the iPhone camera

For even more wallpaper fun, you can create an on-the-fly wallpaper image using the iPhone camera. Here are the steps to follow:

1. **On the Home screen, tap Camera.** The Camera app appears.

2. **Line up your subject and tap the Camera button to take the picture.**

3. **Tap the Camera Roll button.** The Camera Roll photo album appears.

4. **Tap the photo you just took.** A preview of the photo appears, as shown in Figure 1.7.

1.6 Use the Move and Scale screen to set the position and zoom level for the new wallpaper.

1.7 Tap the photo you want to use as wallpaper to see a preview of the photo.

5. **Tap the Action button.** The Action button is the button on the left side of the menu bar. (If you don't see the menu bar, tap the screen.) iPhone displays a list of actions you can perform.

6. **Tap Use as Wallpaper.** The Move and Scale screen appears.

7. **Tap and drag the image so that it's positioned on the screen the way you want.**

8. **Pinch or spread your fingers over the image to set the zoom level you want.**

9. **Tap Set Wallpaper.** iPhone sets the image as the wallpaper.

More Useful iPhone Configuration Techniques

You've seen quite a few handy iPhone customization tricks so far, but you're not done yet, not by a long shot. The next few sections take you through a few more heart-warmingly useful iPhone customization techniques.

Turning sounds on and off

Your iPhone is often a noisy little thing that makes all manner of rings, beeps, and boops, seemingly at the slightest provocation. Consider a short list of the events that can give the iPhone's lungs a workout:

- Incoming calls
- Incoming e-mail messages
- Outgoing e-mail messages
- Incoming text messages
- New voicemail messages
- Calendar alerts
- Locking and unlocking the phone
- Tapping the keys on the on-screen keyboard

What a racket! None of this may bother you when you're on your own, but if you're in a meeting, a movie, or anywhere else where extraneous sounds are unwelcome, you might want to turn off some or all of the iPhone's sound effects.

First, you should know that when a call comes in and you press the Sleep/Wake button once, your iPhone silences the ringer. That's a sweet and useful feature, but the problem is that it may take you one or two rings before you can dig out your iPhone and press Sleep/Wake, and by that time the folks nearby are already glaring at you.

To prevent this phone faux pas, you can switch your iPhone into silent mode, which means it doesn't ring, and it doesn't play any alerts or sound effects. When the sound is turned off, the only alarms that are audible are the ones you've set using the Clock app. The phone still vibrates unless you turn this feature off as well. You switch the iPhone between ring and silent modes using the Ring/Silent switch, which is located on the left side panel of the iPhone, near the top. Use the following techniques to switch between silent and ring modes:

- To put the phone in silent mode, flick the Ring/Silent switch toward the back of the phone. You see an orange bar (on the iPhone 4) or an orange dot (on earlier iPhones) on the switch and the iPhone screen displays a bell with a slash through it. Your iPhone is now in silent mode.

- To resume the normal ring mode, flick the Ring/Silent switch toward the front of the phone. The iPhone screen displays a bell and your iPhone is now in normal ring mode.

If silent mode is a bit too drastic, you can control exactly which sounds your iPhone utters by following these steps:

1. **On the Home screen, tap Settings.** The Settings app appears.

2. **Tap Sounds.** The Sounds screen appears, as shown in Figure 1.8.

3. **In the Silent section, the Vibrate setting determines whether iPhone**

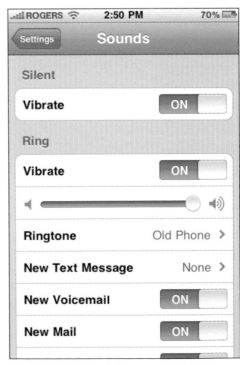

1.8 Use the Auto-Lock Screen to set the Auto-Lock interval or to turn it off.

vibrates when the phone is in silent mode. Vibrating is a good idea in silent mode, so On is a good choice here.

4. **In the Ring section, the Vibrate setting determines whether iPhone vibrates when the phone is in ring mode.** Vibrating probably isn't all that important in ring mode, so feel free to change this setting to Off. The exception is if you reduce the ringer volume (see step 5), in which case setting Vibrate to On might help you notice an incoming call.

5. **Drag the volume slider to set the volume of the ringtone that plays when a call comes in.**

6. **To set a different default ringtone, tap Ringtone to open the Ringtone screen, tap the ringtone you want to use (iPhone plays a preview), and then tap Sounds to return to the Sounds screen.**

7. **To set a different incoming text message sound, tap New Text Message to open the New Text Message screen, tap the sound effect you want to use (iPhone plays a preview), and then tap Sounds to return to the Sounds screen.**

8. **For the rest of the settings, such as New Voicemail and New Mail, tap the On/Off switch to turn each sound on or off.**

Note

If you don't want your iPhone to play a sound when a new text message arrives, tap New Text Message and then tap None.

Adjusting the brightness of the screen

Your iPhone's touchscreen offers a crisp, bright display that's easy to read in most situations. Unfortunately, keeping the screen bright enough to read comfortably extracts a heavy cost in battery power. To help balance screen brightness and battery life, your iPhone comes with a built-in ambient light sensor. That sensor checks the surrounding light levels and adjusts the brightness of the iPhone screen accordingly:

- If the ambient light is dim, the iPhone screen is easier to read, so the sensor dims the screen brightness to save battery power.

- If the ambient light is bright, the iPhone screen is harder to see, so the sensor brightens the screen to improve readability.

This feature is called Auto-Brightness, and it's sensible to let your iPhone handle this stuff for you. However, if you're not happy with how Auto-Brightness works, or if you simply have an uncontrollable urge to tweak things, you can follow these steps to adjust the screen brightness by hand:

Note Even if you leave Auto-Brightness turned on, you still might want to adjust the Brightness slider because this affects the relative brightness of the screen. For example, suppose you adjust the slider to increase brightness by 50 percent and you leave Auto-Brightness turned on. In this case, Auto-Brightness still adjusts the screen automatically, but any brightness level it chooses is 50 percent brighter than it would be otherwise.

1. **On the Home screen, tap Settings.** The Settings app appears.

2. **Tap Brightness.** The Brightness screen appears, as shown in Figure 1.9.

3. **Drag the Brightness slider left (for a dimmer screen) or right (for a brighter screen).**

4. **To prevent iPhone from controlling the brightness automatically, turn the Auto-Brightness setting to Off.**

1.9 Use the Brightness screen to control the iPhone's screen brightness by hand.

Customizing the keyboard

You can type on your iPhone, although don't expect to pound out the prose as easily as you can on your computer. The on-screen keyboard is a bit too small for rapid and accurate typing, but it's still a far sight better than any other phone out there, mostly because the keyboard was thoughtfully designed by the folks at Apple. It even changes depending on the app you use. For example, the regular keyboard features a spacebar at the bottom. However, if you're surfing the Web with your iPhone's Safari browser, the keyboard that appears when you type in the address bar does away with the spacebar. In its place you find a period (.), a slash (/), and a button that enters the characters *.com*. Web addresses don't use spaces so Apple replaced the spacebar with three things that commonly appear in a Web address. Nice!

Another nice innovation you get with the iPhone keyboard is a feature called Auto-Capitalization. If you type a punctuation mark that indicates the end of a sentence — for example, a period (.), a question mark (?), or an exclamation mark (!) — or if you press Return to start a new paragraph, the iPhone automatically activates the Shift key, because it assumes you're starting a new sentence.

On a related note, double-tapping the spacebar activates a keyboard shortcut: instead of entering two spaces, the iPhone automatically enters a period (.) followed by a space. This is a welcome bit of efficiency because otherwise you'd have to tap the Number key (.?123) to display the numbers and punctuation marks, tap the period (.), and then tap the spacebar.

Genius

Typing a number or punctuation mark normally requires three taps: tapping Number (.?123), tapping the number or symbol, and then tapping ABC. Here's a faster way: press and hold the Number key to open the numeric keyboard, slide the *same* finger to the number or punctuation symbol you want, and then release the key. This types the number or symbol and returns to the regular keyboard all in one touch.

One thing the iPhone keyboard doesn't seem to have is a Caps Lock feature that, when activated, enables you to type all-uppercase letters. To do this, you need to tap and hold the Shift key and then use a different finger to tap the uppercase letters. However, the iPhone keyboard actually does have a Caps Lock feature; it's just that it's turned off by default.

To turn on Caps Lock, and to control the Auto-Capitalization and the spacebar double-tap shortcut, follow these steps:

1. **On the Home screen, tap Settings.** The Settings app appears.

2. **Tap General.** The General screen appears.

3. **Tap Keyboard.** The Keyboard screen appears, as shown in Figure 1.10.

4. **Use the Auto-Capitalization setting to turn this feature On or Off.**

5. **Use the Enable Caps Lock setting to turn this feature On or Off.**

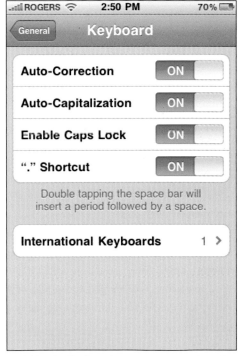

1.10 Use the Keyboard screen to customize a few keyboard settings.

6. **Use the ". " Shortcut setting to turn this feature On or Off.**

7. **To add an international keyboard layout, tap International Keyboards to open the Keyboards screen, and then set the keyboard layout you want to add to On.**

Note When you're using two or more keyboard layouts, the keyboard sprouts a new key to the left of the spacebar (it looks like a stylized globe). Tap that key to run through the layouts (the names of which appear briefly in the spacebar).

Configuring parental controls

If your children have access to your iPhone, or if they have iPhones of their own, then you might be a bit worried about some of the content they might be exposed to on the Web, on YouTube, or in iTunes. Similarly, you might not want them installing apps or giving away their current location.

For all those and similar parental worries, you can sleep better at night by activating the iPhone's parental controls. These controls restrict the content and activities that kids can see and do. Here's how to set them up:

1. **On the Home screen, tap Settings.** The Settings app appears.

2. **Tap General.** The General screen appears.

3. **Tap Restrictions.** The Restrictions screen appears.

4. **Tap Enable Restrictions.** iPhone displays the Set Passcode screen, which you use to specify a four-digit code that you can use to override the parental controls. (Note that this passcode is not the same as the passcode lock code you learned about earlier in the chapter in the section covering how to protect your iPhone with a passcode.)

5. **Tap the four-digit restrictions passcode and then retype the code.** iPhone returns you to the Restrictions screen and enables all the controls, as shown in Figure 1.11.

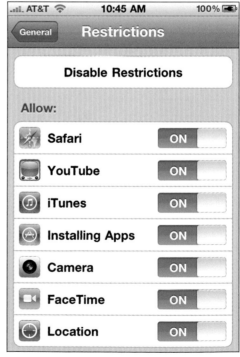

1.11 Use the Restrictions screen to configure the parental controls you want to use.

6. **In the Allow section, for each app or task, tap the On/Off switch to enable or disable the restriction.**

7. **If you don't want your children to be able to make purchases within apps, tap the In-App Purchases switch to Off.**

8. **Tap Ratings For, and then tap the country whose ratings you want to use.**

9. **For each of the content controls — Music & Podcasts, Movies, TV Shows, and Apps — tap the control and then tap the highest rating you want your children to use.**

10. **Tap General.** iPhone puts the new settings into effect.

Customizing app notifications

Lots of apps take advantage of an iOS feature called *push notifications*, which enables the app to send messages and other data to your iPhone. For example, the Facebook app displays an alert on your iPhone when a friend sends you a message; similarly, the Foursquare app, which lets you track where your friends are located, sends you a message when a friend "checks in" at a particular location. There are actually three kinds of push notifications:

- **Sound.** This is a sound effect that plays when some app-related event occurs.
- **Alert.** This is a message that pops up on your iPhone screen.
- **Badge.** This is a small red icon that appears in the upper right corner of an app's icon. The icon usually displays a number, which might be the number of messages you have waiting for you on the service.

If an app supports notifications, the first time you start the app your iPhone will usually display a message like the one shown in Figure 1.12 to ask if you want to allow push notifications for the app. Tap OK if you're cool with that or, if you're not, tap Don't Allow.

Your iPhone also lets you toggle individual notification types (sounds, alerts, and badges) for each app, and you can even turn off notifications altogether if your apps have become too, well, *pushy*. Here's how:

1. **On the Home screen, tap Settings.** The Settings app appears.

2. **Tap Notifications.** The Notifications screen appears, as shown in Figure 1.13. (If you don't see the Notifications item in the Settings screen, it means that none of your apps use push notifications.)

3. **To turn off all push notifications, tap the Notifications switch to Off.** Your iPhone hides the apps, so you can skip the rest of these steps.

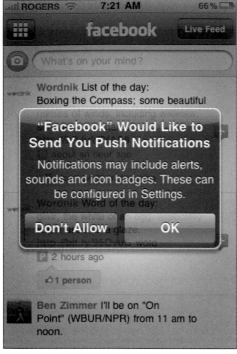

1.12 Your iPhone lets you allow or disallow push notifications for an app.

1.13 Use the Notifications screen to control push notifications on your iPhone.

4. **Tap an app.** The app's notifications page appears.

5. **Control the app's notifications by tapping each of the three switches—Sounds, Alerts, and Badges—to On or Off.**

6. **Tap Notifications to return to the Notifications screen.**

7. **Repeat steps 4 to 6 to customize each app.**

Resetting the iPhone

If you've spent quite a bit of time in the iPhone's Settings app, your phone probably doesn't look much like it did fresh out of the box. That's okay, though, because your iPhone should be as individual as you are. However, if you've gone a bit *too* far with your customizations, your iPhone might feel a bit alien and uncomfortable. That's okay, too, because there's an easy solution to the problem: you can erase all your customizations and revert the iPhone to its default settings.

A similar problem that comes up is when you want to sell or give your iPhone to someone else. Chances are you don't want the new owner to see your data — contacts, appointments, e-mail and text messages, favorite Web sites, music, and so on — and it's unlikely the other person wants to wade through all that stuff anyway (no offense). To solve this problem, you can erase not only your custom settings, but also all of the content you've stored on the iPhone.

Caution If you have any content on your iPhone that isn't synced with iTunes — for example, iTunes music you've recently downloaded or an Apps Store program that you've recently installed — you lose that content if you choose Reset All Content and Settings. First sync your iPhone with your computer to save your content, and then run the reset.

The iPhone's Reset app handles these scenarios and a few more to boot. Here's how it works:

1. **On the Home screen, tap Settings.** The Settings app appears.

2. **Tap General.** The General screen appears.

3. **Tap Reset.** The Reset screen appears, as shown in Figure 1.14.

4. **Tap one of the following reset options:**

   - **Reset All Settings.** Tap this option to reset your custom settings to the factory default settings.

   - **Erase All Content and Settings.** Tap this option to reset your custom settings and remove any data you've stored on the iPhone.

   - **Reset Network Settings.** Tap this option to delete your Wi-Fi network settings, which is often an effective way to solve Wi-Fi problems.

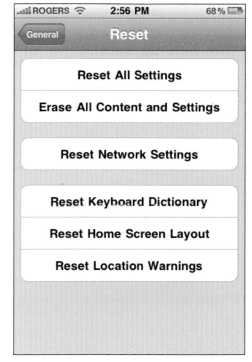

1.14 Use the Reset screen to reset various aspects of your iPhone.

- **Reset Keyboard Dictionary.** Tap this option to reset your keyboard dictionary. This dictionary contains a list of the keyboard suggestions that you've rejected. Tap this option to clear the dictionary and start fresh.

- **Reset Home Screen Layout.** Tap this option to reset your Home screen icons to their default layout.

- **Reset Location Warnings.** Tap this option to wipe out the location preferences for your apps. A location warning is the dialog you see when you start a 6PS-aware app for the first time, and your iPhone asks if the app can use your current location. You tap either OK or Don't Allow, and these are the preferences you're resetting here.

5. **When the iPhone asks you to confirm, tap the red button.** Note that the name of this button is the same as the reset option. For example, if you tapped the Reset All Settings option in step 4, the confirm button is called Reset All Settings. iPhone resets the data.

Note Remember that the keyboard dictionary contains rejected suggestions. For example, if you type "Viv", iPhone suggests "Bob" instead. If you tap the "Bob" suggestion to reject it and keep "Viv," the word "Bob" is added to the keyboard dictionary.

Protecting Your iPhone

These days your iPhones are much more than just phones. You use it to surf the Web, send and receive e-mail and text messages, manage your contacts and schedules, find your way in the world, and much more. This is handy, for sure, but it also means that your iPhone is jammed with tons of information about you. And although you might not store the nuclear launch codes on your iPhone, chances are what *is* on your iPhone is pretty important to you. All of which means that you should take steps to protect your iPhone, and that what's the next few sections are all about.

Protecting your iPhone with a passcode

When your iPhone is asleep, the phone is locked in the sense that tapping the touchscreen or pressing the volume controls does nothing. This sensible arrangement prevents accidental taps when the phone is in your pocket or rattling around in your backpack or handbag. To unlock the phone, you either press the Home button or the Sleep/Wake button, drag the Slide to Unlock slider, and you're back in business.

Unfortunately, this simple technique means that anyone else who gets his or her mitts on your iPhone can also be quickly back in business — *your* business! If you have sensitive or confidential information on your phone, or if you want to avoid digital joyrides that run up massive roaming or data charges, you need to truly lock your iPhone.

Caution You really, really need to remember your iPhone passcode. If you forget it, you're locked out of your own phone and the only way to get back in is to completely reset the iPhone (as described later in Chapter 13).

You do that by specifying a passcode that must be entered before anyone can use the iPhone. In iOS 4.0, you can either set a simple, four-digit passcode, or you can set a longer, more complex passcode that uses any combination of numbers, letters, and symbols. Follow these steps to set up your passcode:

1. **On the Home screen, tap Settings.** The Settings app appears.

2. **Tap General.** The General screen appears.

3. **If you prefer to set a complex passcode, tap the Simple Passcode switch to Off**.

4. **Tap Turn Passcode On.** The Set Passcode screen appears.

5. **Tap your passcode.** For security, the characters appear in the passcode box as dots.

6. **If you're entering a complex passcode, tap Next.** Your iPhone prompts you to reenter the passcode.

7. **Tap your passcode again.**

8. **If you're entering a complex passcode, tap Done.**

With your passcode now active, iPhone displays the Passcode Lock screen, as shown in Figure 1.15. (You can also get to this screen by tapping Settings in the Home screen, then General, then Passcode Lock.) This screen offers six buttons:

- **Turn Passcode Off.** If you want to stop using your passcode, tap this button, and then enter the passcode (for security; otherwise an interloper could just shut off the passcode).

- **Change Passcode.** Tap this button to enter a new passcode. (Note that you first need to enter your old passcode and then enter the new passcode.)

- **Require Passcode.** This setting determines how much time elapses before the iPhone locks the phone and requests the passcode. The default setting is Immediately, which means you see the

1.15 Use the Passcode Lock screen to configure your iPhone's passcode locking.

21

Enter Passcode screen as soon as you finish dragging Slide to Unlock. The other options are After 1 minute, After 5 minutes, After 15 minutes, After 1 hour, and After 4 hours. Use one of these settings if you want to be able to work with your iPhone for a bit before getting locked out. For example, the After 1 minute option is good if you need to quickly check e-mail without having to enter your passcode.

- **Simple passcode.** Use this switch to toggle between a simple four-digit passcode and a complex passcode.

- **Voice Dial.** When this setting is on, you can use the Voice Control feature to dial calls (as explained in Chapter 3) even when your iPhone is locked. If you change this setting to Off, you can no longer voice dial calls when your iPhone is locked, but you can still use Voice Control to play music (as explained in Chapter 7).

- **Erase Data.** When this setting in On, your iPhone will self-destruct, er, I mean erase all of its data when it detects ten incorrect passcode attempts. Ten failed passcodes almost always means that some nasty person has your phone and is trying to guess the passcode. If you have sensitive or private data on your phone, having the data erased automatically is a good idea.

With the passcode activated, when you bring the iPhone out of standby, you drag the Slide to Unlock slider as usual, and then the Enter Passcode screen appears. Type your passcode (and tap OK if it's a complex passcode) to unlock the iPhone.

Note

If an emergency arises and you need to make a call for help, you probably don't want to mess around entering a passcode. Similarly, if something happens to you, another person who doesn't know your passcode may need to use your iPhone to call for assistance. In both cases, you can temporarily bypass the passcode by tapping the Emergency Call button on the Enter Passcode screen.

Configuring your iPhone to sleep automatically

You can put your iPhone into Standby mode at any time by pressing the Sleep/Wake button once. This drops the power consumption considerably (mostly because it shuts off the screen), but you can still receive incoming calls and text messages, and if you have the iPod app running, it continues to play.

However, if your iPhone is on but you're not using it, the phone automatically goes into standby mode after two minutes. This is called Auto-Lock and it's a handy feature because it saves battery power (and prevents accidental taps) when your iPhone is just sitting there. It's also a crucial feature if you've protected your iPhone with a passcode lock, as I described earlier, because if your iPhone never sleeps, it never locks either.

To make sure your iPhone sleeps automatically, or if you're not comfortable with the default 2-minute Auto-Lock interval, you can make it shorter or longer (or turn it off altogether). Here are the steps to follow:

1. **On the Home screen, tap Settings.** The Settings app appears.
2. **Tap General.** The General screen appears.
3. **Tap Auto-Lock.** The Auto-Lock screen appears.
4. **Tap the interval you want to use.** You have six choices: 1 Minute, 2 Minutes, 3 Minutes, 4 Minutes, 5 Minutes, or Never.

Backing up your iPhone

When you sync your iPhone with your computer, iTunes automatically creates a backup of your current iPhone data before performing the sync. Note, however, that iTunes doesn't back up your entire iPhone, which makes sense since most of what's on your phone — music, photos, videos, apps, and so on — is already on your computer. Instead, iTunes only backs up data unique to the iPhone, including your call history, text messages, Web clips, network settings, app settings and data, Safari history and cookies, and so on.

However, what if you've configured iTunes to not sync your iPhone automatically? Is there a way to back up your iPhone without performing a sync? You bet there is:

1. **Connect your iPhone to your computer.**
2. **Open iTunes, if it doesn't launch automatically.**
3. **In the Devices section, right-click (or Control+click on a Mac) your iPhone, and then click Back Up.** iTunes backs up the iPhone data.

Using MobileMe to Find and Protect a Lost iPhone

If there's a downside to using a smartphone, particularly one as smart as the iPhone, it's that you end up with a pretty large chunk of your life on that phone. That sounds like a good thing, I know, but if you happen to lose the phone, you've also lost that chunk of your life, plus you've opened up a gaping privacy hole because anyone can now delve into your data. (I'm assuming here you haven't configured your iPhone with a passcode lock, as described earlier in this Chapter.)

If you've been syncing your iPhone with your computer regularly, then you can probably recover most or even all of that data. However, I'm sure you'd probably rather find your phone because it's expensive and there's just something creepy about the thought of some stranger flicking through your stuff.

The old way of finding your phone consisted of scouring every nook and cranny that you visited before losing the phone and calling up various lost and found departments to see if anyone's turned in your phone. The new way to find your phone is a great new feature that comes with a MobileMe account. It's called Find My iPhone, and I guess the name pretty much says it all. Find My iPhone uses the GPS sensor embedded inside your iPhone to locate the phone. You can also use Find My iPhone to send a message to the phone, remotely lock your phone, and, in a pinch, remotely delete your data. The next few sections provide the details.

Configuring Find My iPhone

Find My iPhone works by looking for a particular signal that your iPhone beams out to the ether. This signal is turned off by default, so you need to turn it on if you ever plan to use Find My iPhone. Here are the steps to follow:

1. **On the Home screen, tap Settings.** The Settings app shows up.
2. **Tap Mail, Contacts, Calendars.** Your iPhone displays the Mail, Contacts, Calendars screen.
3. **Tap Fetch New Data to open the Fetch New Data Screen.**
4. **If the Push setting is Off, tap it to On.**
5. **Tap Mail to return to the Mail, Contacts, Calendars screen.**
6. **Tap your MobileMe account.** Your MobileMe account settings appear.
7. **Tap the Find My iPhone switch to On.** Your iPhone asks you to confirm.
8. **Tap Allow.** Your iPhone activates the Find My iPhone feature.

Caution The only drawback to Find My iPhone is that if someone else finds your phone, he can easily turn off the feature to disable it. To prevent this, turn on the passcode lock as I described earlier in the chapter or, if your iPhone is already lost, use MobileMe to remotely lock the phone, as described later in this chapter.

Locating your iPhone on a map

With push and Find My iPhone now active on your iPhone, you can use MobileMe to locate it at any time. Here's how you do it:

1. **Log in to your MobileMe account.**
2. **Click the Switch Apps icon (the cloud) and then click Find My iPhone.** MobileMe prompts you for your account password to log in to the Find My iPhone application.

3. **Type your password, and then click Continue.** The MobileMe Find My iPhone application appears.

4. **Click your iPhone in the Devices list.** MobileMe locates your phone on a map, as shown in Figure 1.16. MobileMe then tries to refine the location, which usually takes a few minutes.

5. **To see if the location has changed, click the Refresh Location button (the circular arrow to the left of your MobileMe name).**

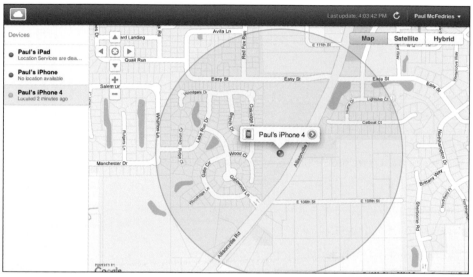

1.16 Log in to the MobileMe Account application and then open the Find My iPhone application to locate your phone on a map.

Sending a message to your iPhone

If you think another person has your phone, then you could try calling your number. That might not work either because you don't have a phone handy, or because the person might have already installed a new SIM card. You can still contact the person by sending a message from MobileMe to the phone using the Find My iPhone feature. Here's how it works:

1. **Log in to your MobileMe account.**

2. **Open the Find My iPhone application, as described in the previous section.**

3. **Click your iPhone in the Devices list.** MobileMe locates your phone on a map.

4. **Click the blue More icon to the right of your phone name.** MobileMe displays information about your phone as well as buttons for various actions you can take.

5. **Click Display Message or Play Sound.** MobileMe displays the Display a Message dialog.

6. **Type your message.** Figure 1.17 shows an example.

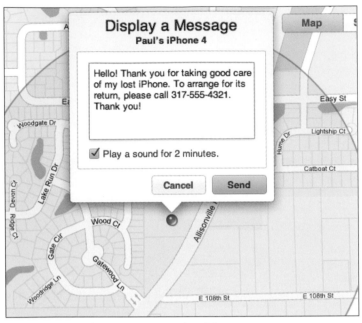

Display a Message
Paul's iPhone 4

Hello! Thank you for taking good care of my lost iPhone. To arrange for its return, please call 317-555-4321. Thank you!

☑ Play a sound for 2 minutes.

Cancel   Send

1.17 You can send a message to your lost iPhone.

7. **Click Send.** MobileMe sends the message, which then appears on the iPhone screen, as shown in Figure 1.18.

Remotely locking the data on your iPhone

While you're waiting for the other person to return your phone, you probably don't want that person rummaging around in your stuff. To prevent that, you can remotely lock the phone. Here's how:

1. **Log in to your MobileMe account.**

2. **Open the Find My iPhone feature, as described in the previous section.**

3. **Click your iPhone in the Devices list.** MobileMe locates your phone on a map.

Important Message

Hello! Thank you for taking good care of my lost iPhone. To arrange for its return, please call 317-555-4321. Thank you!

OK

1.18 The message appears on the iPhone screen.

4. **Click the blue More Icon to the right of your phone name.** MobileMe displays information about your phone as well as buttons for various actions you can take.

5. **Click Lock.** MobileMe displays the Remote Lock dialog shown in Figure 1.19.

6. **Click the numbers in the keypad to enter a four-digit passcode, and then click next.**

7. **Re-enter a four-digit passcode.**

8. **Click Lock.** MobileMe remotely locks the iPhone.

1.19 To prevent anyone from messing with your lost iPhone, you can apply a passcode lock remotely.

Remotely deleting the data on your iPhone

If you can't get the other person to return your phone and your phone contains sensitive or confidential data — or if it just contains that big chunk of your life I mentioned earlier — you can use MobileMe to take the drastic step of remotely wiping all the phone's data. Here's what you do:

1. **Log in to your MobileMe account.**

2. **Open the Find My iPhone application, as described in the previous section.**

3. **Click your iPhone in the Devices list.** MobileMe locates your phone on a map.

27

4. **Click the blue More icon to the right of your phone name.** MobileMe displays information about your phone as well as buttons for various actions you can take.

5. **Click Wipe.** MobileMe displays the warning shown in Figure 1.20.

6. **Select the check box.**

7. **Click Erase All Data.** MobileMe remotely wipes all the data from the iPhone.

1.20 If you're certain your lost iPhone is a lost cause, you can erase all its data from MobileMe.

Using the Find My iPhone app

Apple recently made available an iPhone app called Find My iPhone, which enables you to locate a lost iPhone, send a message to a lost iPhone, and lock or wipe a lost iPhone. Use another iPhone to download the app from the App Store, tap the Find My iPhone icon to launch the app, and then enter your MobileMe username and password. Tap your lost iPhone in the list of devices, and Find My iPhone app locates the phone on a map, as shown in Figure 1.21.

From here, tap the blue More icon to display information about the phone, as well as access the Display Message, Remote Lock, and Remote Wipe commands.

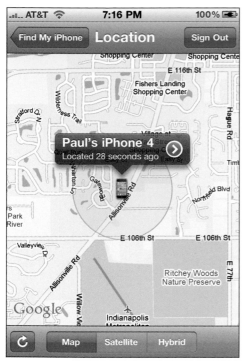

1.21 Use the Find My iPhone app to locate your phone on a map, as well as send a message to, lock, and wipe your phone.

Enhancing Your iPhone with the App Store

Your iPhone is an impressive, eyebrow-raising device right out of the box. It does everything you want it to do, or so you think, but then you find out about some previously unknown feature and you wonder how you ever lived without it. It's hard to imagine that anyone would want to improve upon the iPhone, or even that anyone *could* improve upon it. However, as you see in this chapter, the new App Store can make your iPhone more convenient, more productive, and more, well, anything!

Accessing the App Store on your computer

You've seen that your iPhone comes loaded with not only a basketful of terrific technology, but also a decent collection of truly amazing apps, all of which take advantage of the iPhone's special features. But it won't escape your notice that the iPhone's suite of apps is, well, incomplete. Where are the news and sports headlines? Why isn't there an easy way to post a short note to your blog or a link to your de.licio.us account? And why on Earth isn't there a game in sight?

Fortunately, it's possible to fill in these and many other gaping holes in the iPhone app structure by using the App Store. In the same way that you use the iTunes Store to browse and purchase songs and albums, you use the App Store to browse and purchase apps (although many of them are free for the downloading). It's done using the familiar iTunes software on your Mac or Windows PC. (You can also connect to the App Store directly from your iPhone, which is explained later.)

To access the App Store on your computer, follow these steps:

1. **Launch iTunes.**

2. **Click iTunes Store.** The iTunes Store interface appears.

Note

In most cases you can't tell just by looking whether an app is free. However, the App Store does have a Top Charts section on the right hand side, which includes a handy Free Apps list, so that's often a good place to start if you're looking for free stuff.

3. **Click App Store.** iTunes loads the main App Store page.

4. **Click the iPhone tab.** iTunes loads the iPhone version of the App Store page, as shown in Figure 1.22.

From here, use the links to browse the apps, or use the iTunes Store search box to look for something specific.

1.22 In the App Store, tap the iPhone tab to see the apps that are available for your iPhone.

Syncing apps

After you download an app or two into iTunes, they won't do you much good just sitting there. To actually use the apps, you need to get them on your iPhone. Here's how:

1. **Connect your iPhone to your computer.** iTunes opens and accesses the iPhone.

2. **In iTunes, click your iPhone in the Devices list.**

3. **Click the Apps tab.**

4. **Select the Sync Apps check box.**

5. **In the app list, select the check box beside each app that you want to sync, as shown in Figure 1.23.**

6. **Click Apply.** iTunes syncs the iPhone using your new apps settings.

Genius

By default, any new apps you add to your computer are automatically synced to your iPhone. If you'd rather not have all your new apps synced without your say so, deselect the Automatically sync new apps check box (not shown in Figure 1.23, but it appears just below the app list).

1.23 You can sync selected apps with your iPhone.

Accessing the App Store on Your iPhone

Getting apps synced to your iPhone from iTunes is great, but what if you're away from your desk and you hear about an amazing iPhone game, or you realize that you forgot to download an important app using iTunes? This isn't even remotely a problem because your iPhone can establish a wireless connection to the App Store anywhere you have Wi-Fi access or a cellular signal (ideally 3G for faster downloads). You can browse and search the apps, check for updates, and purchase any app you want (unless it's free, of course). The app downloads to your iPhone and installs itself on the Home screen. You're good to go!

To access the App Store on your iPhone, follow these steps:

1. **Tap the Home button to return to the Home screen.**

2. **Tap the App Store icon.**

As you can see in Figure 1.24, your iPhone organizes the App Store similar to the iTunes Store (as well as the iPod and YouTube apps). That is, you get five browse buttons in the menu bar — Featured, Categories, Top 25, Search, and Updates. You use these buttons to navigate the App Store.

Here's a summary of what each browse button does for you:

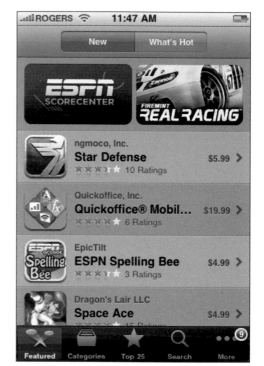

1.24 Use the browse buttons in the App Store's menu bar to locate and manage apps for your iPhone.

● **Featured.** Tap this button to display a list of videos picked by the App Store editors. The list shows each app's name, icon, star rating, number of reviews, and price. Tap New to see the latest apps, and tap What's Hot to see the most popular items.

● **Categories.** Tap this button to see a list of app categories, such as Games and Business. Tap a category to see a list of the apps available.

● **Top 25.** Tap this button to see a list of the 25 most often downloaded apps.

● **Search.** Tap this button to display a Search text box. Tap inside the box, enter a search phrase, and then tap Search. App Store sends back a list of apps that match your search term.

● **Updates.** Tap this button to install updated versions of your apps.

Note Tap an app to get more detailed information about it. The Info screen that appears gives you a description of the app, shows a screen shot, and may even offer some user reviews.

Viewing and updating your apps

When you click Applications in the iTunes Library, you see a list of icons that represent all the apps that you've downloaded from the App Store, as shown in Figure 1.25.

1.25 In the iTunes Library, click the Apps category to see your downloaded apps.

To check for updates to your apps, click x Updates Available (where x is the number of updates you have waiting for you). When the developer releases a new version of an app, App Store compares the new version with what you have. If you have an earlier version, it offers to update the app for you (usually without charge).

When you access the App Store with your iPhone, take a look at the Updates browse button in the menu bar. If you see a red dot with a white number inside it superimposed over the Updates button (see Figure 1.24), it means some of your installed apps have updated versions available. The number inside the dot tells you how many updates are waiting for you. It's a good idea to update your apps whenever a new version becomes available. The new version usually fixes bugs, but it might also supply more features, give better performance, or beef up the app's security.

Follow these steps to install an update:

1. **On the Home screen, tap App Store.** Your iPhone connects to the App Store.

2. **Tap the Updates button.** Remember that you are only able to tap this button if you see the red dot with a number that indicates the available updates. You see the Updates screen, as shown in Figure 1.26.

33

3. **Tap an update.** App Store displays a description of the update.

4. **Tap Free.** The Free button changes to Install. (In the unlikely event that the update isn't free, you'd tap the price, instead, and then tap Buy Now.)

5. **Tap Install.** Your iPhone downloads and installs the app update.

Connecting Your iPhone with Bluetooth Devices

Your iPhone is configured to use a wireless technology called Bluetooth, which enables you to make wireless connections to other Bluetooth-friendly devices. Most Macs come with Bluetooth built in, and they can use it to connect to a wide range of Bluetooth devices, including a mouse, keyboard, cell phone, PDA, printer, digital camera, and even another Mac. Your iPhone can at least connect to a Bluetooth headset, which lets you listen to phone conversations, music, and movies without wires and without disturbing your neighbors.

1.26 Use the Updates screen to choose the app you want to update.

In theory, connecting Bluetooth devices should be criminally easy: You bring them within 33 feet of each other (the maximum Bluetooth range), and they connect without further ado. In practice, however, there's usually at least a bit of further ado (and sometimes plenty of it). This usually takes one or both of the following forms:

- **Making the devices discoverable.** Unlike Wi-Fi devices that broadcast their signals constantly, most Bluetooth devices only broadcast their availability — that is, they make themselves *discoverable* — when you say so. This makes sense in many cases because you usually only want to connect a Bluetooth component such as a headset with a single device. By controlling when the device is discoverable, you ensure that it works only with the device you want it to.

- **Pairing the iPhone and the device.** As a security precaution, many Bluetooth devices need to be *paired* with another device before the connection is established. In most

Rigatoni's Reward
20501 Hesperian Blvd
Hayward CA 94541
510-785-9300

Host: Dine-In Cashier	10/23/2011
#187	6:14 PM
	20087

$8.99 Spaghetti Combo	8.99
Caesar Dressing	
NO Croutons	
Corona	2.99
Corona	2.99

| Subtotal | 14.97 |
| Tax | 1.31 |

| Here Total | 16.28 |

| VISA #XXXXXXXXXXXXX9241 | 16.28 |
| Auth:000098 Exp 0415 | |

| Tent # | 24 |

Rigatoni's now offers
ONLINE ORDERING!
SIMPLE
CONVENIENT
DELICIOUS
www.rigatonis.com

--- Check Closed ---

cases, the pairing is accomplished by entering a multidigit *passkey* — your iPhone calls it a PIN — that you must then enter into the Bluetooth device (assuming, of course, that it has some kind of keypad). In the case of a headset, the device comes with a default passkey that you must enter into your iPhone to set up the pairing.

Making your iPhone discoverable

So your first order of Bluetooth business is to ensure that your iPhone is discoverable by activating the Bluetooth feature. This feature is on by default with new iPhones, so check for that first: On the status bar, look for the Bluetooth logo to the left of the battery status icon, as shown in Figure 1.27.

If you don't see the Bluetooth icon, follow these steps to turn on Bluetooth and make your iPhone discoverable:

1. **On the Home screen, tap Settings.** The Settings screen appears.

2. **Tap General.** The General screen appears.

3. **Tap Bluetooth.** The Bluetooth screen appears.

4. **Tap the Bluetooth On/Off button to change the setting to On, as shown in Figure 1.28.**

1.27 If your iPhone is discoverable, you see the Bluetooth icon in the status bar.

1.28 Use the Bluetooth screen to make your iPhone discoverable.

35

Pairing your iPhone with a Bluetooth keyboard

iOS 4.0 The iPhone virtual keyboard is an ingenious invention, but it's not always a convenient one, particular when you need to type fast or type a lot. Fortunately, iOS 4 supports connections to a Bluetooth keyboard which, while paired, disables the onscreen keyboard. Follow these steps to pair your iPhone with a Bluetooth keyboard:

1. **On the Home screen, tap Settings.** The Settings screen appears.

2. **Tap General.** The General screen appears.

3. **Tap Bluetooth.** The Bluetooth screen appears.

4. **If the keyboard has a separate switch or button that makes the device discoverable, turn on that switch or press that button.** Wait until you see the keyboard appear in the Bluetooth screen, as shown in Figure 1.29.

5. **Tap the name of the Bluetooth keyboard.** Your iPhone displays a passkey, as shown in Figure 1.30.

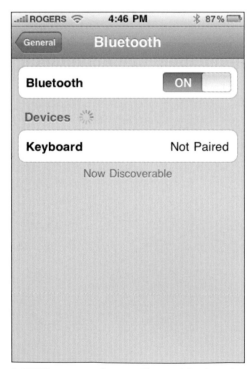

1.29 When you make your Bluetooth keyboard discoverable, the device appears in the Bluetooth screen.

1.30 Your iPhone displays a passkey, which you then type on the Bluetooth keyboard.

6. **On the Bluetooth keyboard, type the passkey and press Return or Enter.** Your iPhone pairs with the keyboard and returns you to the Bluetooth screen, where you now see Connected beside the keyboard.

Pairing your iPhone with a Bluetooth headset

If you want to listen to music, headphones are a great way to go because the sound is often better than with the built-in iPhone speakers, and no one else around is subjected to Weezer at top volume. Similarly, if you want to conduct a hands-free call, a headset (a combination of headphones for listening and a microphone for talking) makes life easier because you can put the phone down and make all the hand gestures you want (providing you aren't driving, of course). Add Bluetooth into the mix, and you've got an easy and wireless audio solution for your iPhone.

Follow these general steps to pair your iPhone with a Bluetooth headset:

1. **On the Home screen, tap Settings.** The Settings screen appears.

2. **Tap General.** The General screen appears.

3. **Tap Bluetooth.** The Bluetooth screen appears.

4. **If the headset has a separate switch or button that makes the device discoverable, turn on that switch or press that button.** Wait until you see the correct headset name appear in the Bluetooth screen.

5. **Tap the name of the Bluetooth headset.** Your iPhone should pair with the headset automatically and you see Connected in the Bluetooth screen, as shown in Figure 1.31; you can skip the rest of these steps. Otherwise you see the Enter PIN screen.

6. **Enter the headset's passkey in the PIN box.** See the headset documentation to get the passkey (it's often 0000).

1.31 When you have paired your iPhone with the Bluetooth headset, you see Connected beside the device in the Bluetooth screen.

7. **Tap Done.** Your iPhone pairs with the headset and returns you to the Bluetooth screen, where you now see Connected beside the headset name.

Selecting a paired headset as the audio output device

Once you've paired a Bluetooth headset, you usually need to configure your iPhone to blast your tunes through the headset rather than the phone's built-in speaker. Here's what you do:

1. **On the Home screen, tap iPod.** The iPod apps loads.

2. **Tap a song to start the playback.** At the bottom of the playback screen, your iPhone shows "Speaker" to indicate the built-in speaker is the current audio output device.

3. **Tap the Bluetooth icon that appears in the lower right corner of the screen.** The Audio Device dialog appears, as shown in Figure 1.32.

4. **Tap your paired Bluetooth headset.** Your iPhone starts playing the song through the headset.

1.32 Use the Audio Device dialog box to select your paired Bluetooth headset.

Unpairing your iPhone from a Bluetooth device

When you no longer plan to use a Bluetooth headset for a long period of time, you should unpair it from your iPhone. Follow these steps:

1. **On the Home screen, tap Settings.** The Settings screen appears.

2. **Tap General.** The General screen appears.

3. **Tap Bluetooth.** The Bluetooth screen appears.

4. **Tap the name of the Bluetooth headset.**

5. **Tap Forget this Device.** Your iPhone unpairs the headset.

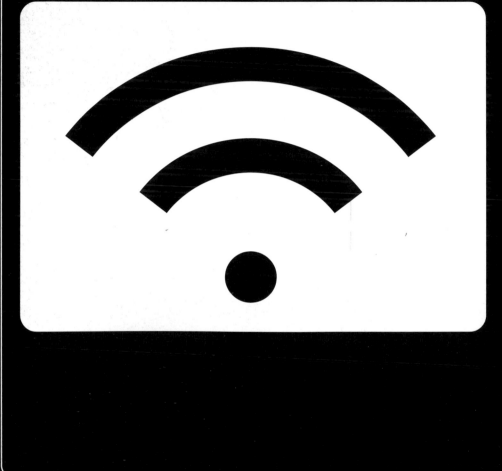

As a standalone device, your iPhone works just fine, thank you, because you can make calls, listen to music, take pictures, record and edit video, work with your contacts and calendars, take notes, play games, and much more. But your iPhone was made to *connect*: to surf the web, exchange email and text messages, watch YouTube videos, navigate with maps, and on and on. To do all of that, your iPhone must first connect to a network, and that's what this chapter is all about. I tell you about the various network types supported by the iPhone, and then I show you how to make, monitor, and control connections to those networks.

Understanding Internet Access Networks

To get on the Web, your iPhone must first connect to a network that offers Internet access. To make this easy and seamless, your iPhone can work with not just a single network, not just two networks (like the original iPhone), but *three* network types:

- **Wi-Fi.** Short for wireless fidelity, and also called 802.11 by the geeks and AirPort by Apple types, you use your iPhone's built-in Wi-Fi antenna to connect to a wireless network that's within range. This usually means within about 115 feet, but some public networks — also called *Wi-Fi hot spots* — boost their signals to offer a greater range. Because most wireless networks are connected to high-speed Internet connections, Wi-Fi is by far your best bet for an Internet connection. You get fast downloads and you don't use up data in whatever Internet connection plan you have with your cellular provider. Plus you get the added bonus of being able to make and receive phone calls while you're online. As long as a Wi-Fi network is within range and you can connect to that network, your iPhone always defaults to using Wi-Fi for Internet access.

Genius

Just about any place you see people set up with their laptops has Wi-Fi that you can use. Another easy way to find Wi-Fi near you is to open the Google Maps app on your iPhone and type your city and **wifi** into the search box. This gives you a map with pushpins representing Wi-Fi hotspots near you.

- **3G.** Short for Third Generation, 3G is slower than Wi-Fi, but Wi-Fi requires you to be within range of a network to use it. The 3G network is a cellular network, so as long as you're in a 3G coverage area, you can access the Internet from anywhere, even a moving car. 3G is currently available in over 280 U.S. metropolitan areas. Most other countries offer widespread 3G coverage, so you won't often find yourself out of 3G service. As a major bonus for cell phone addicts everywhere, 3G lets you access the Internet *and* talk on the phone at the same time, something the original iPhone's EDGE network couldn't do. Plus, the 3G download speeds are anywhere from 2 to 2.5 times as fast as the notoriously pokey EDGE downloads, so you won't grow old waiting for a Web site to open. If your iPhone has no Wi-Fi hot spot in range, it automatically switches to the 3G network, assuming you're in a coverage area.

- **EDGE.** This is short for Enhanced Data rates for GSM (Global System for Mobile communication) Evolution, an absurdly grandiose name for a rightfully maligned cellular network technology. Why the bad press for EDGE? Because in a word, it's *slow*. Paint dries faster than most Web sites download over an EDGE connection. Even worse, EDGE is strictly a monotasking system: If you're on the phone, you can't surf the Web; if you're surfing the Web, you can't send or receive calls. So why bother with EDGE at all? Mostly because although 3G is widespread, it doesn't have as much coverage as EDGE does. So if you don't have a Wi-Fi network nearby, and you're not in a 3G coverage area, your iPhone drops down into EDGE mode so you can at least get a signal.

Connecting to a Wi-Fi Network

Connections to the cellular network are automatic and occur behind the scenes. As soon as you switch on your iPhone, it checks for a 3G signal and if it finds one, it connects to the network and displays the 3G icon in the status bar, as well as the connection strength (the more bars the better). If your current area doesn't do the 3G thing, your iPhone tries to connect to an EDGE network instead. If that works, you see the E icon in the status bar (plus the usual signal strength bars). If none of that works, you see No Signal, so you might as well go home.

Making your first connection

Things aren't immediately automatic when it comes to Wi-Fi connections, at least not at first. As soon as you try to access something on the Internet — a Web site, your e-mail, a Google Map, or whatever — your iPhone scours the surrounding airwaves for Wi-Fi network signals. If you've never connected to a Wi-Fi network, or if you're in an area that doesn't have any Wi-Fi networks that you've used in the past, you see the Select a Wi-Fi Network dialog, as shown in Figure 2.1. (If you don't see the Select a Wi-Fi Network dialog, you can still connect to a wireless network; see the section about how to stop Wi-Fi network prompts later in this chapter.)

This dialog displays a list of the Wi-Fi networks that are within range. For each network, you get three tidbits of data:

- **Network name.** This is the name that the administrator has assigned to the network. If you're in a coffee shop or similar public hot spot and you want to use that network, look for the name of the shop (or a variation on the name).
- **Password-protected.** If a Wi-Fi network displays a lock icon, it means the network is protected by a password, and you need to know that password to make the connection.

- ● **Signal strength.** This icon gives you a rough idea of how strong the wireless signals are. The stronger the signal (the more bars you see, the better the signal), the more likely you are to get a fast and reliable connection.

Follow these steps to connect to a Wi-Fi network:

1. **Tap the network you want to use.** If the network is protected by a password, your iPhone prompts you to enter the password, as shown in Figure 2.2.

2. **Use the keyboard to enter the password.**

3. **Tap Join.** The iPhone connects to the network and adds the Wi-Fi network signal strength icon to the status bar.

To connect to a commercial Wi-Fi operation — such as those you find in airports, hotels, and convention centers, for example — you almost always have to take one more step. In most cases, the network prompts you for your name and credit card data so you can be charged for accessing the network. If you're not prompted right away, you will be as soon as you try to access a Web site or check your e-mail. Enter your information and then enjoy the Internet in all of its Wi-Fi glory.

2.1 If you're just starting out on the Wi-Fi trail, your iPhone displays a list of nearby networks.

2.2 If the Wi-Fi network is secured with a password, use this screen to enter it.

Caution
Because the password box shows dots instead of the actual text for added security, this is no place to demonstrate your iPhone speed-typing prowess. Slow and steady wins the password typing race (or something).

Note
If you're not fortunate enough to be near Wi-Fi you can use, you can still access the Internet via the cellular connection. Your iPhone tries to use the 3G network, but if that's a no go it uses the dreaded EDGE network.

Connecting to known networks

If the Wi-Fi network is one that you use all the time — for example, your home or office network — the good news is that your iPhone remembers any network that you connect to. As soon as a known network comes within range, your iPhone makes the connection without so much as a peep. Thanks!

Stopping the incessant Wi-Fi network prompts

The Select a Wi-Fi Network dialog is a handy convenience if you're not sure whether a Wi-Fi network is available. However, as you move around town, you may find that dialog popping up all over the place as new Wi-Fi networks come within range. One solution is to wear your finger down to the bone with all the constant tapping of the Cancel button, but there's a better way: just tell your iPhone to shut up already with the Wi-Fi prompting. Here's how:

1. **On the Home screen, tap Settings.** The Settings screen appears.

2. **Tap Wi-Fi.** iPhone opens the Wi-Fi Networks screen.

3. **Tap the Ask to Join Networks switch to the Off position, as shown in Figure 2.3.** Your iPhone no longer prompts you with nearby networks. Whew!

2.3 Toggle the Ask to Join Networks switch to Off to put a gag on the network prompts.

Okay, I hear you ask, if I'm no longer seeing the prompts, how do I connect to a Wi-Fi network if I don't even know it's there? That's a good question, and here's a good answer:

1. **On the Home screen, tap Settings.** Your iPhone displays the Settings screen.

2. **Tap Wi-Fi.** The Wi-Fi Networks screen appears, and the Choose a Network list shows you the available Wi-Fi networks.

3. **Tap the network you want to use.** If the network is protected by a password, your iPhone prompts you to enter the password.

4. **Use the keyboard to tap the password.**

5. **Tap Join.** The iPhone connects to the network and adds the Wi-Fi network signal strength icon to the status bar.

Connecting to a hidden Wi-Fi network

Each Wi-Fi network has a network name — often called the Service Set Identifier, or SSID — that identifies the network to Wi-Fi-friendly devices such as your iPhone. By default, most Wi-Fi networks broadcast the network name so that you can see the network and connect to it. However, some Wi-Fi networks disable network name broadcasting as a security precaution. The idea here is that if an unauthorized user can't see the network, he or she can't attempt to connect to it. (However, some devices can pick up the network name when authorized computers connect to the network, so this is not a foolproof security measure.)

You can still connect to a hidden Wi-Fi network by entering the connection settings by hand. You need to know the network name, the network's security type and encryption type, and the network's password. Here are the steps to follow:

1. **On the Home screen, tap Settings to open the Settings screen.**

2. **Tap Wi-Fi.** You see the Wi-Fi Networks screen.

3. **Tap Other.** Your iPhone displays the Other Network screen, as shown in Figure 2.4.

4. **Use the Name text box to enter the network name.**

5. **Tap Security to open the Security screen.**

6. **Tap the type of security used by the Wi-Fi network: WEP, WPA, WPA2, WPA Enterprise, WPA2 Enterprise, or None.**

7. **Tap Other Network to return to the Other Network screen.** If you chose WEP, WPA, WPA2, WPA Enterprise, or WPA2 Enterprise, your iPhone prompts you to enter the password.

8. **Use the keyboard to enter the password.**

9. **Tap Join.** The iPhone connects to the network and adds the Wi-Fi network signal strength icon to the status bar.

Turning off the Wi-Fi antenna to save power

Your iPhone's Wi-Fi antenna is constantly on the lookout for nearby Wi-Fi networks. That's useful because it means you always have an up to date list of networks to check out, but it

2.4 Use the Other Network screen to connect to a hidden Wi-Fi network.

takes its toll on the iPhone battery. If you know you won't be using Wi-Fi for a while, you can save some battery juice for more important pursuits by turning off your iPhone's Wi-Fi antenna. Here's how:

1. **On the Home screen, tap Settings.** The Settings screen appears.

2. **Tap Wi-Fi.** The Wi-Fi Networks screen appears.

3. **Tap the Wi-Fi switch to the Off position.** Your iPhone disconnects from your current Wi-Fi network and hides the Choose a Networks list.

When you're ready to resume your Wi-Fi duties, return to the Wi-Fi Networks screen and tap the Wi-Fi switch to the On position.

Tethering a Computer to Your iPhone's Internet Connection

Here's a scenario you've probably tripped over a time or two when you've been roaming around with both your iPhone and your notebook computer along for the ride. You end up somewhere where you have access to just the cellular network, with no Wi-Fi in sight. This means that your iPhone can access the Internet (using the cellular network), but your notebook can't. That's a real pain if you want to do some work on the computer that involves Internet access.

To work around this problem, you can use a nifty bit of technology called Internet tethering. This means you use your iPhone as a kind of Internet gateway device. That is, you connect your iPhone to your notebook (either directly via a USB cable or wirelessly via Bluetooth), and your notebook can then use the iPhone's cellular Internet connection to get online.

This sounds too good to be true, and to a certain extent it is. That is, your cellular provider will probably charge you extra (anywhere from $30 to $70 per month!) to use tethering, that is *if* your provider even supports tethering. So before you get too excited about this interesting technology, check with your cellular provider and get the details.

If you're ready to check it out, your first chore is to turn on Internet tethering on your iPhone. Follow these steps:

Note

Remember that you won't see the Internet Tethering option if your cellular provider doesn't support Internet tethering.

1. **On the Home screen, tap Settings.** The Settings screen appears.

2. **Tap General to open the General screen.**

3. **Tap Network.** The Network screen opens.

4. **Tap Set Up Internet Tethering.** Note that you might not see this button if your provider sets up Internet tethering automatically. In that case, skip step 6.

5. **Follow the instructions that appear for setting up tethering with your provider.** These steps vary depending on provider. for example, with AT&T in the U.S., you can either call 611 or go to www.att.com/mywireless.

6. **Once tethering has been set up, return to the Network screen and tap Internet Tethering to display the Internet Tethering screen.**

7. **Tap the Internet Tethering switch to the On position, as shown in Figure 2.5.** If you have Bluetooth turned off on your iPhone, you see a warning dialog, and you need to tap either Turn on Bluetooth to use it, or tap USB Only if you plan on making a USB connection to the notebook.

Connect your iPhone to the computer. On a Mac, you see a dialog telling you a new network interface has been detected. Click Network Preferences, and then click Apply to create the tethering connection. You know you were successful when you see two things:

○ In the Network preferences window, the iPhone network interface (for example, iPhone USB, if you're using a USB connection) shows connected, as shown in Figure 2.6.

2.5 To use tethering, first set the Internet Tethering switch to the On position.

2.6 When you successfully set up Internet tethering, the iPhone network interface shows Connected.

49

● On your iPhone, you see a blue Internet Tethering bar just below the status bar, as shown in Figure 2.7.

2.7 When your iPhone is tethered to your computer, you see the blue Internet Tethering bar.

Keeping an Eye on Your Data Usage

The days of having no cap on the amount of cellular network data you use each month — so-called *unlimited* plans — are going the way of the Dodo. Most providers — including AT&T, the iPhone provider in the U.S. — are eliminating (or never had in the first place) unlimited data plans, particularly for new accounts. This means that it's likely you're using your iPhone with a plan that comes with a maximum amount of monthly data. More importantly, if you exceed that monthly cap, you'll almost certainly pay big bucks for the privilege.

To avoid that, most providers are kind enough to send you a message when you approach your cap. However, if you don't trust your provider, or if you're just paranoid about these things (justly, in my view), then you can keep an eye on your data usage yourself. Your iPhone keeps track of the cellular network data your iPhone has sent or received, as well as the Internet tethering data it has sent or received.

First, take a look at your most recent bill from your cellular provider and, in particular, look for the dates the bill covers. For example, the bill might run from the 24th of the one month to the 23rd of the next month. This is important because it tells you when you need to reset the usage data on your iPhone.

Now follow these steps to check your cellular data usage:

1. **On the Home screen, tap Settings.** The Settings screen appears.

2. **Tap General to open the General screen.**

3. **Tap Usage.** The Usage screen opens.

4. **Scroll down to the Cellular Network Data section and read the Sent and Received values, as shown in Figure 2.8.**

5. **If your provider supports Internet tethering and you've been using this feature, also read the Sent and Received values in the Tether Data section.**

6. **If you're at the end of your data period, tap Reset Statistics to start with fresh values for the new period.**

Controlling Network Data

Your iPhone gives you fairly fine-grained control over your network data. For example, you can toggle just the 3G data, all cellular data, data roaming, or all your iPhone antennas. The next few sections provide the details.

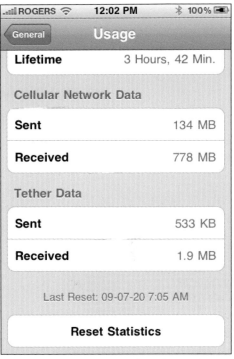

2.8 In the Usage screen, use the values in the Cellular Network Data and Tether Data sections to track your total data usage.

Turning off 3G

Using the 3G cellular network is a real pleasure because it's so much faster than a molasses-in-January EDGE connection. If 3G has a downside, it's that it uses up a lot of battery power. That's true even if you're currently connected to a Wi-Fi network, because the 3G antenna is constantly looking for a 3G signal. If you'll be on your Wi-Fi network for a while, or if you battery is running low and you don't need a 3G cellular connection, you should turn off the 3G antenna to reduce the load on your iPhone's battery. Here's how:

1. **On the Home screen, tap Settings.** The Settings screen appears.

2. **Tap General to open the General screen.**

3. **Tap Network.** The Network screen opens.

4. **Tap the Enable 3G switch to Off, as shown in Figure 2.9.**

Turning off cellular data

If you've reached the limit of your provider's cellular data plan, you almost certainly want to avoid going over the cap because the charges are usually prohibitively expensive. As long as you have a Wi-Fi network in range, or as long as you're disciplined enough not to surf the Web or cruise YouTube when there's no Wi-Fi in sight, you'll be okay. Still, accidents can happen. For example, you might accidentally tap a link in an email message or text message, or someone in your household might use your phone without knowing about your restrictions.

To prevent these sorts of accidents from happening (or if you simply don't trust yourself when it comes to YouTube), you can turn off cellular data altogether, which means your iPhone only accesses Internet data if it has a Wi-Fi signal. Follow these steps to turn off cellular data on your iPhone:

1. **On the Home screen, tap Settings.** The Settings screen appears.

2. **Tap General to open the General screen.**

3. **Tap Network.** The Network screen opens.

4. **Tap the Cellular Data switch (see Figure 2.9) to Off.**

Now, if you try to access the Internet without a Wi-Fi connection, you see the dialog shown in Figure 2.10. If you really *must* connect, you can tap Settings to jump directly to the Network screen.

Turning off data roaming

Data roaming is an often convenient cell phone feature that enables you to make calls — and, with your iPhone, surf the Web, check and send e-mail, and exchange text messages — when you're outside of your provider's normal coverage area. The downside is that roaming charges are almost always eye-poppingly expensive, and you're often talking several dollars per *minute*, depending on where you are and what type of service you're using. Not good!

Unfortunately, if you have your iPhone's Data Roaming feature turned on, you may incur massive roaming charges even if you never use your phone! That's because your iPhone still performs background checks for things like incoming e-mail messages and text messages, so a week in some far-off land could cost you hundreds of dollars without even using your phone.

2.9 Use the Network screen to change the Enable 3G setting to Off.

2.10 With cellular data turned off, you see this dialog when you try to access Internet data without being connected to a Wi-Fi network.

To avoid this insanity, turn off your iPhone's Data Roaming feature when you don't need it. Follow these steps:

1. **On the Home screen, tap Settings.** The Settings screen appears.

2. **Tap General.** The General screen appears.

3. **Tap Network.** The Network screen appears.

4. **Tap the Data Roaming On/Off switch (see Figure 2.9) to Off.**

Switching your iPhone to airplane mode

When you board a flight, aviation regulations in most countries are super strict about cell phones: no calls in and no calls out. In fact, most of those regulations ban wireless signals of *any* kind, which means your iPhone is a real hazard to sensitive airline equipment because it also transmits Wi-Fi and Bluetooth signals, even if there are no Wi-Fi receivers or Bluetooth devices within 30,000 feet of your current position.

If a flight attendant sees you playing around with your iPhone, he or she may ask you to confirm that the phone is off. (One obviously iPhone-savvy attendant even asked me if my phone was in Airplane mode.) Showing the Airplane icon should be sufficient.

Your pilot or friendly flight attendant will suggest that everyone simply turn off their phones. Sure, that does the job, but darn it you've got an iPhone, which means there are plenty of things you can do outside of its wireless capabilities: listen to music or an audiobook, watch a show, view photos, and much more.

So how do you reconcile the no-wireless-and-that-means-you regulations with the iPhone's multitude of wireless-free apps? You put your iPhone into a special state called Airplane mode. This mode turns off the transceivers — the internal components that transmit and receive wireless signals — for the iPhone's phone, Wi-Fi, and Bluetooth features. With your iPhone now safely in compliance of federal aviation regulations, you're free to use any app that doesn't rely on wireless transmissions.

Follow these steps to activate Airplane mode:

1. **On the Home screen, tap Settings.** The Settings screen appears.

2. **Tap the Airplane Mode On/Off switch to turn this setting On, as shown in Figure 2.11.** Your iPhone disconnects your cellular network and your wireless network (if you have a current connection). Notice, as well, that while Airplane mode is on, an Airplane icon appears in the status bar in place of the signal strength and network icons.

2.11 When your iPhone is in Airplane mode, an Airplane icon appears in the status bar.

Creating a VPN Network Connection

What do you do if you want to transfer secure data such as financial information or personnel files between your network and your iPhone? With most connections, that's a problem. A malicious hacker might not be able to access your system directly, but he certainly can use a packet sniffer or similar technology to access your incoming and outgoing data. Because that data isn't encrypted, the hacker can easily read the contents of the packets.

The solution is a tried-and-true technology called *virtual private networking* (VPN), which offers secure access to a private network over a public connection, such as the Internet. VPN is secure because it uses a technique called *tunneling*, which establishes a connection between two computers — a VPN server and a VPN client — using a specific port (such as port 1723). Control-connection packets are sent back and forth to maintain the connection between the two computers (to, in a sense, keep the tunnel open).

When it comes to sending the actual network data — sometimes called the payload — each network packet is encrypted and then encapsulated within a regular IP packet, which is then routed through the tunnel. Any hacker can see this IP packet traveling across the Internet, but even if he intercepts the packet and examines it, no harm is done because the content of the packet — the actual data — is encrypted. When the IP packet arrives on the other end of the tunnel, VPN decapsulates the network packet and then decrypts it to reveal the payload (which is part of the reason why VPN connections tend to be quite slow).

Your iPhone supports VPN and it can use any of the following three tunneling protocols:

- **Point-to-Point Tunneling Protocol (PPTP).** This protocol is the most widely used in VPN setups. It was developed by Microsoft and is related to the Point-to-Point Protocol (PPP) that's commonly used to transport IP packets over the Internet. PPTP sets up the tunnel and encapsulates the encrypted network packets in an IP packet for transport across the tunnel.

- **IP Security (IPSec).** This protocol encrypts the payload (IP packets only), sets up the tunnel, and encapsulates the encrypted network packets in an IP packet for transport across the tunnel.

- **Layer 2 Tunneling Protocol (L2TP).** This protocol goes beyond PPTP by allowing VPN connections over networks other than just the Internet (such as networks based on X.25, ATM, or Frame Relay). L2TP uses the encryption portion of IPSec to encrypt the network packets.

If you have a VPN server set up at work, your administrator can supply you with the necessary data for the connection: the type of protocol, the server name or address, your account username and password, and so on. With all that in hand, follow these steps to set up a VPN network connection on your iPhone:

1. **On the Home screen, tap Settings.** The Settings screen appears.

2. **Tap General.** The General screen appears.

3. **Tap Network.** The Network screen appears.

4. **Tap VPN.** The VPN screen appears.

5. **Tap Add VPN Configuration.** The Add Configuration screen appears.

6. **Tap the protocol you want to use.** Figure 2.12 shows the PPTP tab.

7. **Type the connection data provided by your administrator.**

8. **Tap Save.** Your iPhone adds the connection to the VPN screen.

9. **Tap the VPN switch to On.** Your iPhone connects to the VPN server.

2.12 Tap the VPN protocol used by your network, then enter the connection details.

How Can I Get More Out of the Phone App?

The iPhone is chock full of great apps that enable you to surf the Web, send and receive e-mail messages, listen to music, take photos, organize your contacts, schedule appointments, and much, much more. These features put the "smart" into the iPhone's status as a smartphone, but let's not forget the "phone" part! So while you're probably familiar with the basic steps required to make and answer calls, the iPhone's powerful phone component is loaded with amazing features that can make the cell phone portion of your life easier, more convenient, and more efficient. This chapter takes you through these features.

Working with Outgoing Calls

You can do much more with your iPhone than just make a call the old-fashioned way — by dialing the phone number. There are speedy shortcuts you can take, and even settings to alter the way your outgoing calls look on the receiver's phone.

Making calls quickly

The iPhone has a seemingly endless number of methods you can use to make a call. It's nice to have the variety, but in this have-your-people-call-my-people world, the big question is not how many ways can you make a call, but how *fast* can you make a call? Here are my favorite iPhone speed-calling techniques:

- **Favorites list.** This list acts as a kind of speed dial for the iPhone because you use it to store the phone numbers you call most often, and you have space to add your top 20 numbers. To call someone in your Favorites list, double-click the Home button to leap immediately to the Favorites screen, and then tap the number you want to call. I show you how to manage your Favorites later in this chapter.

- **Visual Voicemail.** If you're checking your voicemail messages (from the Home screen, tap Phone, and then tap Voicemail) and you want to return someone's call, tap the message and then tap Call Back.

- **Text message.** If someone enters a phone number in a text message, iPhone handily converts that number into a kind of link: The number appears in blue, underlined text, much like a link on a Web page, as shown in Figure 3.1. Tap the phone number to call that number. You can also use a similar technique to call numbers embedded in Web pages (see Chapter 4) and e-mail messages (see Chapter 5).

3.1 Your iPhone is kind enough to convert a text message phone number into a link that you can tap to call the number.

Caution The stainless steel band that runs around the outside edges of your iPhone is part of the phone's antenna system: one part is for Bluetooth, Wi-Fi, and GPS, and the rest is for cellular signals. Be careful though: On the left edge of the phone, near the bottom, you'll see a thin line, which separates the two antennas. If you cover that gap with any part of your hand, you'll reduce your signal or lose it completely. You can fix the problem either by applying a bit of electrical tape (or, really, any tape) to cover the gap, or purchase one of Apple's bumper cases designed for the iPhone 4.

● **Recent numbers.** The Recent Calls list (from the Home screen, tap Phone and then tap Recents) shows your recent phone activity: the calls you've made, the calls you've received, and the calls you've missed. Recent Calls is great because it enables you to quickly redial someone you've had recent contact with. Just tap the call and away you go. (If you want to return a missed call, tap Missed and then tap the call.) To call the person using a different phone number, tap the More Info icon (the arrow) to the right of the name or number, and then tap the phone number you want to use to make the call.

Genius If your Recent Calls list is populated with names or numbers that you know you won't ever call back, you should clear the list and start fresh. In the Recent Calls screen, tap Clear and then tap Clear All Recents.

Voice dialing a call

Tapping a favorite number, a recent number, or a text message phone number link are all pretty easy methods to launch a phone call, but if you have an iPhone 3GS, you get an even easier method that doesn't require even a single tap on your part. I speak, of course, of voice dialing, which is part of the Voice Control feature in the iPhone 3GS. With voice dialing, you tell the iPhone 3GS the name of the person you want to call (if that person's in your Contacts list) or the number you want to call (for everyone else), and Voice Control does the rest. Here are the details (such as they are):

1. **Tap and hold the Home button.** You can also press and hold the center button of the iPhone 3GS headset. The Voice Control screen appears.

2. **Say "Call" or "Phone" and then specify who or what:**

   ● If the person is in your Contacts list, say the person's name. If you have multiple numbers for that person, also include the label of that number (such as "mobile" or "home"). If you're not sure of the correct label, skip that part and Voice Control will let you know which labels are available.

   ● For anyone else, say the full phone number you want to dial.

3. **If the person has multiple numbers and you didn't specify a label, you see the Multiple Numbers version of the Voice Control screen, shown in Figure 3.2, and you now need to say the label of the number you want to dial.** Conveniently, Voice Control also responds verbally by listing the available labels for that person, so you don't have to guess which one to use.

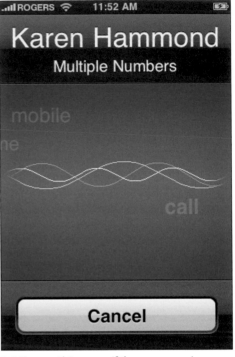

That's it. For a contact, the iPhone 3GS responds with "Calling *name label*", where *name* is the person's name and *label* is the phone number label; for a phone number, the iPhone responds with "Calling *number,*" where *number* is the phone number you specified.

Configuring your iPhone to not show your caller ID

3.2 You see this screen if the person you're calling has multiple numbers and you don't specify a label.

When you use your iPhone to call someone, and the called phone supports Caller ID, your number and often your name appear. If you'd rather hide your identity for some reason, you can configure your iPhone to not show your caller ID:

1. **On the Home screen, tap Settings.** The Settings screen appears.
2. **Tap Phone.** The Phone screen appears.
3. **Tap Show My Caller ID.** The Show My Caller ID screen appears.
4. **Tap the Show My Caller ID On/Off button to change this setting to Off.** Your iPhone disables the Caller ID feature.

Handling Incoming Calls

When a call comes into your iPhone, you answer it, right? What could be simpler? You'd be surprised. Your iPhone gives you quite a few options for dealing with that call, aside from just answering it. After all, you don't want to talk to everyone all the time, do you?

Silencing an incoming call

When you're in a situation where the ringing of a cell phone is inappropriate, bothersome, or just plain rude, you, as a good cell phone citizen, practice "celliquette" (cell etiquette) and turn off your ringer. (On your iPhone, flick the Silent/Ring switch on the left side panel to the silent position.) However, we're merely human and so we all forget to turn off our phone's ringer once in a while. Hey, it happens.

Your job in that situation is to grab your phone and answer it as quickly as possible. However, what if you're in a situation where answering the call is bad form? Or what if you'd prefer to delay answering the call until you can leave the room or get out of earshot? That's a stickier cell wicket, for sure, but the iPhone designers have been there and they've come up with a simple solution: press either the Sleep/Wake button on the phone's top panel, or either volume button on the left side panel. Either way, your iPhone stops ringing (and vibrating). The ringing is still going on (your caller hears it on her end), so you've still got the usual four rings to answer the call should you decide to.

Genius

If you don't want someone to know you are ignoring his or her call, just silence the ring. The caller will still hear the standard four rings before the voicemail and be none the wiser that you just didn't pick up your phone.

Sending an incoming call directly to voicemail

Sometimes you just don't want to talk to someone. Whether this person is your significant other calling to complain, a friend who never seems to have anything to say and just talks in circles for ten minutes, or if you're just indisposed at the moment, you might prefer to ignore the call.

That's not a problem on your iPhone:

- If the phone isn't locked, tap the red Decline button on the touchscreen.
- If you're using the earbuds you just need to squeeze and hold the microphone/clicker for two seconds.
- Press the Sleep/Wake button twice in quick succession.

Any of these methods sends the call directly to voicemail.

Turning off the iPhone Call Waiting feature

If you're already on a call and another call comes in, your iPhone springs into action and displays the person's name or number as well as three options: Ignore, Hold Call + Answer, and End

Call + Answer. (See the section about handling multiple calls later in this chapter for more info on these options.) This is part of your iPhone's Call Waiting feature, and it's great if you're expecting an important call or if you want to add the caller to a conference call that you've set up.

However, the rest of the time you might just find it annoying and intrusive (and anyone who you put on hold or hang up on to take the new call probably finds it rude and insulting). In that case, you can turn off Call Waiting by following these steps:

1. **On the Home screen, tap Settings.** The Settings screen appears.

2. **Tap Phone.** The Phone screen appears.

3. **Tap Call Waiting.** The Call Waiting screen appears.

4. **Tap the Call Waiting On/Off button to change this setting to Off.** Your iPhone disables the Call Waiting feature.

Caution

If you ignore a call, as with any phone, the caller will know that you've ignored the call when voicemail kicks in before the normal four rings.

Forwarding iPhone calls to another number

What do you do about incoming calls if you can't use your iPhone for a while? For example, if you're going on a flight, you must either turn off your iPhone or put it into Airplane mode, as described in this chapter, so incoming calls won't go through. Similarly, if you have to return your iPhone to Apple for repairs or battery replacement, the phone won't be available if anyone tries to call you.

For these and other situations where your iPhone can't accept incoming calls, you can work around the problem by having your calls forwarded to another number, such as your work number or your home number. Here's how it's done:

1. **On the Home screen, tap Settings.** The Settings screen appears.

2. **Tap Phone.** The Phone screen appears.

3. **Tap Call Forwarding.** The Call Forwarding screen appears.

4. **Tap the Call Forwarding On/Off button to change this setting to On.** Your iPhone displays the Forwarding To screen.

5. **Tap the phone number to use for the forwarded calls.**

6. **Tap Call Forwarding to return to the Call Forwarding screen.** Figure 3.3 shows the Call Forwarding screen set up to forward calls. In the status bar at the top of the screen, note the little phone icon with an arrow that appears to the right of the time to let you know that call forwarding is on.

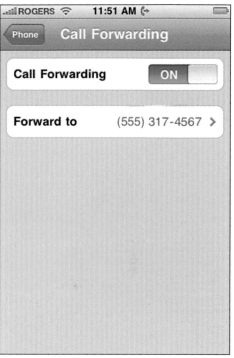

Juggling Multiple Calls and Conference Calls

We all juggle multiple tasks and duties these days, so it's not surprising that sometimes that involves juggling multiple phone calls:

3.3 Activate Call Forwarding to have your iPhone calls forwarded to another number.

- You might need to call two separate people on a related issue, and then switch back and forth between the callers as the negotiations (or whatever) progress.

- You might already be on a call and another call comes in from a person you need to speak to, so you put the initial person on hold, deal with the new caller, and then return to the first person.

- You might need to speak to two separate people at the same time on the same phone call — in other words, a conference call.

In the real world, juggling multiple calls and setting up conference calls often requires a special phone or a fancy phone system. In the iPhone world, however, these things are a snap. In fact, the way the iPhone juggles multiple calls really is something spectacular. Jumping back and forth between calls is simple; putting someone on hold to answer an incoming call is a piece of cake; and creating a conference call from incoming or outgoing calls is criminally easy.

When you're on an initial call, your iPhone displays the Call Options screen, as shown in Figure 3.4. To make another call, tap Add Call and then use the Phone app to place your second call.

Note

If you have an iPhone 4, you don't see the hold icon shown in Figure 3.4 unless you turn off the FaceTime video calling feature. To do that, return to the home screen, tap Settings, tap Phone, and then tap the FaceTime switch to Off.

Once the second call goes through, the Call Options screen changes: The top of the screen shows the first caller's name or number, with HOLD beside it, and below that you see the name or number of the second call and the duration of that call. Figure 3.5 shows the new screen layout. To switch to the person on hold, tap the Swap button. iPhone puts the second caller on hold and returns you to the first caller. Congratulations: You now have two calls going at once!

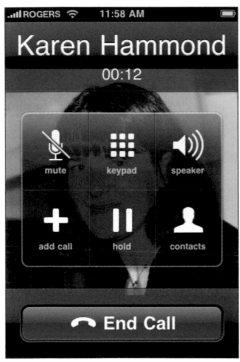

3.4 When you're on a call, your iPhone displays these call options.

3.5 The iPhone Call Options screen with two phone calls on the go.

If you're already on the phone and another call comes in, your iPhone displays the number (and the name, if the caller is in your Contacts list), and gives you three ways to handle the call (see Figure 3.6):

- **Ignore.** Tap this option to send the incoming call directly to voicemail.

- **Hold Call + Answer.** Tap this option to put the first call on hold and answer the incoming call. You're working with two calls again in this scenario, so you can tap Swap to switch between the callers.

- **End Call + Answer.** Tap this option to drop the first call and answer the incoming call.

If you have two calls on the go, you might prefer that all three of you be able to talk to each other in a conference call. Easier done than said: tap the Merge option and iPhone combines everyone into a single conference call and displays Conference at the top of the Call Options screen. Click the More Info arrow and iPhone displays the participants' names or numbers in the Conference screen, as shown in Figure 3.7.

From here, there are a few methods you can use to manage your conference call:

- To speak with one of the callers privately, tap the green Private key next to that person's name or number you want to talk with. This places you in a one-on-one call with that person and places the other caller on hold.

- To drop someone from the conference call, tap the red phone icon to the left of the person's name or number, and then tap End Call to confirm. iPhone drops the caller and you resume a private call with the other caller.

3.6 The iPhone displays this screen if a call comes in while you are on another call.

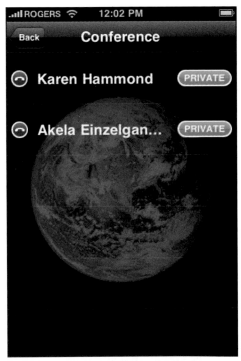

3.7 When you merge two phone calls, the participants' names or numbers appear in the Conference screen.

- To add someone else to the conference call, tap Back to return to the Call Options screen, tap Add Call, and then make the call. Once the call goes through, tap Merge Calls.

- To add an incoming caller to the conference call, tap Hold Call + Answer. Once you're connected, tap Merge Calls.

Clearly, juggling multiple calls on a phone has never been easier. The iPhone does a remarkable job of organizing the calls and giving you an admirably easy process to follow to swap calls, add or drop calls, and combine calls in conference.

Caution

You can hold a conference call with up to five people at once by repeating the steps outlined for conference calls. However, remember, conference calls use up your minutes faster — two callers use them up twice as fast, three callers use them up three times as fast, and so on — so you may want to be judicious when using this feature.

Using Other iPhone Features While On a Call

We live in a multitasking age, and your iPhone can multitask with the best of them. For example, suppose you're on a call and the other person needs someone's phone number or e-mail address. No sweat: with your iPhone, you can switch to the Contacts list, get the info you seek, and recite it to your caller, all without interrupting the call. In fact, you can switch to any iPhone app during the call: you can look up information on the Web using Safari; set up an appointment; look up a map location; send an e-mail; check your text messages; even crank up a tune using the iPod!

Here are the steps to follow:

1. **Initiate the phone call.**

2. **Tap the Speaker icon.** This ensures that you can still converse with the caller while using the other app.

3. **When you need to use a different app, press the Home button.** iPhone displays the Home screen, but you remain connected to the caller. iPhone displays a bar across the top of the screen (below the status bar) that says Touch to return to call, as shown in Figure 3.8.

4. **Tap the icon of the app you want to use.**

5. **When you complete your chores in the app, tap the Touch to return to call bar.** iPhone returns you to the Call Options screen.

6. **Tap the Speaker icon to turn it off and then continue with the call.**

Managing Your Favorites List

The iPhone's Favorites list is great for making quick calls because you can often get someone on the horn in just two finger gestures (double-click the Home button and then tap the number). Of course, this only works if the numbers you call most often appear on your Favorites list. Fortunately, your iPhone gives you lots of different ways to populate the list. Here are the easiest methods to use:

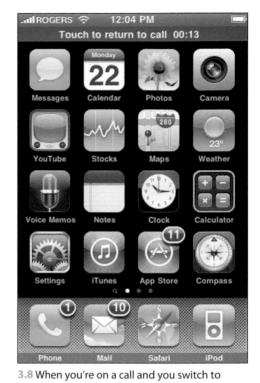

3.8 When you're on a call and you switch to another app, you see "Touch to return to call" below the status bar.

- In the Favorites list, tap + to open the All Contacts screen and then tap the person you want to add. If that person has multiple phone numbers, tap the number you want to use as a favorite.

Note

This is a good place to remind you that the Favorites list isn't a list of people, it's a list of *numbers*. That's why the list shows both the person's name and the type of phone number (work, home, mobile, and so on).

- In the Recent Calls list, tap the More Info icon to the right of the call from (or to) the person you want to add and then tap Add to Favorites. If the person has multiple phone numbers, tap the number you want to use as the favorite. iPhone adds a star beside the phone number to remind you that it's a favorite.

- In Visual Voicemail, tap the More Info icon beside a message and then tap Add to Favorites.

◉ In the Contacts list, tap the person you want to add and then tap Add to Favorites. If the person has multiple phone numbers, tap the number you want to use as the favorite. iPhone adds a star beside the phone number to remind you that it's a favorite.

You can add up to 20 numbers in the Favorites list, but the iPhone screen only shows eight numbers at a time. This means that if you want to call someone who doesn't appear in the initial screen, then you need to scroll down to bring that number into view. Therefore, your Favorites list is most efficient when the people you call most often appear in the first eight numbers. Your iPhone adds each new number to the bottom of the Favorites list, so chances are that at least some of your favorite numbers aren't showing up in the top eight. Follow these steps to fix that:

1. **In the Favorites list, tap Edit.** iPhone displays delete icons to the left of each favorite and drag icons to the right, as shown in Figure 3.9.

2. **If you want to get rid of a favorite, tap its Delete icon, tap Remove, and then tap Edit to return to Edit mode.**

3. **To move a favorite to a new location, tap and drag the icon up or down until the favorite is where you want it, and then release the icon.**

4. **Click Done.**

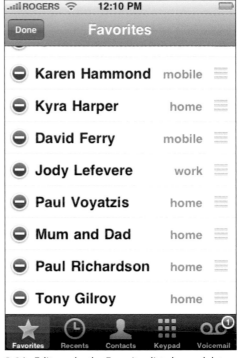

3.9 In Edit mode, the Favorites list shows delete icons on the left and drag icons on the right.

Working with Contacts from the Phone App

As you learn later in this book, you can enter all your contacts into your iPhone — either by syncing with your computer or by adding them on the fly. You do all that using your iPhone's Contacts app, but the Phone app also has a couple of useful tricks you can use. You can convert a phone number into a contact and even assign specific ringtones to various contacts.

Converting a phone number into a contact

Your iPhone is at its most efficient when the numbers you call are part of your Contacts list, because not only can you add contacts to the Favorites list for quick, speed-dial-like access, but also because you can use the index (the letters A, B, C, and so on that run down the right side of the Contacts list) and a few finger flicks to rapidly find and tap the person you want to chinwag with.

I talk about ways to add contacts in Chapter 9. For now, here's a quick way to add a contact right from your iPhone's phone keypad:

1. **In the Home screen, tap Phone.** The Phone app appears.

2. **In the menu bar, tap Keypad.** The Keypad screen appears.

3. **Type the phone number of a person you want to add as a contact.**

4. **Tap the Add Contact icon, to the left of the Call button, as shown in Figure 3.10.**

5. **Tap Create New Contact.** The New Contact screen appears.

6. **Fill in the other contact info as needed.**

7. **Tap Save.** Your iPhone adds the new contact and returns you to the Keypad screen.

8. **Tap Call to proceed with the phone call.**

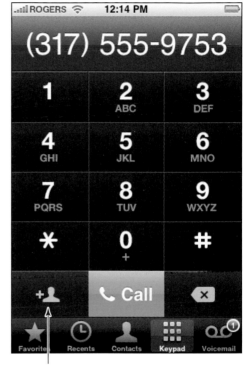

Add Contact

3.10 After you enter a phone number using the Keypad, tap the Add Contact icon to create a contact for the number.

Note

The phone number you're dialing might be an alternative number of an existing contact. For example, you may already have set up the contact with a home number, but now you're dialing that person's cell number. In that case, tap the Add Contact icon and then tap Add to Existing Contact. Use the Contacts list to tap the contact, choose the phone type (such as mobile), and then tap Save.

Genius You can also convert a phone number on your Recent Calls list to a contact. On the Home screen, tap Phone, and then tap Recents to open the Recent Calls list. Locate the name or phone number you want to convert to a contact and then tap the blue More Info arrow. Tap Create New Contact, fill in the other contact info, and then tap Save.

Assigning a ringtone to a contact

Your iPhone has a default ringtone that it plays whenever a call comes in. You grab your phone, check the name (if the person's in your Contacts list) or the number, and then decide whether to answer or let the call go to voicemail. However, what if you're busy or concentrating on something and you'd prefer not to break off just to check the incoming call? Wouldn't it be nice to *know* whether the call is important?

Your iPhone smartphone isn't quite smart enough to know that, but you can help it along by assigning different ringtones to different contacts. There are a couple of ringtone routes you can take:

- **You can assign a different ringtone to each of the people who call you most often.** That way, you can know exactly who's calling you just by hearing the ringtone.

- **You can assign a single different ringtone to all of the people who you consider important.** That way, when you hear that ringtone, you know that it's okay to interrupt whatever you're doing; if you hear the regular ringtone, just keep working (or whatever).

Here are the steps to follow to assign a ringtone to a contact:

1. **On the Home screen, tap Contacts.** Alternatively, if you're currently in the Phone app, tap Contacts in the menu bar.

2. **Tap the contact you want to work with.** The contact's Info screen appears.

3. **Tap the Ringtone setting.** The iPhone displays the Ringtones screen.

4. **Tap the ringtone you want to use.** iPhone plays a preview. If that's not the tone you want, tap another until you find the right one.

5. **Tap Info.** iPhone returns you to the contact's Info screen with the new ringtone selected.

Video Calling with FaceTime

iOS 4.0 One of the welcome new features in the iPhone 4 is a front-mounted camera, which means you can finally take pictures of yourself without guessing where the shutter button is! Fortunately, that's not all the front camera is good for. With Apple's new FaceTime feature, you can use your iPhone 4 to make video calls where you can actually see the other person face-to-face. It's an awesome new feature, but the first version of the software does have a couple of restrictions:

- The other person must also be using an iPhone 4.
- Both of you must be on a Wi-Fi connection.

The good news about FaceTime (besides how cool it is), is that it's a complete no-brainer to use. You don't have to activate any options, configure any settings, download any software, or connect to any servers.

To initiate a FaceTime call, you have three choices:

- Call the other person normally, and once you're connected, tap the FaceTime icon, shown in Figure 3.11.
- If the other person is in your Contacts list, open the contact and tap the FaceTime button, shown in Figure 3.12.
- If you've recently made a FaceTime call to someone, tap the Phone app's Recents icon, and then tap the FaceTime call (which the Phone app indicates with a FaceTime icon).

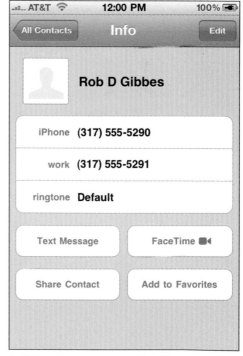

3.11 To convert the current call to a FaceTime video call, tap the FaceTime icon.

3.12 To call a contact using FaceTime, open the contact and tap the FaceTime button.

If an iPhone 4 user on a Wi-Fi connection calls you (and you're on a Wi-Fi connection yourself), you see the message "*Name* would like FaceTime" (where *Name* is the caller's name, if he or she is in your Contacts list), as shown in Figure 3.13. Tap Accept and your video call connects, just like that. You see your caller's (hopefully) smiling face in the full iPhone screen, and your own mug in a picture-in-picture (PIP) window, as shown in Figure 3.14.

Genius

Your PIP window shows up by default in the upper right corner. If you prefer a different position, tap and drag the PIP window to any corner of the screen.

The FaceTime calling screen includes three buttons in the menu bar:

- **Mute.** Tap this icon (it's the one on the left) to mute the sound from your end of the conversation (you can still hear sound from the other person's end).

3.13 When a Wi-Fi-connected iPhone 4 user calls you, tap Accept to initiate a FaceTime video call.

3.14 Face-to-face calling on the iPhone 4: The future is finally here!

Caution

Mute is the FaceTime equivalent of hold. Note, however, that there's no way to put a FaceTime caller on hold while you answer another call. If a new call comes in while you're on FaceTime and you accept the call, your iPhone disconnects the FaceTime call.

- **End.** Tap this button (it's the one in the middle) to end the call.
- **Switch cameras.** Tap this button to switch your video output to the rear camera (for example, to show your caller something in front of you).

How Can I Make the Most of Web Surfing with My iPhone?

One of the most popular modern pastimes is Web surfing, and now you can surf sites even when you're out and about thanks to your iPhone's large screen and support for speedy networks such as 3G and Wi-Fi. You perform theƏse surfin' safaris using, appropriately enough, the Mobile Safari Web browser. This is a trimmed-down version of Safari, one of the world's best browsers, and out of the box it's easy to use and intuitive. However, Mobile Safari offers quite a few options and features, many of which are hidden in obscure nooks and crannies of the iPhone interface. If you think your surfing activities could be faster, more efficient, more productive, or more secure, this chapter shows you a bunch of techniques that can help.

Touchscreen Tips for Web Sites

The touchscreen operates much the same way in Safari as it does in the other iPhone apps. You can use the touchscreen to scroll pages, zoom in and out, click links, fill in forms, enter addresses, and more. The screen is remarkably fluid in its motion and its response to your touch is neither hyperactive nor sluggish. It actually makes surfing the Web a pleasure, which isn't something you can say about most smartphones.

To make it even more pleasurable, here's a little collection of touchscreen tips that ought to make your Web excursions even easier:

- **Precision zooming.** Zooming on the iPhone is straightforward: to zoom in, spread two fingers apart; to zoom out, pinch two fingers together. However, when you zoom in on a Web page, it's almost always because you want to zoom in on something. It might be an image, a link, a text box, or just a section of text. To ensure that your target ends up in the middle of the zoomed page, pinch your thumb and forefinger together on the screen as if you are pinching the target you want to zoom in on. Spread your thumb and forefinger apart to zoom in.

- **The old pan-and-zoom.** Another useful technique for getting a target in the middle of a zoomed page is to zoom and pan at the same time. That is, as you spread (or pinch) your fingers, you also move them up, down, left, or right to pan the page at the same time. This takes a bit of practice, and often the iPhone only allows you to pan either horizontally or vertically (not both), but it's still a useful trick.

- **Double-tap.** A quick way to zoom in on a page that has various sections is to double-tap on the specific section — it could be an image, a paragraph, a table, or a column of text — that you want magnified. Your iPhone zooms the section to fill the width of the screen. Double-tap again to return the page to the regular view.

Note

The double-tap-to-zoom trick only works on pages that have identifiable sections. If a page is just a wall of text, you can double-tap until the cows come home (that's a long time) and nothing much happens.

- **One tap to the top.** If you're reading a particularly long-winded Web page and you're near the bottom, you may have quite a long way to scroll if you need to head back to the top to get at the address bar or tap the Search icon. Save the wear and tear on your flicking finger! Instead, tap the status bar; Safari immediately transports you to the top of the page.

Tap and hold to see where a link takes you. You "click" a link in a Web page by tapping it with your finger. In a regular Web browser, you can see where a link takes you by hovering the mouse pointer over the link and checking out the link address in the status bar. That doesn't work in your iPhone, of course, but you can still find out the address of a link before tapping it. Hold your finger on the link for a few seconds and Safari displays a pop-up screen that shows the link text and, more importantly, the link address, as shown in Figure 4.1. If the link looks legit, either tap Open to surf there in the current browser page, or tap Open in New Page to start a fresh page (see the section about opening and managing multiple browser pages later in this chapter for more info on browser pages); if you decide not to go there, click Cancel.

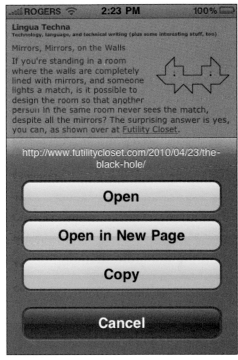

4.1 Hold your finger on a link to see the link address and several link options.

Tap and hold to make a copy of a link address. If you want to include a link address in another app, such as a note or an e-mail message, you can copy it. Tap and hold your finger on the link for a few seconds and Safari displays the pop-up screen shown in Figure 4.1. Tap Copy to place the link address into memory, switch to the other app, tap the cursor, and then tap Paste.

Use the portrait view to navigate a long page. When you rotate your iPhone 90 degrees, the touchscreen switches to landscape view, which gives you a wider view of the page. Return the iPhone to its upright position, and you return to portrait view. If you have a long way to scroll in a page, first use the portrait view to scroll down then switch to the landscape view to increase the text size. I find that scrolling in the portrait view goes much faster than in landscape.

Two-fingered frame scrolling. Some Web sites are organized using a technique called frames, where the overall site takes up the browser window, but some of the site's pages appear in a separate rectangular area — called a *frame* — usually with its own scroll bar. In such sites, you may find that the usual one-fingered scroll technique only scrolls the entire browser window, not the content within the frame. To scroll the frame stuff, you must use two fingers to do the scrolling. Weird!

- **Getting a larger keyboard.** The on-screen keyboard appears when you tap into a box that allows typing. However, the keyboard you get in landscape view uses noticeably larger keys than the one you see in portrait view. For the fumble-fingered among us, larger keys are a must, so always rotate the iPhone into landscape mode to enter text.

- **Quick access to common top-level domains.** A top-level domain (TLD) is the part of the domain name that comes after the last dot. For example, in wiley.com, the .com part is the TLD. The most common TLD is com, so your iPhone thoughtfully includes a .com key on the Safari keyboard. The next most common TLDs are net, edu, and org, and if you regularly use any of those, you might think you have to type them out the old-fashioned way. Nope! Tap and hold the .com key, and after a second or two, you see a pop-up that includes keys for: .net, .edu, and .org, another key for .us, and the usual .com key. Just tap the one you want.

Note

Remember that rotating the iPhone only changes the view if your iPhone is upright. The iPhone uses gravity to sense the change in orientation, so if it's lying flat on a table, rotating the iPhone won't do anything. So rotate it first before you put it on the table.

Filling in Online Forms

Many Web pages include forms where you fill in some data and then submit the form, which sends the data off to some server for processing. Filling in these forms in your iPhone's Safari browser is mostly straightforward:

- **Text box.** Tap inside the text box to display the touchscreen keyboard, tap out your text, and then tap Done.

- **Text area.** Tap inside the text area, and then use the keyboard to tap your text. Most text areas allow multiline entries, so you can tap Return to start a new line. When you finish, tap Done.

- **Check box.** Tap the check box to toggle the check mark on and off.

- **Radio button.** Tap a radio button to activate it.

- **Command button.** Tap the button to make it do its thing (usually submit the form).

Many online forms consist of a bunch of text boxes or text areas. If the idea of performing the tap-type-Done cycle over and over isn't appealing to you, fear not. Your iPhone's Safari browser offers an easier method:

1. **Tap inside the first text box or text area.** The keyboard appears.

2. **Tap to type the text you want to enter.** Above the keyboard, notice the Previous and Next buttons, as shown in Figure 4.2.

3. **Tap Next to move to the next text box or text area.** If you need to return to a text box, tap Previous instead.

4. **Repeat steps 2 and 3 to fill in the text boxes.**

5. **Tap Done.** Safari returns you to the page.

I haven't yet talked about selection lists, and that's because your iPhone's browser handles them in an interesting way. When you tap a list, Safari displays the list items in a separate box, as shown in Figure 4.3. Tap the item you want to select. As with text boxes and text areas, if the form has multiple lists, you see the Previous and Next buttons, which you can tap to navigate from one list to another. After you make all your selections, tap Done to return to the page.

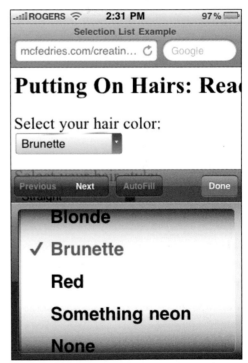

4.2 If the form contains multiple text boxes or text areas, you can use the Previous and Next buttons to navigate them.

4.3 Tap a list to see its items in a separate box for easier selecting.

Turning on AutoFill for faster forms

The iPhone's Safari browser makes it relatively easy to fill in online forms, but it can still be slow going, particularly if you have to do lots of text box or text area typing. To help make forms less of a chore, Safari supports a welcome feature called AutoFill. Just as with the desktop version of Safari (or just about any other mainstream browser), AutoFill remembers the data you enter into forms and then enables you to fill in similar forms with a simple tap of a button. You can also configure AutoFill to remember usernames and passwords.

To take advantage of this nifty feature, you first have to turn it on by following these steps:

1. **In the Home screen, tap Settings.** Your iPhone opens the Settings screen.

2. **Tap Safari.** The Safari screen appears.

3. **Tap AutoFill to open the AutoFill screen.**

4. **Tap the Use Contact Info switch to the On position.** This tells Safari to use your item in the Contacts app to grab data for a form. For example, if a form requires your name, Safari uses your contact name.

5. **The My Info field should show your name, but if it doesn't tap the field and then tap your item in the Contacts list.**

6. **If you want Safari to remember the usernames and passwords you use to log in to sites, tap the Names and Passwords switch to the On position.** A completed AutoFill screen appears in Figure 4.4.

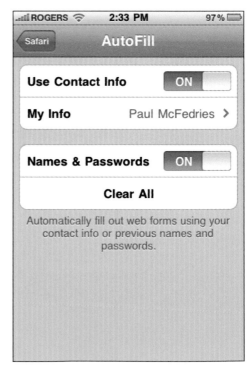

Now when you visit an online form, and access any text field in the form, the AutoFill button becomes enabled. Tap AutoFill to fill in those portions of the form that correspond to your contact data, as shown in Figure 4.5. Notice that the fields Safari was able to automatically fill in display with a colored background.

4.4 Fill in the AutoFill screen to make online forms less of a chore.

Saving Web site login passwords

If you enabled the Names & Passwords option in the AutoFill screen, each time you fill in a username and password to log in to a site, Safari displays the dialog shown in Figure 4.6 that asks if you want to remember the login data, and it gives you three choices:

- **Yes.** Tap this button to have Safari remember your username and password.

- **Never for this Website.** Tap this button to tell Safari not to remember the username and password, and to never again prompt you to save the login data.

- **Not Now.** Tap this button to tell Safari not to remember the username and password this time, but to prompt you again next time you log in to this site.

4.5 Tap the AutoFill button to fill in form fields with your contact data.

4.6 If you configured Safari to remember usernames and passwords, you see this dialog when you log in to a site.

Note

Your iPhone is cautious about this password stuff, so it doesn't offer to save *all* the passwords you enter. In particular, if the login form is part of a secure site, then your iPhone doesn't ask if you want to save the password. This means you won't be tempted to store the password for your online bank, corporate Web site, or any other site where you save your credit card data (such as Amazon and similar shopping sites).

Using Bookmarks for Faster Surfing

Although you've seen that your iPhone's Safari browser offers a few tricks to ease the pain of typing Web page addresses, it's still slower and quite a bit more cumbersome than a full-size, physical keyboard, which lets even inexpert typists rattle off addresses lickety-split. All the more reason that you should embrace bookmarks with all your heart. After all, a bookmark lets you jump to a Web page with precisely no typing; just a tap or three and you're there.

Adding bookmarks by hand

You probably want to get your iPhone bookmarks off to a flying start by copying a bunch of existing bookmarks from your Mac or Windows PC. That's a good idea, and I show you how to do that in Chapter 6.

But even if you've done the sync and now have a large collection of bookmarks at your beck and call, it doesn't mean your iPhone bookmark collection is complete. After all, you might find something interesting while you're surfing with the iPhone. If you think you'll want to pay that site another visit down the road, you can create a new bookmark right on the iPhone. Here are the steps to follow:

1. **On the iPhone, use Safari to navigate to the site you want to save.**

2. **Tap the + button in the menu bar.**

3. **Tap Add Bookmark.** This opens the Add Bookmark screen, as shown in Figure 4.7.

4.7 Use the Add Bookmark screen to specify the bookmark name and location.

4. **Tap into the top box and enter a name for the site that helps you remember it.** This name is what you see when you scroll through your bookmarks.

5. **Tap Bookmarks.** This displays a list of your bookmark folders.

6. **Tap the folder you want to use to store the bookmark.** Safari returns you to the Add Bookmark screen.

7. **Tap Save.** Safari saves the bookmark.

Note Syncing bookmarks is a two-way street, which means that any site you bookmark in your iPhone is added to your desktop Safari (or Internet Explorer) the next time you sync.

Getting Firefox bookmarks into your iPhone

iTunes bookmark syncing only works with Safari and Internet Explorer. So are you out of luck if your entire Web life is bookmarked in Firefox? Nope. Fortunately Firefox has a feature that lets you export your bookmarks to a file. You can then import those bookmarks to Safari or Internet Explorer, and then sync with your iPhone. It's a bit of a winding road, we know, but it's better than starting from scratch. Here are the details:

1. **Crank up Firefox and start the export procedure like so:**

   - **Firefox 3 (Mac).** Choose Bookmarks ⇨ Organize Bookmarks (or press Shift+⌘+B) to open the Library. Click the Import and Backup button, and then click Export HTML.

   - **Firefox 3 (Windows).** Choose Bookmarks ⇨ Organize Bookmarks (or press Ctrl+Shift+B) to open the Library. Click the Import and Backup button, and then click Export HTML.

   - **Firefox 2 (Windows).** Choose Bookmarks ⇨ Organize Bookmarks to open the Bookmarks Manager, and then choose File ⇨ Export.

2. **In the Export Bookmarks File dialog, choose a location for the file, and then click Save.** Firefox saves its bookmarks to a file named bookmarks.html.

3. **Import the Firefox bookmarks file to your browser of choice:**

   - **Safari.** Choose File ⇨ Import Bookmarks, locate and click the bookmarks.html file, and then click Import.

   - **Internet Explorer.** In versions 8 and 7, press Alt+Z and then click Import and Export; in version 6, choose File ⇨ Import and Export. In the Import/Export Wizard, click Next, click Import Favorites, and then follow the wizard's instructions to import the bookmarks.html file.

85

4. **Connect your iPhone to your computer.** iTunes opens, connects to the iPhone, and syncs the bookmarks, which now include your Firebox bookmarks.

Managing your bookmarks

Once you have a few bookmarks stashed away in the bookmarks list, you may need to perform a few housekeeping chores from time to time, including changing a bookmark's name, address, or folder; reordering bookmarks or folders; or getting rid of bookmarks that have worn out their welcome.

Before you can do any of this, you need to get the Bookmarks list into Edit mode by following these steps:

1. **In Safari, tap the Bookmarks icon in the menu bar (see Figure 4.8).** Safari opens the Bookmarks list.

2. **If the bookmark you want to mess with is located in a particular folder, tap to open that folder.** For example, if you've synced with Safari, then you should have a folder named Bookmarks Bar, which includes all the bookmarks and folders that you've added to the Bookmarks Bar in your desktop version of Safari.

3. **Tap Edit.** Your iPhone switches the Bookmarks list to Edit mode, as shown in Figure 4.9. With Edit mode on the go, you're free to toil away at your bookmarks. Here are the techniques to master:

   - **Edit bookmark info.** Tap the bookmark to fire up the Edit Bookmark screen. From here, you can edit the bookmark name, change the bookmark address, and change the bookmark folder. When you're done, tap the name of the current bookmark folder in the top-left corner of the screen.

Bookmark icon

4.8 Tap the Bookmarks icon to display the Bookmarks list.

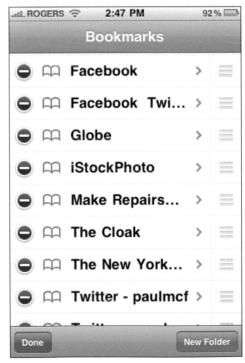

4.9 With the Bookmark list in Edit mode, you can edit, rearrange, and delete bookmarks to your heart's content.

- **Change the bookmark order.** Use the drag icon on the right to tap-and-drag a bookmark to a new position in the list. Ideally, you should move your favorite bookmarks near the top of the list for easiest access.

- **Add a bookmark folder.** Tap New Folder to launch the Edit Folder screen, then tap a folder title and select a location. Feel free to use bookmark folders at will because they're a great way to keep your bookmarks neat and tidy (if you're into that kind of thing).

- **Delete a bookmark.** No use for a particular bookmark? No problem. Tap the Delete icon to the left of the bookmark, and then tap the Delete button that appears.

When the dust settles and your bookmark chores are done for the day, tap Done to get out of Edit mode.

Retracing your steps with the handy History list

Bookmarking a Web site is a good idea if that site contains interesting or fun content that you want to revisit in the future. Sometimes, however, you may not realize that a site had useful data until a day or two later. Similarly, you might like a site's stuff, but decide against bookmarking it, only to regret that decision down the road. You could waste a big chunk of your day trying to track down the site, but then you may run into Murphy's Web Browsing Law: A cool site that you forget to bookmark is never found again.

Fortunately, your iPhone has your back. As you navigate the nooks and crannies of the Web, iPhone keeps track of where you go and stores the name and address of each page in the History list. The iPhone's limited memory means that it can't store tons of sites, but it might have what you're looking for. Here's how to use it:

1. **In Safari, tap the Bookmarks icon in the menu bar.** Safari opens the Bookmarks list.

2. **If you see the Bookmarks screen (shown earlier in Figure 4.8), skip to step 3.** Otherwise, tap the folder names that appear in the upper-left corner of the screen until you get to the Bookmarks screen.

3. **Tap History.** Safari opens the History screen, as shown in Figure 4.10. The screen shows the sites you've visited today at the top, followed by a list of previous surfing dates.

4. **If you visited the site you're looking for on a previous day, tap the day.** Safari displays a list of the sites you visited on that day.

5. **Tap the site you want to revisit.** Safari loads the site.

Maintaining your privacy by deleting the History list

Your iPhone's History list of sites you've recently surfed is a great feature when you need it, and it's an innocuous feature when you don't. However, there are times when the History list is just plain uncool. For example, suppose you shop online to get a nice gift for your spouse's birthday. If he or she also uses your iPhone, your surprise might get ruined if the purchase page accidentally shows up in the History list. Similarly, if you visit a private corporate site, a financial site, or any other site you wouldn't want others to see, the History list might betray you.

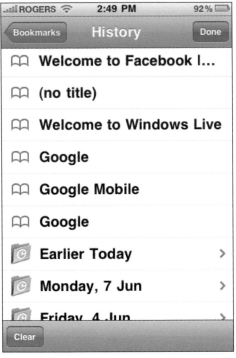

4.10 Safari stores your recent browsing past in the History list.

And sometimes unsavory sites can end up in your History list by accident. For example, you might tap a legitimate-looking link in a Web page or e-mail message, only to end up in some dark, dank Net neighborhood. Of course, you high-tailed it out of there right away with a quick tap of Safari's Back button, but that nasty site is now lurking in your History.

Whether you've got sites on the History list that you wouldn't want anyone to see, or if you just find the idea of your iPhone tracking your movements on the Web to be a bit sinister, follow these steps to wipe out the History list:

1. **In Safari, tap the Bookmarks icon in the menu bar.** Safari opens the Bookmarks list.

2. **Tap the folder names that appear in the upper-left corner of the screen until you get to the Bookmarks screen.**

3. **Tap History.** Safari opens the History screen.

4. **Tap Clear.** Safari prompts you to confirm.

5. **Tap Clear History.** Safari deletes every site from the History list.

Genius

Here's another way to clear the History, and it might be faster if you're not currently working in Safari. In the Home screen, tap Settings, tap Safari, and then tap Clear History. When your iPhone asks you to confirm, tap Clear History.

Getting Even More Out of Safari on Your iPhone

You've seen lots of great Safari tips and techniques so far in this chapter, but I hope you're up for even more, because you've got a ways to go. In the rest of this chapter, you learn such useful techniques as managing multiple pages, changing the default search engine, viewing RSS feeds, and configuring Safari's security options.

Opening and managing multiple browser pages

When you're perusing Web pages, what do you do when you're on a page that you want to keep reading, but you also need to leap over to another page for something? On your computer's Web browser, you probably open another tab, use that tab to open the other page, and then switch back to the first page when you finish. It's an essential Web browsing technique, but can it be done with your iPhone's Safari browser?

Well, Mobile Safari may not have tabs, but it has the next best thing: *pages*. With this feature, you can open a second browser "window" and load a different page into it, and then it's a quick tap and flick to switch between them. And you're not restricted to a meager two pages, no sir. Your iPhone lets you open up to eight — count 'em, *eight* — pages, so you can throw some wild Web page parties.

Here are the steps to follow to open and load multiple pages:

1. **In Safari, tap the Pages icon in the menu bar (see Figure 4.11).** Safari displays a thumbnail version of the current page.

2. **Tap New Page.** Safari opens a blank page using the full screen.

3. **Load a Web site into the new page.** You can do this by selecting a book-mark, entering an address, or whatever.

4. **Repeat steps 1 to 3 to load as many pages as you need.** As you add pages, Safari keeps track of how many are open and displays the number in the Pages icon, as shown in Figure 4.12.

Once you have two or more pages fired up, here are a couple of techniques you can use to impress your friends:

- **To switch to another page.** Tap the Pages icon to get to the thumbnail view (see Figure 4.13), flick right or left to bring the page into view, and then tap the page.

- **When you no longer need a page.** Tap the Pages icon, flick right or left to bring the page into view, and then tap the X in the upper-left corner. Safari trashes the page without a whimper of protest.

Pages icon

4.11 Tap the Pages icon to create a new page.

4.12 The Pages icon tells you how many pages you've got on the go.

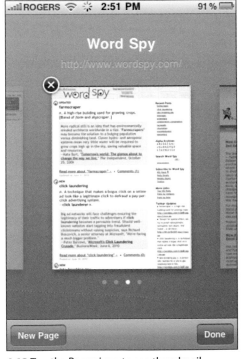

4.13 Tap the Pages icon to see thumbnail versions of your open pages.

Note

Some Web page links are configured to automatically open the page in a new window, so you might see a new page being created when you tap a link. Also, if you add a Web Clip to your Home screen (as described in Chapter 1), tapping the icon opens the Web Clip in a new Safari page.

Note

Below the page thumbnails you see several dots, one for each open page, with the current page shown as a white dot. Rather than flicking through the pages, tap to the right of the current dot to navigate to the next page, or tap to the left of the current dot to see the previous page.

Changing the default search engine

When you tap the Search icon at the top of the Safari screen, your iPhone loads the Address Bar screen and places the cursor inside the Search box so that you can enter your search text and then run the search. The button you tap to launch the search is named Google, which is appropriate as Google is the iPhone's default search engine. We all love Google, of course, but if you have something against it, for some reason, you can switch to using either Yahoo! or Bing as your search engine of choice. Here's how:

1. **In the Home screen, tap Settings.** Your iPhone opens the Settings screen.

2. **Tap Safari.** The Safari screen appears.

3. **Tap Search Engine.** Your iPhone opens the Search Engine screen.

4. **Tap the search engine you want to use.** You have three choices: Google, Yahoo!, or Bing.

Viewing an RSS feed

Some Web sites remain relatively static over time, so you only need to check in every once in a while to see if anything's new. Other sites change content regularly, such as once a day or once a week, so you know in advance when to check for new material. However, there are the more verbose sites — particularly blogs — where the content changes frequently, although not regularly. For these sites, keeping up with new content can be time consuming, and it's criminally easy to miss new information. (Murphy's Blog Reading Law: You always miss the post that everyone's talking about.)

To solve this problem, tons of Web sites now maintain RSS feeds (RSS stands for Real Simple Syndication). A *feed* is a special file that contains the most recent information added to the site. The bad news is that your iPhone's Safari browser doesn't give you any way to subscribe to a site's feed like you can with desktop Safari or Internet Explorer. The good news is that your iPhone can use a Web-based RSS reader app (http://reader.mac.com/) that can interpret a site's RSS feed and display the feed in the comfy confines of SafariHere's how it works:

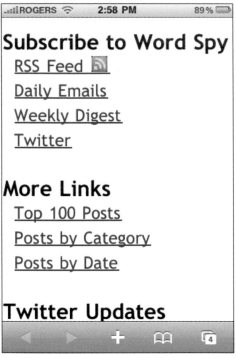

1. **In Safari, navigate to a Web page that you know has an RSS feed.**

2. **Pan and zoom the page until you find the link to the RSS feed.** The link is often accompanied by (or consists entirely of) an icon that identifies it as leading to a feed. Look for an XML icon, an RSS icon, or an orange feed icon, as shown in Figure 4.14.

3. **Tap the link.** Safari loads the RSS file into the reader.mac.com feed reader app, as shown in Figure 4.15.

4.14 Most feed links are identified by a standard feed icon.

Note

Like other links, such as Web pages, you can bookmark RSS feed links and save them to the home screen.

Dialing a phone number from a Web page

Your iPhone's membership in the smartphone club is fully confirmed with this next feature. A common chore when you're surfing business or retail sites is to hunt down a phone number for a person, a department, customer service, technical support, or whatever. In a regular browser, you note the phone number, head for the nearest phone, and then dial. Hah, the iPhone laughs at all that extra work! Why? Because when its Safari browser comes upon a phone number in a Web page, Safari conveniently converts that number into a link, as shown in Figure 4.16. Tap the number, tap Call in the dialog that pops up, and you're immediately switched to the Phone app, which dials the number for you. Sweet!

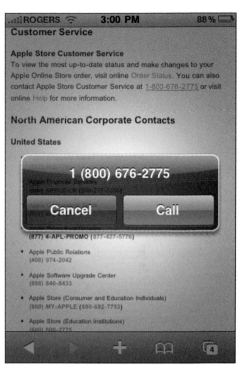

4.15 When you tap an RSS feed link, Safari loads the RSS file into the reader.mac.com feed reader app.

4.16 Your iPhone smartly converts a Web page phone number into a link that you can tap to call the number.

Setting the Web browser security options

It's a jungle out there in cyberspace, with nasty things lurking in the digital weeds. The folks at Apple are well aware of these dangers, of course, so they've clothed your iPhone in protective gear to help keep the bad guys at bay. Safari, in particular, has four layers of security:

- **Phishing protection.** A *phishing* site is a Web site that on the surface appears to belong to a reputable company, such as an online bank or major corporation. In reality, some dark-side hackers have cobbled the site together to fool you into providing your precious login data, credit card data, social security number, or other private information. Many of these sites either are well-known or sport tell-tale signs that mark them as fraudulent. The Safari app comes with a Fraud Warning setting that, when activated, displays a warning about such sites.

- **JavaScript.** This is a programming language that Web site developers commonly use to add features to their pages. However, programmers who have succumbed to the dark side of The Force can use JavaScript for nefarious ends. Your iPhone comes with JavaScript support turned on, but you can turn it off if you're heading into an area of the Web where you don't feel safe. However, many sites won't work without JavaScript, so we don't recommend turning it off full time.

- **Pop-up blocking.** Pop-up ads (and their sneakier cousins, the pop-under ads) are annoying at the best of times, but they really get in the way on the iPhone because the pop-up not only creates a new Safari page, but it immediately switches to that page. So now you have to tap the Pages icon, delete the pop-up page, and then (if you already had two or more pages running) tap the page that generated the pop-up. Boo! So you can thank your preferred deity that not only does your iPhone come with a pop-up blocker that stops these pop-up pests, but it's turned on by default, to boot. However, there are sites that use pop-ups for legitimate reasons: media players, login pages, important site announcements, and so on. For those sites to work properly you may need to turn off the pop-up blocker temporarily.

- **Cookies.** These are small text files that many sites store on the iPhone, and they use those files to store information about your browsing session. The most common example is a shopping cart, where your selections and amounts are stored in a cookie. However, for every benign cookie there's at least one not-so-nice cookie used by a third-party advertiser to track your movements and display ads supposedly targeted to your tastes. Yuck. By default, your iPhone doesn't accept third-party cookies, so that's a good thing. However, you can configure Safari to accept every cookie that comes its way or no cookies at all (neither of which I recommend).

Follow these steps to customize your iPhone's Web security options:

1. **In the Home screen, tap Settings.** The Settings screen slides in.
2. **Tap Safari.** Your iPhone displays the Safari screen, as shown in Figure 4.17.
3. **Tap the Fraud Warning setting to toggle phishing protection On and Off.**
4. **Tap the JavaScript setting to toggle JavaScript support On and Off.**

5. **Tap the Block Pop-ups setting to toggle pop-up blocking On and Off.**

6. **To configure the cookies that Safari allows, tap Accept Cookies, tap the setting you want — None, From visited, or Always — and then tap Safari.** The From visited setting (the default) means that Safari only accepts cookies directly from the sites you surf to; it spits out any cookies from third-party sites such as advertisers.

7. **If you want to get rid of all the cookies that have been stored on your iPhone, tap Clear Cookies and, when you're asked to confirm, tap Clear Cookies.** It's a good idea to clear cookies if you're having trouble accessing a site or if you suspect some unwanted cookies have been stored on your iPhone (for example, if you surfed for a while with Accept Cookies set to Always.)

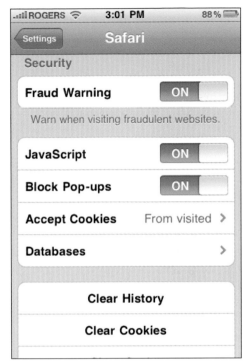

4.17 Use the Safari screen to set your iPhone's Web security settings.

How Do I Maximize
E-mail on My iPhone?

E-mail has been called the "killer app" of the Internet, and it certainly deserves that title. Yes, chat and instant messaging are popular; social networks such as Facebook, Twitter, and LinkedIn get lots of press; and blogging sites appeal to a certain type of person. However, while not everyone uses these services, it's safe to say that almost *everyone* uses e-mail. You probably use e-mail all day, particularly when you're on the go with your iPhone in tow, so learning a few useful and efficient e-mail techniques can make your day a bit easier and save you time for more important pursuits.

Managing Your iPhone E-mail Accounts

Your iPhone comes with the Mail app, which is a radically slimmed-down version of the Mail application that's the default e-mail program on Mac machines. Mail in iPhone may be a pale shadow of its OS X cousin, but that doesn't mean it's a lightweight, far from it. It has a few features and settings that make it ideal for your traveling e-mail show. First, however, you've got to set up your iPhone with one or more e-mail accounts.

Adding an account by hand

The Mail application on your iPhone is most useful when it's set up to use an e-mail account that you also use on your computer. That way, when you're on the road or out on the town, you can check your messages and rest assured that you won't miss anything important (or even anything unimportant, for that matter). This is most easily done by syncing an existing e-mail account between your computer and your iPhone, and I show you how that's done in Chapter 6.

Caution For some accounts, you need to be careful that your iPhone doesn't delete incoming messages from the server before you have a chance to download them to your computer. I show you how to set this up later in this chapter.

However, you might also prefer to have an e-mail account that's iPhone-only. For example, if you join an iPhone mailing list, you might prefer to have those message sent to just your iPhone. That's a darn good idea, but it means that you have to set up the account on the iPhone itself, which, as you soon see, requires a fair amount of tapping.

Genius You might think you can avoid the often excessive tapping required to enter a new e-mail account into your iPhone by creating the account in your computer's e-mail program and then syncing with your iPhone. That works, but there's a hitch: You *must* leave the new account in your e-mail program. If you delete it or disable it, iTunes also deletes the account from the iPhone.

How you create an account on your iPhone with the sweat of your own brow depends on the type of account you have. First, there are the five e-mail services that your iPhone recognizes:

- **Microsoft Exchange.** Your iPhone supports accounts on Exchange servers, which are common in large organizations like corporations or schools. Exchange uses a central server to store messages, and you usually work with your messages on the server, not your iPhone. However, one of the great new features in the iPhone is support for Exchange ActiveSync, which automatically keeps your phone and your account on the server synchronized. I discuss the ActiveSync settings later in this chapter.

⬤ **MobileMe.** This is Apple's replacement for its venerable .Mac online service. I give you the details in Chapter 12.

⬤ **Google Gmail.** This is a Web-based e-mail service run by Google.

⬤ **Yahoo! Mail.** This is a Web-based e-mail service run by Yahoo!.

⬤ **AOL.** This is a Web-based e-mail service run by AOL.

Your iPhone knows how to connect with these services, so to set up any of these e-mail accounts you only need to know the address and the account password.

Otherwise, your iPhone Mail app supports the following e-mail account types:

⬤ **POP.** Short for Post Office Protocol, this is the most popular type of account. Its main characteristic for our purposes is that incoming messages are only stored temporarily on the provider's mail server. When you connect to the server, the messages are downloaded to iPhone and removed from the server. In other words, your messages (including copies of messages you send) are stored locally on your iPhone. The advantage here is that you don't need to be online to read your e-mail. Once it's downloaded to your iPhone, you can read it or delete it at your leisure.

⬤ **IMAP.** Short for Internet Message Access Protocol, this type of account is most often used with Web-based e-mail services. It's the opposite of POP (sort of) because all your incoming messages, as well as copies of messages you send, remain on the server. In this case, when Mail works with an IMAP account, it connects to the server and works with the messages on the server itself, not on your iPhone (although it *looks* like you're working with the messages locally). The advantage here is that you can access the messages from multiple devices and multiple locations, but you must be connected to the Internet to work with your messages.

Your network administrator or your e-mail service provider can let you know what type of e-mail account you have. Your administrator or provider can also give you the information you need to set up the account. This includes your e-mail address; the username and password you use to check for new messages (and perhaps also the security information you need to specify to send messages); the host name of the incoming mail server (typically something like mail.*provider*.com, where *provider*.com is the domain name of the provider); and the host name of the outgoing mail server (typically either mail.*provider*.com or smtp.*provider*.com).

With your account information at the ready, follow these steps to forge a brand-new account:

1. **On the Home screen, tap Settings.** Your iPhone opens the Settings screen.

2. **Tap Mail, Contacts, Calendars.** The Mail, Contacts, Calendars screen appears.

3. **Tap Add Account.** This opens the Add Account screen, as shown in Figure 5.1.

4. **You have two ways to proceed:**

   - If you're adding an account for Microsoft Exchange, MobileMe, Google Gmail, Yahoo! Mail, or AOL, tap the corresponding logo. In the account information screen that appears, enter your name, e-mail address, password, and an account description. Tap Save and you're done!

   - If you're adding another account type, tap Other and continue with step 5.

5. **Tap Add Mail Account to open the New Account screen.**

6. **Use the Name, Address, and Description text boxes to enter the corresponding account information, and then tap Next.**

5.1 Use the Add Account screen to choose the type of e-mail account you want to add.

7. **Tap the type of account you're adding: IMAP or POP.**

8. **In the Incoming Mail Server section, use the Host Name text box to enter the host name of your provider's incoming mail server, as well as your username and password.**

9. **In the Outgoing Mail Server (SMTP) section, use the Host Name text box to enter the host name of your provider's outgoing (SMTP) mail server.** If your provider requires a username and password to send messages, enter those as well.

10. **Tap Save.** Your iPhone verifies the account info and then returns you to the Mail settings screen with the account added to the Accounts list.

Specifying the default account

If you've added two or more e-mail accounts to your iPhone, Mail specifies one of them as the default account. This means that Mail uses this account when you send a new message, when you reply to a message, and when you forward a message. The default account is usually the first account you add to your iPhone. However, you can change this by following these steps:

1. **On the Home screen, tap Settings.** The Settings screen appears.

2. **Tap Mail, Contacts, Calendars.** Your iPhone displays the Mail, Contacts, Calendars screen.

3. **At the bottom of the Mail section, tap Default Account.** This opens the Default Account screen, which displays a list of your accounts. The current default account is shown with a check mark beside it, as shown in Figure 5.2.

4. **Tap the account you want to use as the default.** Your iPhone places a check mark beside the account.

5. **Tap Mail to return to the Mail settings screen.**

5.2 Use the Default Account screen to set the default account that you want Mail to use when sending messages.

Switching to another account

When you open the Mail app — in your iPhone's Home screen, tap Mail in the menu bar — you usually see the Inbox folder of your default account. If you have multiple accounts set up on your iPhone and you want to see what's going on with a different account, follow these steps to make the switch:

1. **On the Home screen, tap Mail to open the Mail app.**

2. **Tap the account button that appears in the top-left corner of the screen (but below the status bar).** The Mailboxes screen appears, as shown in Figure 5.3.

3. **Tap the account you want to work with:**

   - If you only want to see the account's Inbox folder, tap the account name in the Inboxes section of the Mailboxes screen.

   - If you want to see all the account's available folders, tap the account name in the Accounts section of the Mailboxes screen. Mail displays a list of the account's folders, and you then tap the folder you want to work with.

Temporarily disabling an account

The Mail app checks for new messages at a regular interval. (I show you how to configure this interval a bit later in this chapter.) If you have several accounts configured in Mail, this incessant checking can put quite a strain on your iPhone battery. To ease up on the juice, you can disable an account temporarily to prevent Mail from checking it for new messages. Here's how:

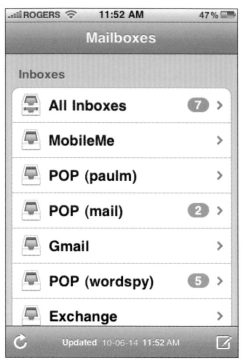

5.3 Use the Accounts screen to choose the e-mail account you want to play with.

1. **On the Home screen, tap Settings.** Your iPhone displays the Settings screen.

2. **Tap Mail, Contacts, Calendars to see the Mail settings.**

3. **Tap the account you want to disable.** Your iPhone displays the account's settings.

4. **Depending on the type of account, use one of the following techniques to temporarily disable the acocunt:**

   - **For a MobileMe, Exchange, Gmail, Yahoo!, or AOL account, tap the Mail switch to Off, as shown in Figure 5.4.** If the account syncs other type of data, such as contacts and calendars, you can also turn off those switches, If you want.

   - **For a POP or IMAP account, tap the Account switch to Off.**

When you're ready to work with the account again, repeat these steps to turn the Account switch back to On.

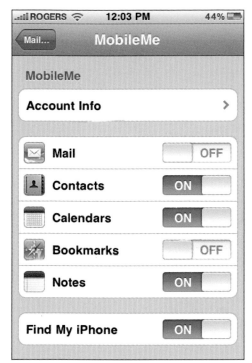

5.4 For a MobileMe, Exchange, Gmail, Yahoo!, or AOL account, tap the Mail switch to Off.

Deleting an account

If an e-mail account has grown tiresome and boring (or you just don't use it anymore), you should delete it to save storage space, speed up sync times, and save battery power. Follow these steps:

1. **On the Home screen, tap Settings.** The Settings screen appears.

2. **Tap Mail, Contacts, Calendars to get to the Mail settings.**

3. **Tap the account you want to delete.** This opens the account's settings.

4. **At the bottom of the screen, tap Delete Account.** Your iPhone asks you to confirm.

5. **Tap Delete Account.** Your iPhone returns you to the Mail settings screen, and the account no longer graces the Accounts list.

Configuring E-mail Accounts

Setting up an e-mail account on your iPhone is one thing, but making that account do useful things — or sometimes, anything at all! — is quite another. The next few sections take you through a few useful settings that help you get more out of e-mail and troubleshoot e-mail problems.

Managing multiple devices by leaving messages on the server

In today's increasingly mobile world, it's not unusual to find you need to check the same e-mail account from multiple devices. For example, you might want to check your business account not only using your work computer, but also using your home computer, or using your iPhone while commuting or traveling.

If you need to check e-mail on multiple devices, you can take advantage of how POP e-mail messages are delivered over the Internet. When someone sends you a message, it doesn't come directly to your computer. Instead, it goes to the server that your ISP (or your company) has set up to handle incoming messages. When you ask Apple Mail to check for new messages, it communicates with the POP server to see if any messages are waiting in your account. If so, Mail downloads those messages to your computer and then instructs the server to delete the copies of the messages that are stored on the server.

The trick, then, is to configure Mail so that it leaves a copy of the messages on the POP server after you download them. That way, the messages are still available when you check messages using another device. Fortunately, the intuitive folks who designed the version of Mail on your iPhone must have understood this, because the program automatically sets up POP accounts to do just that. Specifically, after you download any messages from the POP server to your iPhone, Mail leaves the messages on the server.

Here's a good overall strategy that ensures you can download messages on all your devices, but prevents messages from piling up on the server:

- **Let your main computer be the computer that controls deleting the messages from the server.** In OS X, Mail's default setting is to delete messages from the server after one week, and that's fine.

- **Set up all your other devices — particularly your iPhone — to not delete messages from the server.**

Note

Outlook, Outlook Express, and Windows Live Mail always configure POP accounts to delete messages from the server as soon as you retrieve them. You need to fix that. In Outlook, choose Tools ⇨ Account Settings, click the account, click Change, and then click More Settings. Click the Advanced tab and select the Leave a copy of messages on the server check box. In Outlook Express or Windows Live Mail, choose Tools ⇨ Accounts, click your e-mail account, and click Properties. Click the Advanced tab and then select the Leave a copy of messages on server check box.

It's a good idea to check your iPhone POP accounts to ensure they're not deleting messages from the server. To do that, or to use a different setting — such as deleting messages after a week or when you delete them from your Inbox — follow these steps:

1. **On the Home screen, tap Settings.** The Settings screen appears.

2. **Tap Mail, Contacts, Calendars.** Your iPhone opens the Mail, Contacts, Calendars settings screen.

3. **Tap the POP account you want to work with.** The account's settings screen appears.

4. **Near the bottom of the screen, tap Advanced.** Your iPhone displays the Advanced screen.

5. **Tap Delete from server.** The Delete from server screen appears, as shown in Figure 5.5.

6. **Tap Never.** If you prefer that your iPhone delete messages from the server automatically, tap either Seven days or When removed from Inbox.

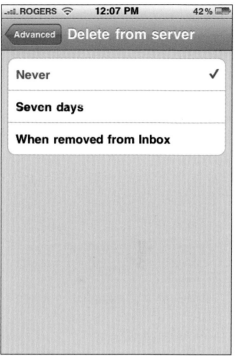

.ıtıl. ROGERS 🛜   12:07 PM   42% 🔋

Advanced Delete from server

Never   ✓

Seven days

When removed from Inbox

Fixing outgoing e-mail problems by using a different server port

For security reasons, some Internet service providers (ISPs) insist that all their customers' outgoing mail must be routed through the ISP's Simple Mail Transport Protocol (SMTP) server. This usually isn't a big deal if you're using an e-mail account maintained by the ISP, but it can lead to the following problems if you are

5.5 Use the Delete from Server screen to ensure your iPhone is leaving messages on your POP server.

using an account provided by a third party (such as your Web site host):

- Your ISP might block messages sent using the third-party account because it thinks you're trying to relay the message through the ISP's server (a technique often used by spammers).

- You might incur extra charges if your ISP allows only a certain amount of SMTP bandwidth per month or a certain number of sent messages, whereas the third-party account offers higher limits or no restrictions at all.

- You might have performance problems, with the ISP's taking much longer to route messages than the third-party host.

- You might think you can solve the problem by specifying the third party host's outgoing mail is sent by default through port 25. When you use this port, the outgoing mail goes through the ISP's SMTP server.

To work around the problem, many third-party hosts offer access to their SMTP server via a port other than the standard port 25. For example, the MobileMe SMTP server (smtp.me.com) also accepts connections on ports 465 and 587. Here's how to configure an e-mail account to use a nonstandard SMTP port.

1. **On the Home screen, tap Settings.** You see the Settings screen.

2. **Tap Mail, Contacts, Calendars.** The Mail, Contacts, Calendars settings screen appears.

3. **Tap the POP account you want to work with.** The account's settings screen appears.

4. **Near the bottom of the screen, tap SMTP.** Your iPhone displays the SMTP screen.

5. **In the Primary Server section, tap the server.** Your iPhone displays the server settings.

6. **In the Outgoing Mail Server section, tap Server Port.** Your iPhone displays a keypad so you can enter the port number, as shown in Figure 5.6.

5.6 In the Server settings screen's Outgoing Mail Server area, tap Server Port to enter the new port number to use for outgoing messages.

Configuring authentication for outgoing mail

Because spam is such a big problem these days, many ISPs now require SMTP authentication for outgoing mail, which means that you must log on to the SMTP server to confirm that you're the person sending the mail (as opposed to some spammer spoofing your address). If your ISP requires authentication on outgoing messages, you need to configure your e-mail account to provide the proper credentials.

If you're not too sure about any of this, check with your ISP. If that doesn't work out, by far the most common type of authentication is to specify a username and password (this happens behind the scenes when you send messages). Follow these steps to configure your iPhone e-mail account with this kind of authentication:

1. **On the Home screen, tap Settings.** Your iPhone displays the Settings screen.

2. **Tap Mail, Contacts, Calendars.** The Mail settings screen appears.

3. **Tap the POP account you want to work with.** The account's settings screen appears.

4. **Near the bottom of the screen, tap SMTP, and then tap Primary Server.** Your iPhone displays the server's settings screen.

5. **In the Outgoing Mail Server section, tap Authentication.** Your iPhone displays the Authentication screen.

6. **Tap Password.**

7. **Tap the server address to return to the server settings screen.**

8. **In the Outgoing Mail Server section, enter your account username in the User Name box and the account password in the Password box.**

Configuring E-mail Messages

The rest of this chapter takes you through a few useful and time-saving techniques for handling e-mail messages on your iPhone.

Configuring iPhone to automatically check for new messages

By default, your iPhone only checks for new messages when you tell it to:

1. **On the Home screen, tap Mail to open the Mail app.**

2. **Tap your account button that appears in the top-left corner of the screen (but below the status bar).** Mail displays the Mailboxes screen.

3. **In the Inboxes section, tap the account you want to work with.** Mail opens the folder and checks for messages.

Note
While you have an account's Inbox folder open, you can check for messages again by tapping the Refresh icon on the left side of the menu bar.

This is usually the behavior you want, because it limits bandwidth if you're using the cellular network, and it saves battery life. However, if you're busy with something else and you're expecting an important message, you might prefer to have your iPhone check for new messages automatically. Easy money! The Auto-Check feature is happy to handle everything for you. Here's how you set it up:

1. **On the Home screen, tap Settings to display the Settings screen.**

2. **Tap Mail, Contacts, Calendars.** The Mail settings screen appears.

3. **Tap Fetch New Data.** Your iPhone opens the Fetch New Data screen.

4. **For your MobileMe, Exchange, Gmail, Yahoo!, and AOL accounts, tap the Push switch to On.** Note that you must also tap the Mail switch to On for each account (see the section on temporarily desabling an account earlier in this chapter).

5. **For your POP and IMAP accounts, in the Fetch section, tap the interval you want to use.** For example, if you tap Every 15 minutes (see Figure 5.7), your iPhone checks all your accounts for new messages every 15 minutes.

When you're ready to return to checking for new messages on your own time, repeat these steps, and when you get to the Fetch New Data screen, tap the Push switch to Off and tap Manually in the Fetch section.

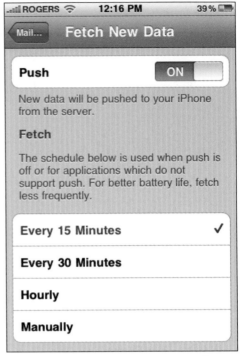

5.7 Use the Fetch New Data screen to configure your iPhone to check for new messages automatically.

Displaying more messages in your Inbox message list

When you open an account's Inbox folder, initially you only see the first four messages (actually four and a bit). As you can see in Figure 5.8, the reason you see so few messages is that Mail displays for each message the sender, the subject line, and a two-line preview of the message. Of course, it's not a big whoop to flick through the rest of your messages (it's kind of fun, actually), but if you're looking for (or waiting for) a particular message, it would be nice to see more messages on the screen at once.

Can this be done? Of course! The secret is to reduce the number of lines that Mail uses for the message preview. Reduce the preview to a single line, and you now see five full messages on the screen; get rid of the preview altogether, and you see a whopping eight messages per screen. (Well, I fibbed: it's actually seven and a half, because the final message shows only the sender's name.) Follow these steps to reduce the preview size:

1. **On the Home screen, tap Settings.** The Settings screen appears.

2. **Tap Mail, Contacts, Calendars to open the Mail screen.**

3. **Tap Preview.** Your iPhone displays the Preview screen, as shown in Figure 5.9.

4. **Tap the number of lines you want to use.** To reduce the preview to a single line, tap 1 Line; to see no preview at all, tap None.

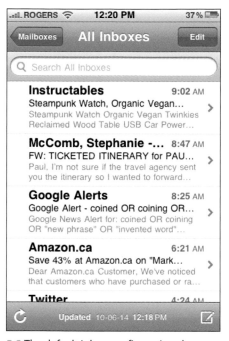

5.8 The default Inbox configuration shows only a maximum of five messages at a time.

5.9 Use the Preview screen to set the number of lines used to preview the Inbox messages.

Processing e-mail faster by identifying messages sent to you

In your iPhone's Mail app, the Inbox folder tells you who sent you each message, but it doesn't tell you to whom the message was sent (that is, which addresses appeared on the To line or the Cc line). No big deal, right? Maybe, maybe not. You see, bulk mailers — I'm talking newsletters, mailing lists, and, notoriously, spammers — often don't send messages directly to each person on their subscriber lists. Instead, they use a generic bulk address, which means, significantly, that your e-mail address doesn't appear on the To or Cc lines. That's significant because most newsletters and mailing lists — and all spam — are low-priority messages that you can ignore when you're processing a stuffed Inbox.

109

Okay, great, but what good does all this do you if Mail doesn't show the To and Cc lines? No, it doesn't show those lines, but you *can* configure Mail to show a little icon for messages that were sent directly to you.

- If the message includes your address in the To field, you see a "To" icon beside the message.

- If the message includes your address in the Cc field, you see a "Cc" icon beside the message.

Neat! Here's how to make this happen:

1. **On the Home screen, tap Settings.** The Settings screen appears.

2. **Tap Mail, Contacts, Calendars.** The Mail, Contacts, Calendars screen appears.

3. **Tap the Show To/Cc Label switch to the On position.**

When you examine your Inbox, you see the To and Cc icons on messages addressed to you, and you don't see either icon on bulk messages, as shown in Figure 5.10.

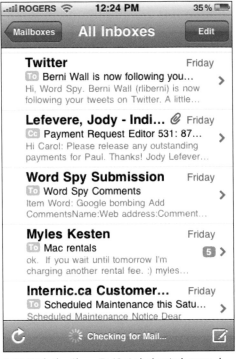

5.10 With the Show To/Cc Label switch turned on, Mail shows you which messages were addressed directly to you.

Placing a phone call from an e-mail message

E-mail messages often include a signature — a line or three of text that appears at the bottom of the message. In business e-mail, a person's signature often includes contact information — what hipster business types like to refer to as their "coordinates" — such as their address (e-mail and postal) and their phone numbers (land and cell). (I show you how to create your own custom iPhone signature a bit later in this chapter.)

In a run-of-the-mill e-mail program, if you wanted to call one of your correspondents based on this signature information, you'd open the message, perhaps jot down the number if there was no phone nearby, and then make the call. As you know, your iPhone isn't run-of-the-mill *anything*, so you can just forget all that rigmarole. Why? Because when it sees a phone number in an e-mail message, your

Genius

Your iPhone's Mail app converts phone numbers into fake links that you can tap, so it's not even remotely surprising that Mail also converts Web addresses into actual links. That is, when you tap an address that appears in an e-mail message, your iPhone fires up Safari and takes you to that address. Even better, if the sender includes a link in the message, you can tap and hold the link to see a pop-up bubble that tells you the link address.

iPhone does something quite smart: it converts that number into a kind of link — the number appears in blue, underlined text, much like a link on a Web page. Figure 5.11 shows an example. Tap the number, tap Call in the dialog that appears, and your iPhone immediately dials the number for you. Thanks!

E-mailing a link to a Web page

The Web is all about finding content that's interesting, educational, and, of course, fun. And if you stumble across a site that meets one or more of these criteria, then the only sensible thing to do is share your good fortune with someone else, right? So, how do you do that? Some sites are kind enough to include an Email This Page link (or something similar), but you can't count on having one of those around. Instead, the usual method is to copy the page address, switch to your e-mail program, paste the address into the message, choose a recipient, and then send the message.

5.11 Your iPhone is savvy enough to convert an e-mail message phone number into a link that you can tap to call the number.

And, yes, with your iPhone's copy-and-paste feature, you can do all that on your iPhone, but boy, that sure seems like a ton of work. So are stuck using this unwieldy method? Not a chance (you probably knew that). Your iPhone includes a great little feature that enables you to plop the address of the current Safari page into an e-mail message with just a couple of taps. You then ship out the message and you've made the world a better place.

Here's how it works:

1. **Use Safari to navigate to the site you want to share.**

2. **Tap the + button in the menu bar.** Safari displays a dialog with several options.

3. **Tap Mail Link to this Page.** This opens a new e-mail message. As you can see in Figure 5.12, the new message already includes the page title as the Subject and the page address in the message body.

4. **Choose a recipient for the message.**

5. **Edit the message text as you see fit.**

6. **Tap Send.** Your iPhone fires off the message and returns you to Safari.

5.12 When you tap the Mail Link to this Page option, your iPhone creates a new e-mail message with the page title and address already inserted.

Setting a minimum message font size

Some people who send e-mails must have terrific eyesight because the font they use for the message text is positively microscopic. Such text is tough to read even on a big screen, but when it's crammed into the iPhone's touchscreen, you'll be reaching for the nearest magnifying glass. Of course, that same touchscreen can also solve this problem: a quick finger spread magnifies the text accordingly.

That's easy enough if you just get the occasional message with nanoscale text, but if a regular correspondent does this, or if your eyesight isn't quite what it used to be (so *all* your messages appear ridiculously teensy), then a more permanent solution might be in order. Your iPhone rides to the rescue once again by letting you configure a minimum font size for your messages. This means that if the message font size is larger than what you specify, your iPhone displays the message as is; however, if the font size is smaller than your specification, your iPhone scales up the text to your minimum size. Your tired eyes will be forever grateful.

Follow these steps to set your minimum font size:

1. **On the Home screen, tap Settings.** The Settings screen appears.

2. **Tap Mail, Contacts, Calendars.** Your iPhone displays the Mail, Contacts, Calendars settings screen.

3. **Tap Minimum Font Size.** The Minimum Font Size screen appears, as shown in Figure 5.13.

4. **Tap the minimum font size you want to use: Small, Medium, Large, Extra Large, or Giant.** Mail uses the font size you select (or larger) when displaying your messages.

Creating a custom iPhone signature

E-mail signatures can range from the simple — a signoff such as "Cheers," or "All the best," followed by the sender's name — to baroque masterpieces filled with contact information, snappy quotations, even text-based artwork! On your iPhone, the Mail app takes the simple route by adding the following signature to all your outgoing messages (new messages, replies, and forwards):

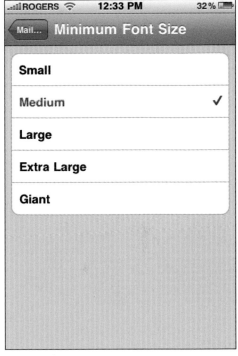

5.13 Use the Minimum Font Size screen to set the smallest text size that you want Mail to use when it displays a message.

```
Sent from my iPhone
```

Caution Mail doesn't give any way to cancel your edits and return to the original signature, so enter your text carefully. If you make a real hash of things, tap Clear to get a fresh start.

I really like this signature because it's short, simple, and kinda cool (I, of course, want my recipients to know that I'm using my iPhone!). If that default signature doesn't rock your world, you can create a custom one that does. Follow these steps:

1. **On the Home screen, tap Settings.** Your iPhone opens the Settings screen.

2. **Tap Mail, Contacts, Calendars.** You see the Mail, Contacts, Calendars settings screen.

3. **Tap Signature.** The Signature screen appears, as shown in Figure 5.14.

4. **Enter the signature you want to use.**

5. **Tap Mail.** Mail saves your new signature and uses it on all outgoing messages.

Disabling remote images in messages

Lots of messages nowadays come not just as plain text, but also with fonts, colors, images, and other flourishes. This fancy formatting, called either *rich text* or *HTML*, makes for a more pleasant e-mail experience, particularly when using images in messages, because who doesn't like a bit of eye candy to brighten their day?

Unfortunately, however, getting images in your e-mail messages can sometimes be problematic:

5.14 Use the Signature screen to create your custom iPhone e-mail signature.

- **A cellular connection might cause trouble.** For example, it might take a long time to load the images, or if your data plan has an upper limit, you might not want a bunch of e-mail images taking a big bite out of that limit.

- **Not all e-mail images are benign.** A *Web bug* is an image that resides on a remote server and is added to an HTML-formatted e-mail message by referencing an address on the remote server. When you open the message, Mail uses the address to download the image for display within the message. That sounds harmless enough, but if the message is junk e-mail, it's likely that the address also contains either your e-mail address or a code that points to your e-mail address. So when the remote server gets a request to load the image, it knows not only that you've opened the message, but also that your e-mail address is legitimate. So, not surprisingly, spammers use Web bugs all the time because, for them, valid e-mail addresses are a form of gold.

HTML stands for Hypertext Markup Language and is a set of codes that folks use to put together Web pages.

Note

The iPhone Mail app displays remote images by default. To disable remote images, follow these steps:

1. **On the Home screen, tap Settings.** Your iPhone opens the Settings screen.

2. **Tap Mail, Contacts, Calendars.** You see the Mail, Contacts, Calendars settings screen.

3. **Tap the Load Remote Images switch to the Off position.** Mail saves the setting and no longer displays remote images in your e-mail messages.

4.0 Preventing Mail from organizing messages by thread

iOS 4.0 In the iOS 4 version of the Mail app, your messages get grouped by thread, which means the original message and all of the replies you've received are grouped together in the account's Inbox folder. This is usually remarkably handy, because it means you don't have to scroll through a million messages to locate the reply you want to read.

Mail indicates a thread by displaying the number of messages in the thread on the right side of the latest thread message, as shown in Figure 5.15. Tap the message to see a list of the messages in the thread, and then tap the message you want to read.

Organizing messages by thread is usually convenient, but not always. For example, when you're viewing your messages and scrolling through them by tapping the Next and Previous buttons, when you come to a thread, Mail jumps into the thread and you then scroll through each message in the thread, which can be a real hassle if the thread contains a large number of replies.

If you find that threads are more hassle than they're worth, you can follow these steps to configure Mail to no longer organize messages by thread:

1. **On the Home screen, tap Settings.** Your iPhone opens the Settings screen.

2. **Tap Mail, Contacts, Calendars.** You see the Mail, Contacts, Calendars settings screen.

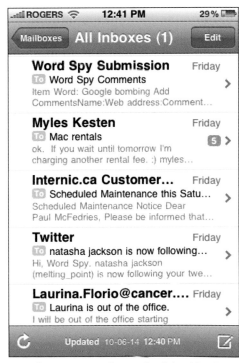

5.15 If you see a number on the right side of a message, that number tells you how many messages are in the thread.

3. **Tap the Organize By Thread switch to the Off position.** Your iPhone saves the setting and no longer organizes your images by thread.

4.0 Deleting Gmail messages instead of archiving them

iOS 4.0 With most email accounts, you can tidy up the Inbox folder by tapping Edit, choosing one or more messages you no longer need, and then tapping Delete. Not so in your Google Gmail account. However, when you open your Gmail Inbox, tap Edit, and then select one or more messages, you see an Archive button, instead of a Delete button, as shown in Figure 5.16. Tapping Archive moves the selected messages to the All Mail folder.

If you'd really prefer to delete your Gmail messages instead of archiving them, follow these steps to knock some sense into the Mail app:

1. **On the Home screen, tap Settings.** Your iPhone opens the Settings screen.

2. **Tap Mail, Contacts, Calendars.** You see the Mail, Contacts, Calendars settings screen.

3. **Tap your Gmail account. Your iPhone opens the Gmail settings.**

4. **Tap the Archive Messages switch to the Off position.** Your iPhone saves the setting and no longer archives your Gmail messages.

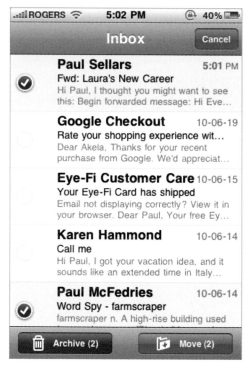

5.16 By default, Mail archives Gmail messages instead of deleting them.

Configuring your Exchange ActiveSync settings

If you have an account on a Microsoft Exchange Server 2003 or 2007 network, and that server has deployed Exchange ActiveSync, then you're all set to have your iPhone and Exchange account synchronized automatically. That's because ActiveSync supports wireless push technology, which means that if anything changes on your Exchange server account, that change is immediately synced with your iPhone:

- **E-mail.** If you receive a new message on your Exchange account, ActiveSync immediately displays that message in your iPhone's Mail app.

- **Contacts.** If someone at work adds or edits data in the server address book, those changes are immediately synced to your iPhone Contacts list.

- **Calendar.** If someone at work adds or edits an appointment in your calendar, or if someone requests a meeting with you, that data is immediately synced with your iPhone's Calendar app.

ActiveSync works both ways, too, so if you send e-mail messages, add contacts or appointments, or accept meeting requests, your server account is immediately updated with the changes. And all this data whizzing back and forth is safe, because it's sent over a secure connection.

Your iPhone also gives you a few options for controlling ActiveSync, and the following steps show you how to set them:

1. **On the Home screen, tap Settings.** Your iPhone opens the Settings screen.

2. **Tap Mail, Contacts, Calendars to open the Mail, Contacts, Calendars settings.**

3. **Tap your Exchange account.** The Exchange account settings screen appears, as shown in Figure 5.17.

4. **To sync your Exchange e-mail account, tap the Mail On/Off switch to the On position.**

5. **To sync your Exchange address book, tap the Contacts On/Off switch to the On position, and then click Sync.**

6. **To sync your Exchange calendar, tap the Calendars On/Off switch to the On position, and then click Sync.**

7. **To control the amount of time that gets synced on your e-mail account, tap Mail Days to Sync, and then tap the number of days, weeks, or months you want to sync.**

8. **If you want more folders pushed to you, tap Mail Folders to push, then tap each folder you want: Sent items, Deleted Items, or Junk E-Mail.**

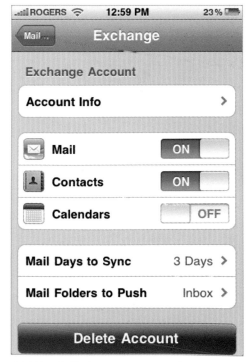

5.17 Use the Exchange account settings screen to customize your iPhone's ActiveSync support.

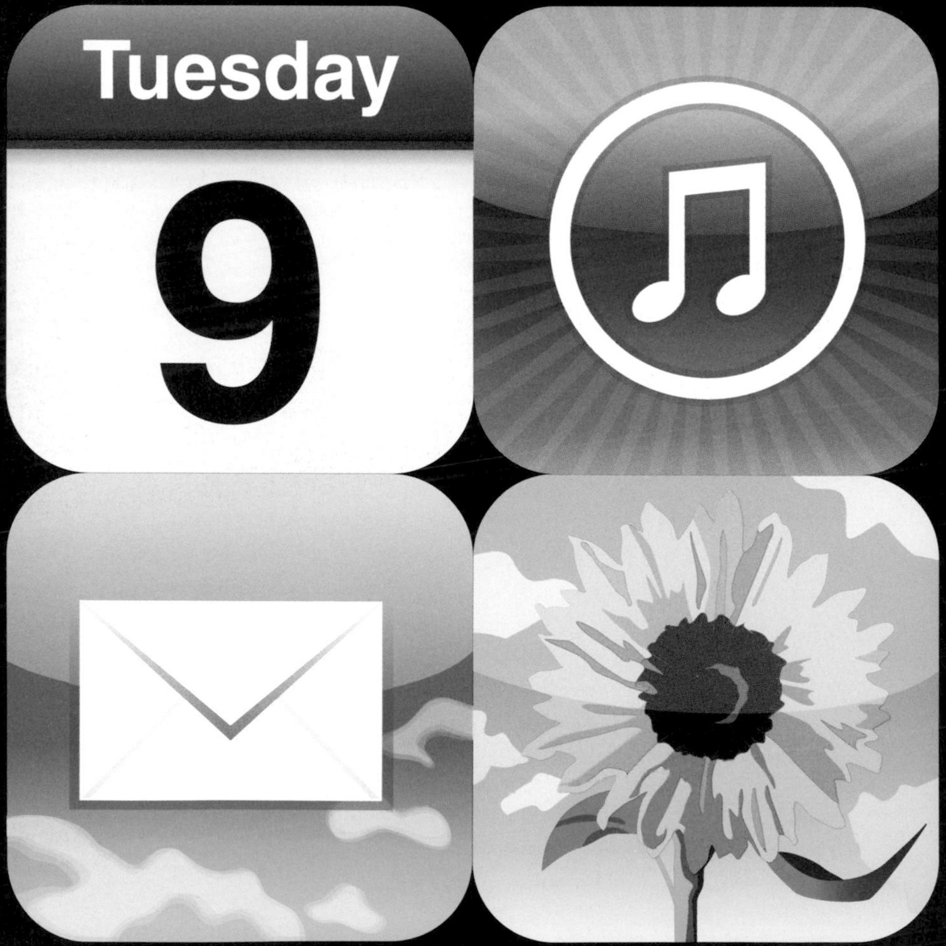
Tuesday
9

Your iPhone can function perfectly well on its own. After all, you can use it to create your own bookmarks, e-mail accounts, contacts, and appointments; you can download music and other media from the iTunes store; and you can take your own photos using the iPhone's built-in camera. If you want to use your iPhone as a stand-alone device, no one can stop you, not even Steve Jobs himself (I think). Yes, you can do that, but I'm not sure *why* you'd want to. With all of the iPhone's great synchronization features, tons of that useful and fun content on your computer can also be shared with your iPhone. This chapter shows you how to master syncing your iPhone and your Mac or Windows computer.

Syncing Your iPhone Automatically

Start with the look-ma-no-hands syncing scenario where you don't have to pay any attention in the least: automatic syncing. If the amount of iPhone-friendly digital content you have on your Mac or Windows PC is less than the capacity of your iPhone, then you have no worries because you know it's all going to fit. So all you have to do is turn on your iPhone, and then connect it to your computer.

That's it! iTunes opens automatically and begin syncing your iPhone (and, as an added bonus, also begins charging your iPhone's battery). Your iPhone displays the Sync in Progress screen while the sync runs, and then returns you to the Home screen when the sync is complete. Note that you can't use your iPhone while the sync is running.

Note If a call comes in while you're syncing, your iPhone cancels the sync automatically so that you can take the call.

However, one of the iPhone's nicest features is its willingness to be rudely interrupted in midsync. Figure 6.1 shows the Sync in Progress screen. Check out the slide to cancel slider at the bottom. If you ever need to bail out of the sync to, say, make a call, drag the slider to the right. iTunes dutifully cancels the sync so you can go about your business. To restart the sync, click the Sync button in iTunes.

Bypassing the automatic sync

What do you do if you want to connect your iPhone to your computer, but you don't want it to sync? I'm not talking here about switching to manual syncing full time (I get to that in a second). Instead, I'm talking about bypassing the sync one time only. For example, you might want to connect your iPhone to your computer just to charge it (assuming you either don't have the optional dock or you

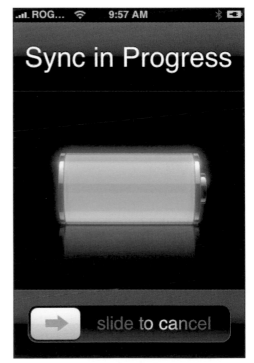

6.1 If you need to use your iPhone in midsync, drag the slide to cancel slider to the right to stop the sync.

don't have it with you). Or perhaps you just want to use iTunes to eyeball how much free space is left on your iPhone or to check for updates to the iPhone software.

Whatever the reason, you can tell iTunes to hold off the syncing this time only by using one of the following techniques:

- **Mac.** Connect the iPhone to the Mac and then quickly press and hold the Option and ⌘ keys.

- **Windows.** Connect the iPhone to the Windows PC and then quickly press and hold the Ctrl and Shift keys.

When you see that iTunes has added your iPhone to the Devices list, you can release the keys.

Genius

You don't need to use iTunes to see how much free space is left on your iPhone. On the Home screen, tap Settings, tap General, and then tap About. In the About screen that slides in, the Available value tells you how many gigabytes (or megabytes) of free space you have to play with.

Troubleshooting automatic syncing

Okay, so you connect your iPhone to your computer and then nothing. iTunes doesn't wake from its digital slumbers or, if iTunes is already running, it sees the iPhone but refuses to start syncing. What's up with that?

It could be a couple of things. First, connect your iPhone, switch to iTunes on your computer, and then click your iPhone in the Devices list. On the Summary tab (see Figure 6.2), make sure the Open iTunes when this iPhone is connected check box is selected.

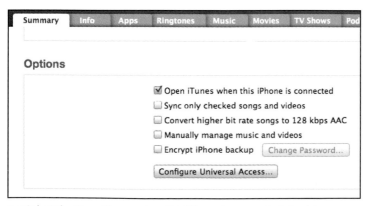

6.2 Select the Open iTunes when this iPhone is connected check box.

121

Giving Your iPhone a Snappy Name

This isn't necessarily a syncing topic, but I thought that while you're in iTunes, you might want to give your iPhone a proper name, one that's a tad more interesting than the boring "iPhone" that passes for the default name. (Similarly, if you already renamed your iPhone during the setup procedure that appears when you first connect your phone, you might want to change that name.) Here's what you do:

1. **Double-click your iPhone in the Devices list.** iTunes forms a text box around the name.

2. **Type the name you want to use.** You can use any characters you want, and the name can be as long as you want (although you might want to use no more than about 15 or 16 characters to ensure the name doesn't get cut off in the Devices list).

3. **Press Return or Enter to save the new name.**

As soon as you press Return or Enter, iTunes connects to your iPhone and saves the name on the phone. This way, even if you connect your iPhone to another computer, that machine's version of iTunes shows your custom iPhone name.

If that check box was already selected, then you need to delve a bit deeper to solve the mystery. Follow these steps:

1. **Open the iTunes preferences:**
   - **Mac.** Choose iTunes ➪ Preferences, or press ⌘ +. (period).
   - **Windows.** Choose Edit ➪ Preferences, or press Ctrl+. (period).

2. **Click the Devices tab.**

3. **Deselect the Prevent iPods, iPhones and iPads from syncing automatically check box.**

4. **Click OK to put the new setting into effect and enable automatic syncing once again.**

Syncing Your iPhone Manually

One fine day, you'll be minding your own business and performing what you believe to be a routine sync operation when a dialog like the one shown in Figure 6.3 rears its nasty head.

Groan! This most unwelcome dialog means just what it says: There's not enough free space on your iPhone to sync all the content from your computer. You've got a couple of ways to handle this:

The iPhone "Paul's iPhone" cannot be synced because there is not enough free space to hold all of the items in the selected playlists (1.25 GB required, 805.6 MB available).

☐ Do not warn me again

OK

6.3 You see this dialog if iTunes can't fit all of your stuff on your iPhone.

- **Remove some of the content from your computer.** This is a good way to go if your iPhone is really close to having enough space. For example, the dialog says your computer wants to send 100MB of data, but your iPhone has only 98MB of free space. Get rid of a few megabytes of stuff on your computer, and you're back in the sync business.

- **Synchronize your iPhone manually.** This means that you no longer sync everything on your computer. Instead, you handpick which playlists, podcasts, audiobooks, and so on are sent to your iPhone. It's a bit more work, but it's the way to go if there's a big difference between the amount of content on your computer and the amount of space left on your iPhone.

The rest of this chapter shows you how to manually sync the various content types: contacts, calendars, e-mail, bookmarks, documents, music, podcasts, audiobooks, movies, TV shows, eBooks, photos, and videos.

Syncing Information with Your iPhone

If you step back a pace or two to take in the big picture, you see that your iPhone deals with two broad types of data: media — all that audio and video stuff — and information such as contacts, appointments, e-mail, Web sites, and notes. You need both types of data to get the most out of your iPhone investment, and happily, both types of data are eminently syncable. I'll get to the media syncing portion of the show a bit later. For now, the next few sections show you how to take control of syncing your information between your iPhone and your computer.

Syncing your contacts

Although you can certainly add contacts directly on your iPhone — and I show you how to do just that in Chapter 9 — adding, editing, grouping, and deleting contacts is a lot easier on a computer. So a good way to approach contacts is to manage them on your Mac or Windows PC, and then sync your contacts with your iPhone.

However, do you really need to sync *all* your contacts? For example, if you only use your iPhone to contact friends and family, then why clog your phone's Contacts list with work contacts? I don't know!

You can control which contacts are sent to your iPhone by creating groups of contacts, and then syncing only the groups you want. Here are some quickie instructions for creating groups:

- **Address Book (Mac).** Choose File ⇨ New Group, type the group name, and then press Return. Now populate the new group by dragging and dropping contacts on it.

- **Contacts (Windows 7 and Windows Vista).** Click New Contact Group, type the group name, and then click Add to Contact Group. Choose all the contacts you want in the group and then click Add. Click OK.

- **Windows Live Contacts (Windows 7).** Drop down the New menu, click Category, and type the group name. Click each contact you want in the group and then click Save.

Note

If you're an Outlook user, note that iTunes doesn't support Outlook-based contact groups, so you're stuck with syncing everyone in your Outlook Contacts folder.

With your group (or groups) all figured out, follow these steps to sync your contacts with your iPhone:

1. **Connect your iPhone to your computer.**

2. **In iTunes, click your iPhone in the Devices list.**

3. **Click the Info tab.**

4. **Turn on contacts syncing by using one of the following techniques:**

    - **Mac.** Select the Sync Address Book Contacts check box.

    - **Windows.** Select the Sync Contacts with check box, and then use the list to choose the program you want to use (such as Outlook).

5. **Select an option:**

    - **All contacts.** Select this option to sync all your Address Book contacts.

    - **Selected groups**. Select this option to sync only the groups you pick. In the group list, select the check box beside each group that you want to sync, as shown in Figure 6.4.

6. **If you want to make the sync a two-way street, select the Add contacts created outside of groups on this iPhone to option, and then choose a group from the menu.**

7. **(Mac only) If you have a Yahoo! account and you also want your Yahoo! Address Book contacts in on the sync, select the Sync Yahoo! Address Book contacts check box, type your Yahoo! ID and password, and click OK.**

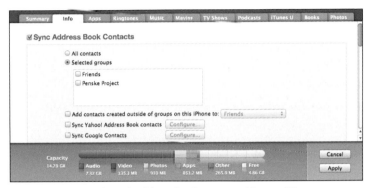

6.4 You can sync selected Address Book groups with your iPhone.

8. **(Mac only) If you have a Google account and you also want your Google Contacts in on the sync, select the Sync Google Contacts check box, type your Google and password, and click OK.**

9. **Click Apply.** iTunes syncs the iPhone using your new contacts settings.

Syncing your calendar

When you're tripping around town with your trusty iPhone at your side, you certainly don't want to be late if you've got a date. The best way to ensure that you don't miss an appointment, meeting, or rendezvous is to always have the event details at hand, which means adding those details to your iPhone's Calendar. You could add the appointment to Calendar right on the iPhone (a technique I take you through in Chapter 9), but it's easier to create it on your computer and then sync it to your iPhone. This gives you the added advantage of having the appointment listed in two places, so you're sure to arrive on time.

Most people sync all the appointments, but it's not unusual to keep track of separate schedules — for example, business and personal. You can control which schedule is synced to your iPhone by creating separate calendars and then syncing only the calendars you want. In your Mac's iCal application, choose File ➪ New Calendar, type the calendar name, and then press Return.

Note Although you can create extra calendars in Outlook, iTunes doesn't recognize them, so you have to sync everything in your Outlook Calendar folder. Also, iTunes doesn't support Windows Calendar (available with Windows Vista), so you're out of luck if you use that to manage your schedule.

Now follow these steps to sync your calendar with your iPhone:

1. **Connect your iPhone to your computer.**

2. **In iTunes, click your iPhone in the Devices list.**

3. **Click the Info tab.**

4. **Turn on calendar syncing by using one of the following techniques:**

   - **Mac.** Select the Sync iCal Calendars check box.

   - **Windows.** Select the Sync Calendars with check box, and then use the list to choose the program you want to use (such as Outlook).

5. **Select an option:**

   - **All calendars.** Select this option to sync all your calendars.

   - **Selected calendars.** Select this option to sync only the calendars you pick. In the calendar list, select the check box beside each calendar that you want to sync, as shown in Figure 6.5.

6.5 You can sync selected calendars with your iPhone.

6. **To control how far back the calendar sync goes, select the Do not sync events older than X days check box, and then type the number of days of calendar history you want to see on your iPhone.**

7. **Click Apply.** iTunes syncs the iPhone using your new calendar settings.

Syncing your e-mail account

By far the easiest way to configure your iPhone with an e-mail account is to let iTunes do all the heavy lifting for you. That is, if you've got an existing account already up and running — whether it's a Mail account on your Mac, or an Outlook or Windows Mail account on your Windows PC — you can convince iTunes to gather all the account details and pass them along to your iPhone. Here's how it works:

1. **Connect your iPhone to your computer.**

2. **In the iTunes sources list, click the iPhone.**

3. **Click the Info tab.**

4. **In the Mail Accounts section, use one of the following techniques:**

   - **Mac.** Select the Sync Mail Accounts check box, and then select the check box beside each account you want to add to iPhone, as shown in Figure 6.6.

   - **Windows.** Select the Sync Mail Accounts from check box, select your e-mail program from the drop-down list, and then select the check box beside each account you want to add to iPhone.

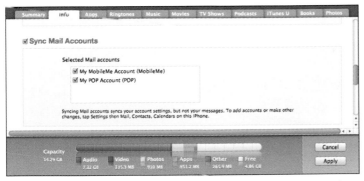

6.6 Make sure you select the Sync selected Mail account check box and at least one account in the list.

5. **Click Apply.** You may see a message asking if AppleMobileSync can be allowed access to your keychain (your Mac's master password list).

6. **If you see that message, click Allow.** iTunes begins syncing the selected e-mail account settings from your computer to your iPhone.

Syncing your bookmarks

The easiest way to get bookmarks for your favorite sites in your iPhone is to take advantage of your best bookmark resource: the Safari browser on your Mac (or Windows), or the Internet Explorer browser on your Windows PC (which calls them favorites). You've probably used those browsers for a while and have all kinds of useful and fun bookmarked sites at your metaphorical fingertips. To get those bookmarks at your literal fingertips — that is, on your iPhone — you need to include bookmarks as part of the synchronization process between the iPhone and iTunes.

Note

Having used Safari or Internet Explorer for a while means having lots of great sites bookmarked, but it likely also means that you've also got lots of digital dreck — sites you no longer visit, or that have gone belly-up. Before synchronizing your bookmarks with the iPhone, consider taking some time to clean up your existing bookmarks. You'll thank yourself in the end.

Genius

What's that? You've already synced your bookmarks to your iPhone and you now have a bunch of useless sites clogging up Mobile Safari's bookmark arteries? Not a problem! Return to your desktop Safari (or Internet Explorer), purge the bogus bookmarks, and then sync your iPhone using the following steps. Any bookmarks you blew away will also get trashed from iPhone.

Follow these steps to activate bookmark syncing:

1. **Connect your iPhone to your computer.**

2. **In the iTunes sources list, click the iPhone.**

3. **Click the Info tab.**

4. **Scroll down to the Other section, and then use one of the following techniques:**

    - **Mac.** Select the Sync Safari bookmarks check box, as shown in Figure 6.7.

    - **Windows.** Select the Sync bookmarks with check box, and then select your Web browser from the drop-down list.

5. **Click Apply.** iTunes begins syncing the bookmarks from your computer to your iPhone.

6.7 Make sure the Sync Safari bookmarks check box is selected.

Syncing your notes

If you use the Notes app on your iPhone to jot down quick thoughts, ideas, and other mental tid-bits, you might want to transfer thought notes to your computer so you can incorporate them into another document, add them to a to-do list, or whatever. To do this in early versions of the iPhone OS, you had to e-mail the notes to yourself, which wasn't exactly convenient. Now, however, notes are full-fledged members of the iPhone information pantheon, which means you can sync your notes to your computer.

Note

To sync notes on your Mac, you must be running Mac OS X 10.5.7 or later.

Follow these steps to activate notes syncing:

1. **Connect your iPhone to your computer.**

2. **In the iTunes sources list, click the iPhone.**

3. **Click the Info tab.**

4. **Scroll down to the Notes section (see Figure 6.7), and then use one of the following techniques:**

   - **Mac.** Select the Sync notes check box.

   - **Windows.** Select the Sync notes with check box, and then select an application from the drop-down list (such as Outlook).

5. **Click Apply.** iTunes begins syncing the notes from your computer to your iPhone.

Merging data from two or more computers

Long gone are the days when our information resided on a single computer. Now it's common to have a desktop computer (or two) at home, a work computer, and perhaps a notebook to take on the road. It's nice to have all that digital firepower, but it creates a big problem: You end up with contacts, calendars, and other information scattered over several machines. How are you supposed to keep track of it all?

Apple's latest solution is MobileMe, which provides seamless information integration across multiple computers (Mac and Windows) and, of course, the iPhone, and that's the topic I cover in Chapter 12.

If you don't have a MobileMe account, you can still achieve a bit of data harmony. That's because iTunes offers the welcome ability to *merge* information from two or more computers on the iPhone. For example, if you have contacts on your home computer, you can sync them with your iPhone. If you have a separate collection of contacts on your notebook, you can also sync them with your iPhone, but iTunes gives you two choices:

- **Merge Info.** With this option, your iPhone keeps the information synced from the first computer and merges it with the information synced from the second computer.

- **Replace Info.** With this option, your iPhone deletes the information synced from the first computer and replaces it with the information synced from the second computer.

Here are the general steps to follow to set up your merged information:

1. **Sync your iPhone with information from one computer.** This technique works with contacts, calendars, e-mail accounts, and bookmarks.

2. **Connect your iPhone to the second computer.**

3. **In iTunes, click your iPhone in the Devices list.**

4. **Click the Info tab.**

5. **Select the Sync check boxes that correspond to information already synced on the first computer.** For example, if you synced contacts on the first computer, select the Sync Address Book contacts check box.

6. **Click Apply.** iTunes displays a dialog like the one shown in Figure 6.8.

7. **Click Merge Info.** iTunes syncs your iPhone and merges the computer's information with the existing information from the first computer.

Handling sync conflicts

When you sync information between your iPhone and a computer, any edits you make to that information are included in the sync. For example, if you change someone's e-mail address on your iPhone, the next time you sync, iTunes updates the e-mail address on the computer, which is exactly what you want.

However, what if you already changed that person's address on the computer? If you made the same edit, then it's no biggie because there's nothing to sync. But what if you made a different edit? Ah, that's a problem, because now iTunes doesn't know which version has the correct information. In that case, it shrugs its digital shoulders and passes off the problem to a program called Conflict Resolver, which displays the dialog shown in Figure 6.9.

If you want to deal with the problem now, click Review Now. Conflict Resolver then offers you the details of the conflict. For example, in Figure 6.10 you can see that a contact's company name and picture are different in Address Book and on the iPhone. To settle the issue once and for all (you hope), click the correct version of the information, and click continue to move on to the next conflict. When you've gone through all the conflicts, click Done. When Conflict Resolver tells you it will fix the problem during the next sync, click Sync Now to make it happen right away.

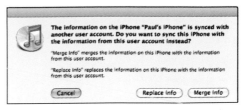

6.8 You can merge contacts, calendars, e-mail accounts, bookmarks, and notes from two or more computers.

6.9 If you make different edits to the same bit of information on your iPhone and your computer, the Conflict Resolver springs into action.

6.10 Review Now shows you the details of any conflicts.

131

Handling large iPhone-to-computer sync changes

Syncing works both ways, meaning that not only does your iPhone receive content from your computer, but your computer also receives content from your iPhone. For example, if you create any bookmarks, contacts, or appointments on your iPhone, those items get sent to your computer during the sync.

However, it's implied that the bulk of the content flows from your computer to your iPhone, which makes sense because for most things it's easier to add, edit, and delete stuff on the computer. So that's why if you make lots of changes to your iPhone content, iTunes displays a warning that the sync is going to make lots of changes to your computer content. The threshold is five percent, which means that if the sync changes more than five percent of a particular type of content on your computer — such as bookmarks or calendars — the warning appears. For example, Figure 6.11 shows the Sync Alert dialog you see if the sync will change more than five percent of your computer's bookmarks.

6.11 iTunes warns you if the sync will mess with more than five percent of your computer's content.

If you're expecting this (because you *did* change lots of stuff on your iPhone), click the Sync *Whatever* button (where *Whatever* is the type of data: Bookmarks, Calendars, and so on). If you're not sure, click Show Details to see what the changes are. If you're still scratching your head, click Cancel to skip that part of the sync.

If you're running iTunes for Windows, you can either turn off this warning or adjust the threshold. (For some unfathomable reason, iTunes for the Mac doesn't offer this handy option.) Follow these steps:

1. **Choose Edit ⇨ Preferences, or press Ctrl+, (comma).** The iTunes dialog box comes aboard.

2. **Click the Devices tab.**

3. **If you want to disable the sync alerts altogether, deselect the Warn when check box.** Otherwise, leave that check box selected and move on to step 4.

4. **Use the Warn when percent of the data on the computer will be changed list to set the alert threshold, where percent is one of the following:**

   - **any.** Select this option to see the sync alert whenever syncing with the iPhone will change data on your computer. iPhone syncs routinely modify data on the computer, so be prepared to see the alerts every time you sync. (Of course, that may be exactly what you want.)

   - **more than X%.** Select one of these options — your choices are 5% (the default), 25%, or 50% — to see the alert only when the sync will change more than *X* percent of some data type on the computer.

5. **Click OK to put the new settings into effect.**

Replacing your iPhone's data with fresh info

After you know what you're doing, syncing contacts, calendars, e-mail accounts, and bookmarks to your iPhone is a relatively bulletproof procedure that should happen without a hitch each time. Of course, this is technology we're dealing with here, so hitches do happen every now and then, and as a result you might end up with corrupt or repeated information on your iPhone.

Or perhaps you've been syncing your iPhone with a couple of different computers, and you decide to cut one of the computers out of the loop and revert to just a single machine for all your syncs.

In both these scenarios, what you need to do is replace the existing information on your iPhone with a freshly baked batch of data. Fortunately, iTunes has a feature that lets you do exactly that. Here's how it works:

1. **Connect your iPhone to your computer.**

2. **In the iTunes sources list, click the iPhone.**

3. **Click the Info tab.**

4. **Select the Sync check boxes for each type of information you want to work with (contacts, calendars, e-mail accounts, bookmarks, or notes).** If you don't select a check box, iTunes won't replace that information on your iPhone. For example, if you like your iPhone bookmarks just the way they are, don't select the Sync bookmarks check box.

5. **In the Advanced section, select the check box beside each type of information you want to replace.** As shown in Figure 6.12, there are five check boxes: Contacts, Calendars, Bookmarks, Notes, and Mail Accounts.

6. **Click Apply.** iTunes replaces the selected information on your iPhone.

6.12 Use the check boxes in the Advanced section to decide which information you want replaced on your iPhone.

Note

If a check box in the Advanced section is disabled, it's because you didn't select the corresponding Sync check box. For example, in Figure 6.12 you see that the Sync notes check box is deselected, so in the Advanced section the Notes check box is disabled.

Syncing Media with Your iPhone

The brainy Phone app and the sleek Safari browser may get the lion's share of kudos for the iPhone, but many people reserve their rave reviews for its iPod app. The darn thing is just so versatile: It can play music, of course, but it also happily cranks out audiobooks and podcasts on the audio side, and music videos, movies, and TV shows on the video side. Ear candy and eye candy in one package!

If there's a problem with this digital largesse, it's that the iPod app might be too versatile. Even if you have a big 32GB iPhone, you may still find its confines a bit cramped, particularly if you're also loading up your iPhone with photos, contacts, and calendars, and you just can't seem to keep your hands out of the App Store cookie jar.

All this means that you probably have to pay a bit more attention when it comes to syncing your iPhone, and the following sections show you how to do just that.

Syncing music and music videos

The iPod app is a digital music player at heart, so you've probably loaded up your iPhone with lots of audio content and lots of music videos. To get the most out of the iPod app's music and video capabilities, you need to know all the different ways you can synchronize these items. For example, if you use the iPod app primarily as a music player and the IPhone has more disk capacity than you need for all of your digital audio, feel free to throw all your music onto the player. On the other hand, your iPhone might not have much free space, or you might only want certain songs and videos on the player to make it easier to navigate. Not a problem! You need to configure iTunes to sync only the songs that you select.

Before getting to the specific sync steps, you need to know that there are three ways to manually sync music and music videos:

Genius

Something I like about syncing playlists is that you can estimate in advance how much space your selected playlists will usurp on the iPhone. In iTunes, click the playlist and then examine the status bar, which tells you the number of songs in the playlist, the total duration, and, most significantly for our purposes, the total size of the playlist.

- **Playlists.** With this method, you specify the playlists that you want iTunes to sync. Those playlists also appear on your iPhone's iPod app. This is by far the easiest way to manually sync music and music videos, because you usually just have a few playlists to select. The downside is that if you have large playlists and you run out of space on your iPhone, the only way to fix the problem is to remove an entire playlist. Another bummer: with this method, you can only sync all of your music videos, or none of your music videos.

- **Check boxes.** With this method, you specify which songs and music videos get synced by selecting the little check boxes that appear beside every song and video in iTunes. This is fine-grained syncing for sure, but because your iPhone can hold thousands of songs, it's also a lot of work.

- **Drag-and-drop.** With this method, you click and drag individual songs and music videos, and drop them on your iPhone's icon in the iTunes Devices list. This is an easy way to get a bunch of tracks on your iPhone quickly, but iTunes doesn't give you any way of tracking which tracks you've dragged and dropped.

Genius

What do you do if you only want to select a few tracks from a large playlist? Waste a big chunk of your life deselecting a few hundred check boxes? Pass. Here's a better way: Press ⌘+A (Mac) or Ctrl+A (Windows) to select every track, right-click (or Control+click on your Mac) any track, and then click Uncheck Selection. Voila! iTunes deselects every track in seconds flat. Now you can select just the tracks you want. You're welcome.

Here are the steps to follow to sync music and music videos using playlists:

1. **In iTunes, click your iPhone in the Devices list.**

2. **Click the Music tab.**

3. **Select the Sync Music check box.** iTunes asks you to confirm that you want to sync music.

4. **Click Sync Music.**

5. **Select the Selected playlists, artists, and genres option.**

6. **Select the check box beside each playlist, artist, and genre you want to sync, as shown in Figure 6.13.**

6.13 Select the Selected playlists option and then select the playlists you want to sync.

7. **Select the Include music videos check box if you also want to add your music videos into the sync mix.**

8. **Select the Include voice memos check box if you also want to sync voice memos that you recorded on your iPhone.**

Genius

If you have lots of music that has been ripped at a high bit rate (say, 256 kbps or higher), those songs will take up lots of disk space on your iPhone. To fix this, click the Summary tab and then select the Convert higher bit rate songs to 128 kbps AAC.

9. **If you want iTunes to fill up any remaining free space on your iPhone with a selection of related music from your library, select the Automatically fill free space with songs check box.**

10. **Click Apply.** iTunes syncs your iPhone using the new settings.

Genius

If you download a music video from the Web and then import it into iTunes (by choosing File@@-->Import), iTunes adds the video to its Movies library. To display it in the Music library instead, open the Movies library, right-click (or Control+click on the Mac) the music video, and then click Get Info. Click the Video tab and use the Kind list to choose Music Video. Click OK. iTunes moves the music video to the Music folder.

Here are the steps to follow to sync using the check boxes that appear beside each track in your iTunes Music library:

1. **Click your iPhone in the Devices list.**

2. **Click the Summary tab.**

3. **Select the Sync only checked songs and videos check box.**

4. **Click Apply.** If iTunes starts syncing your iPhone, drag the Slide to cancel slider on the iPhone to stop it.

5. **Either click Music in the Library list or click a playlist that contains the tracks you want to sync.** If a track's check box is selected, iTunes syncs the track with your iPhone. If a track's check box is deselected, iTunes doesn't sync the track with your iPhone; if the track is already on your iPhone, iTunes removes the track.

6. **In the Devices list, click your iPhone.**

7. **Click the Summary tab.**

8. **Click Sync.** iTunes syncs just the checked tracks.

137

You can also configure iTunes to let you drag tracks from the Music library (or any playlist) and drop them on your iPhone. Here's how this works:

1. **Click your iPhone in the Devices list.**

2. **Click the Summary tab.**

3. **Select the Manually manage music and videos check box.**

4. **Click Apply.** If iTunes starts syncing your iPhone, drag the slide to cancel slider on the iPhone to stop it.

5. **Either click Music in the Library list or click a playlist that contains the tracks you want to sync.**

6. **Choose the tracks you want to sync:**

   - If all the tracks are together, Shift+click the first track, hold down Shift, and then click the last track.

   - If the tracks are scattered all over the place, hold down ⌘ (Mac) or Ctrl (Windows) and click each track.

7. **Click and drag the selected tracks to the Devices list and drop them on the iPhone icon.** iTunes syncs the selected tracks.

Note When you select the Manually manage music and videos check box, iTunes automatically deselects the Sync music check box in the Music tab. However, iTunes doesn't mess with the music on your iPhone. Even when it syncs after a drag and drop, it only adds the new tracks, it doesn't delete any of your phone's existing music.

Caution If you decide to return to playlist syncing by selecting the Sync music check box in the Music tab, iTunes removes all tracks that you added to your iPhone via the drag-and-drop method.

Syncing podcasts

In many ways, podcasts are the most problematic of the various media you can sync with your iPhone. Not that the podcasts themselves pose any concern. Quite the contrary: They're so addictive that it's not unusual to collect them by the dozens. Why is that a problem? Because most professional podcasts are at least a few megabytes in size, and many are tens of megabytes. A large enough collection can put a serious dent in your iPhone's remaining storage space.

All the more reason to take control of the podcast syncing process. Here's how you do it:

1. **Click your iPhone in the Devices list.**

2. **Click the Podcasts tab.**

3. **Select the Sync Podcasts check box.**

4. **If you want iTunes to choose some of the podcasts automatically, select the Automatically include check box and proceed to steps 5 and 6.** If you prefer to choose all the podcasts manually, deselect the Automatically include check box and skip to step 7.

5. **Choose an option from the first pop-up menu:**

   - **All.** Choose this item to sync every podcast.

   - **X Most Recent.** Choose this item to sync the X most recent podcasts.

   - **All Unplayed.** Choose this item to sync all the podcasts you haven't yet played.

   - **X Most Recent Unplayed.** Choose this item to sync the X most recent podcasts that you haven't yet played.

   - **X Least Recent Unplayed.** Choose this item to sync the X oldest podcasts that you haven't yet played.

   - **All New.** Choose this item to sync all the podcasts published since the last sync.

   - **X Most Recent New.** Choose this item to sync the X most recent podcasts published since the last sync.

   - **X Least Recent New.** Choose this item to sync the X oldest podcasts published since the last sync.

6. **Choose an option from the second pop-up menu:**

   - **All podcasts.** Select this option to apply the option from step 4 to all your podcasts.

   - **Selected podcasts.** Select this option to apply the option from step 4 to just the podcasts you select, as shown in Figure 6.14.

7. **Select the check box beside any podcast or podcast episode you want to sync.**

8. **Click Apply.** iTunes syncs the iPhone using your new podcast settings.

Genius

To mark a podcast episode as unplayed, in iTunes choose the Podcasts library, right-click (or Control+click on your Mac) the episode, and then choose Mark as New.

6.14 To sync specific podcasts, choose the Selected podcasts option and then select the check boxes for each podcast you want synced.

Note A podcast episode is unplayed if you haven't yet played at least part of the episode either in iTunes or your iPhone. If you play an episode on your iPhone, the player sends this information to iTunes when you next sync. Even better, your iPhone also lets iTunes know if you paused in the middle of an episode; when you play that episode in iTunes, it starts at the point where you left off.

Syncing audiobooks

The iTunes sync settings for your iPhone have tabs for Music, Photos, Podcasts, and Video, but not one for Audiobooks. What's up with that? It's not, as you might think, some sort of anti-book conspiracy, or even forgetfulness on Apple's part. Instead, iTunes treats audiobook content as a special type of book (not surprisingly). To get audiobooks on your iPhone, follow these steps:

1. **Click your iPhone in the Devices list.**

2. **Click the Books tab.**

3. **Select the Sync Audiobooks check box.**

4. **Select the Selected audiobooks option.**

5. **Select the check box beside each audiobook you want to sync.**

6. **Click Apply.** iTunes syncs your audiobooks to your iPhone.

Syncing movies

It wasn't all that long ago when technology prognosticators and pundits laughed at the idea of people watching movies on a 2-inch by 3-inch screen. Who could stand to watch even a music video on such a tiny screen? The pundits were wrong, of course, because now it's not at all unusual for people to use their iPhones to watch not only music videos, but also short films, animated shorts, and even full-length movies.

The major problem with movies is that their file size tends to be quite large — even short films lasting just a few minutes weigh in at dozens of megabytes, and full-length movies are several gigabytes. Clearly there's a compelling need to manage your movies to avoid filling up your iPhone and leaving no room for the latest album from your favorite band.

Follow these steps to configure and run the movie synchronization:

1. **Click your iPhone in the Devices list.**

2. **Click the Movies tab.**

3. **Select the Sync Movies check box.** iTunes asks you to confirm that you want to sync movies.

4. **Click Sync Movies.**

5. **If you want iTunes to choose some of the movies automatically, select the Automatically include check box and proceed to step 6.** If you prefer to choose all the movies manually, deselect the Automatically include check box and skip to step 7.

6. **Choose an option from the pop-up menu:**

    - **All.** Choose this item to sync every movie.

    - **X Most Recent.** Choose this item to sync the **X** most recent movies you've added to iTunes.

    - **All Unwatched.** Choose this item to sync all the movies you haven't yet played.

    - **X Most Recent Unwatched.** Choose this item to sync the **X** most recent movies you haven't yet played.

    - **X Least Recent Unwatched.** Choose this item to sync the **X** oldest movies you haven't yet played.

Note A movie is unwatched if you haven't yet viewed it either in iTunes or on your iPhone. If you watch a movie on your iPhone, the player sends this information to iTunes when you next sync.

7. **Select the check box beside any other movie you want to sync.**

8. **If you want to watch rented movies on your iPhone, in the Rented Movies section, click the Move button beside the rented movie you want to shift to your iPhone.** iTunes adds the movie to the On *iPhone* list (where *iPhone* is the name of your iPhone).

9. **Click Apply.** iTunes syncs the iPhone using your new movie settings.

Genius

If you download a music video from the Web and then import it into iTunes (by choosing File ➪ Import), iTunes adds the video to its Movies library. To display it in the Music library instead, open the Movies library, right-click (or Ctrl+click on the Mac) the music video, and then click Get Info. Click the Video tab and then use the Kind list to choose Music Video. Click OK. iTunes moves the music video to the Music folder.

Syncing TV show episodes

If the average iPhone is at some risk of being filled up by a few large movie files, it probably is at grave risk of being overwhelmed by a large number of TV show episodes. A single half-hour episode will eat up approximately 250MB, so even a modest collection of shows will consume multiple gigabytes of precious iPhone disk space.

This means it's crucial to monitor your collection of TV show episodes and keep your iPhone synced with only the episodes you need. Fortunately, iTunes gives you a decent set of tools to handle this:

1. **Click your iPhone in the Devices list.**

2. **Click the TV Shows tab.**

3. **Select the Sync TV Shows check box.** iTunes asks you to confirm that you want to sync TV Shows.

4. **Click Sync TV Shows.**

5. **If you want iTunes to choose some of the episodes automatically, select the Automatically include check box and proceed to steps 6 and 7.** If you prefer to choose all the episodes manually, deselect the Automatically include check box and skip to step 8.

6. **Choose an option from the drop-down menu.**
   - **All.** Choose this item to sync every TV show episode.
   - **X Most Recent.** Choose this item to sync the X most recent episodes.
   - **All unwatched.** Choose this item to sync all the episodes you haven't yet viewed.

- **X Most Recent Unwatched.** Choose this item to sync the *X* most recent episodes that you haven't yet viewed.

- **X Least Recent Unwatched.** Choose this item to sync the *X* oldest episodes that you haven't yet viewed.

Note

A TV episode is unwatched if you haven't yet viewed it either in iTunes or your iPhone. If you watch an episode on your iPhone, the player sends this information to iTunes when you next sync.

7. **Choose an option from the second pop-up menu:**

- **All shows.** Select this option to apply the choice from step 5 to all your TV shows with your iPhone.

- **Selected Shows.** Select this option to apply the choice from step 5 just the TV Shows you select, as shown in Figure 6.15.

8. **Select the check box beside any TV Show or episode you want to sync.**

9. **Click Apply.** iTunes syncs the iPhone using your new TV show settings.

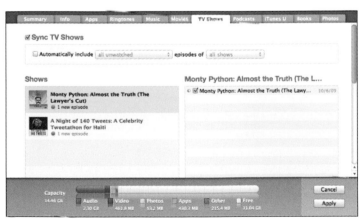

6.15 To sync specific TV shows, select the Sync TV shows option, and then select the check boxes for each show you want synced.

Genius

To mark a TV episode as unwatched, in iTunes choose the TV Shows library, right-click (or Control+click on the Mac) the episode, and then choose Mark as New.

Syncing eBooks

If you've used your computer to add some downloaded eBooks to the iTunes library, you'll want to get those books onto your iPhone as soon as possible. Similarly, if you've grabbed some eBooks from the iBookstore on your iPhone, it's a good idea to back them up to your computer.

You can do both by syncing eBooks between your computer and your iPhone:

1. **In iTunes, click your iPhone in the Devices list.**

2. **Click the Books tab.**

3. **Select the Sync Books check box.**

4. **In the book list, select the check box beside each book that you want to sync, as shown in Figure 6.16.**

5. **Click Apply.** iTunes syncs the iPhone using your new book's settings.

6.16 You can sync selected books with your iPhone.

Syncing computer photos to your iPhone

No iPhone's media collection is complete without a few choice photos to show off around the water cooler. One way to get those photos is to take them with your iPhone's built-in digital camera. However, if you have some good pics on your computer, you can use iTunes to send those images to the iPhone. Note that Apple supports a number of image file types — the usual TIFF and JPEG formats that you normally use for your photos as well as BMP, GIF, JPG2000 or JP2, PICT, PNG, PSD, and SGI.

Note

If you have another photo-editing application installed on your computer, chances are it will also appear in the Sync photos from list.

If you use your computer to process lots of photos, and you want to take copies of some or all of those photos with you on your iPhone, then follow these steps to get synced:

1. **Click your iPhone in the Devices list.**

2. **Click the Photos tab.**

3. **Select the Sync Photos from check box.**

4. **Choose an option from the drop-down menu:**

   - **iPhoto (Mac only).** Choose this item to sync the photos, albums, and events you've set up in iPhoto.

   - **Choose folder.** Choose this command to sync the images contained in a folder you specify.

   - **My Pictures (or Pictures on Windows Vista).** Choose this item to sync the images in the My Pictures (or Pictures) folder.

5. **Select the photos you want to sync.** The controls you see depend on what you chose in step 4:

   - **If you chose either My Pictures or Choose folder.** In this case, select either the All photos option or the Selected folders option. If you select the latter, select the check box beside each subfolder you want to sync.

   - **If you chose iPhoto.** In this case, you get two further options: Select the All photos, albums, events, and faces option to sync your entire iPhoto library; select the Selected photos, albums, events, and faces option and select the check box beside each album, event, and face you want to sync, as shown in Figure 6.17.

6. **Click Apply.** iTunes syncs the iPhone using your new photo settings.

Note

iTunes doesn't sync exact copies of your photos to the iPhone. Instead, it creates what Apple calls TV-quality versions of each image. These are copies of the images that have been reduced in size to match the iPhone's screen size. This not only makes the sync go faster, but it also means the photos take up much less room on your iPhone.

6.17 If you have iPhoto '09 on your Mac, you can sync specified albums, events, and faces to your iPhone.

Syncing iPhone photos to your computer

If you create a Safari bookmark on your iPhone and then sync with your computer, that bookmark is transferred from the iPhone to the default Web browser on your computer. That's a sweet deal that also applies to contacts and appointments, but unfortunately it doesn't apply to media files, which, with one exception, travel along a one-way street from your computer to your iPhone.

Ah, but then there's that one exception, and it's a good one. If you take any photos using your iPhone's built-in (and pretty good) camera, the sync process reverses itself and enables you to send some or all of those images to your computer. Sign us up!

Note

Actually, there's a second exception. If you use the iTunes app on your iPhone to purchase or download music, those files are transferred to your computer during the next sync. iTunes creates a Store category called Purchased on *iPhone*, where *iPhone* is the name of your iPhone. When the sync is complete, you can find your music there, as well as in the Music Library.

The iPhone-to-computer sync process bypasses iTunes entirely. Instead, your computer deals directly with iPhone, and treats it just as though it was some garden-variety digital camera. How this works depends on whether your computer is a Mac or a Windows PC, so I use separate sets of steps.

To sync your iPhone camera photos to your Mac, follow these steps:

1. **Connect your iPhone to your Mac.** iPhoto opens, it adds your iPhone to the Devices list, and it displays the photos from your iPhone's Camera Roll album, as shown in Figure 6.18.

2. **Use the Event Name text box to name the event that these photos represent.**

Genius

If you've imported some of your iPhone photos in the past, you probably don't want to import them again. That's very sensible of you, and you can prevent that by hiding those photos. Select the Hide photos already imported check box.

3. **Choose how you want to import the photos:**

   - If you want to import every photo, click Import All.

   - If you want to import only some of the photos, select the ones you want to import and then click Import Selected.

6.18 When you connect your iPhone to your Mac, iPhoto shows up to handle the import of the photos.

4. **If you want to leave the photos on your iPhone, click Keep Originals.** Otherwise, click Delete Originals to clear the photos from your iPhone.

Here's how things work if you're syncing with a Windows 7 PC (these steps assume you've installed Windows Live Photo Gallery from the Windows Live Essentials site):

Genius

If you don't have Windows Live Photo Gallery installed, you can still access your iPhone photos in Windows 7. Choose Start ⇨ Computer, and then double-click your iPhone in the Portable Devices group. Open the Internal Storage folder, then the DCIM folder, and then the folder that appears (which will have a name such as 800AAAAA). Your iPhone's photos appear, and you can then copy them to your computer.

1. **Connect your iPhone to your Windows PC.**

2. **Open Windows Live Photo Gallery.**

3. **Choose File ⇨ Import from a camera or scanner.** The Import Photos and Videos dialog box appears.

4. **Click the icon for your iPhone, and then click Import.** Windows Live Photo Gallery connects to your iPhone to gather the photo Information.

5. **Select the Import all new Items now option.** If you'd prefer to select the photos you want to Import, select the Review, organize and group Items to import option, click Next and use the dialog box to choose the photos, and then skip to step 7.

6. **Type a tag for the photos.** A tag is a word or short phrase that identifies the photos.

7. **Click Import.** Windows Live Photo Gallery imports the photos.

Here's how things work if you're syncing with a Windows Vista PC:

1. **Connect your iPhone to your Windows PC.** The AutoPlay dialog box appears.

2. **Click Import pictures using Windows.** The rest of these steps assume you selected this option. However, if you have another photo management application installed, it should appear in the AutoPlay list, and you can click it to import the photos using that program.

3. **Type a tag for the photos.** A tag is a word or short phrase that identifies the photos.

4. **Click Import.** Vista imports the photos and then opens Windows Photo Gallery to display them.

Note

Configuring your computer to not download photos from your iPhone means that in the future you either need to reverse the setting to get photos or manually import your photos.

Preventing your iPhone from sending photos to your computer

Each and every time you connect your iPhone to your computer, you see iPhoto (on your Mac), the AutoPlay dialog box (in Windows Vista), or the Scanner and Camera Wizard (in Windows XP). (Windows 7 doesn't display the AutoPlay dialog box when you connect to your iPhone.) This is certainly convenient if you actually want to send photos to your computer, but you might find that you do that only once in a blue moon. In that case, having to deal with iPhoto or a dialog box every time could cause even the most mild mannered among us to start pulling out our hair.

If you prefer to keep your hair, you can config-ure your computer to not pester you about getting photos from your iPhone.

Here how you set this up on your Mac:

1. **Choose Finder ⇨ Applications to open the Applications folder.**

2. **Double-click Image Capture.** The Image Capture application opens.

3. **In the Devices list, click your iPhone.**

4. **Click the Connecting this iPhone opens menu, and then click No appli-cation, as shown in Figure 6.19.**

5. **Choose Image Capture ⇨ Quit Image Capture.** Image Capture saves the new setting and then shuts down. The next time you connect your iPhone, iPhoto ignores it.

6.19 In the Image Capture Preferences window, choose No application to prevent iPhoto from starting when you connect your iPhone.

149

Follow these steps to convince Windows Vista not to open the AutoPlay dialog box each time you connect your iPhone:

1. **Choose Start ⇨ Default Programs to open the Default Programs window.**

2. **Click Change AutoPlay settings.** The AutoPlay dialog box appears.

3. **In the Devices section, open the Apple iPhone list and choose Take no action, as shown in Figure 6.20.**

4. **Click Save.** Vista saves the new setting. The next time you connect your iPhone, you won't be bothered by the AutoPlay dialog box.

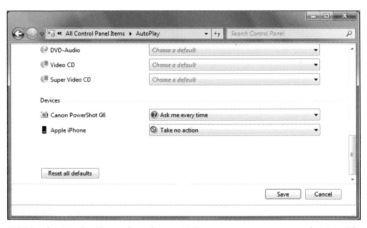

6.20 In the Apple iPhone list, choose Take no action to prevent the AutoPlay dialog box from appearing when you connect your iPhone.

Syncing media with two or more computers

It's a major drag, but you can't sync the same type of content to your iPhone from more than one computer. For example, suppose you're syncing photos from your desktop computer. If you then connect your iPhone to another computer (your notebook, for example), crank up iTunes, and then select the Sync photos from check box, iTunes coughs up the dialog in Figure 6.21. As you can see, iTunes is telling you that if you go ahead with the photo sync on this computer, it will blow away all your existing iPhone photos and albums!

6.21 Syncing the same type of content from two different computers is a no-no in the iTunes world.

So there's no chance of syncing the same iPhone with two different computers, right? Not so fast, my friend! Let's try another thought experiment. Suppose you're syncing your iPhone with your desktop computer, but you're not syncing Movies. Once again, you connect your iPhone to your notebook computer (or whatever), crank up iTunes, and then select the Sync movies check box. Hey, no ominous warning dialog! What gives?

The deal here is that if iTunes sees that you don't have any examples of a particular type of content (such as movies) on your iPhone, it lets you sync that type of content, no questions asked.

In other words, you *can* sync your iPhone with multiple computers, although in a roundabout kind of way. The secret is to have no overlapping content types on the various computers you use for the syncing. For example, let's say you have a home desktop computer, a notebook computer, and a work desktop computer. Here's a sample scenario for syncing your iPhone with all three machines:

- **Home desktop (music and video only).** Select the Sync music check box in the Music tab, and select all the Sync check boxes in the Video tab. Deselect the Sync check boxes on the Photos and Podcasts tabs.
- **Notebook (photos only).** Select the Sync photos from check box on the Photos tab. Deselect all the Sync check boxes in the Music, Podcasts, and Video tabs.
- **Work desktop (podcasts only).** Select the Sync box in the Podcasts tab. Deselect the Sync check boxes in the Music, Photos, and Video tabs.

The eye candy of the iPhone 4's gorgeous screen garners the lion's share of kudos and huzzahs, but your iPhone offers quite a bit of ear candy, as well. With numerous audio accessories available, and with the built-in iPod and iTunes apps, your iPhone packs a real audio punch. This chapter takes you on a tour of your iPhone's audio features and shows you how to get the most out of them to maximize your listening pleasure.

Using Audio Accessories with Your iPhone

As soon as the original iPhone was announced, a rather large cottage industry of iPhone accessories formed, seemingly overnight. Suddenly the world was awash in headsets (wired and Bluetooth), external speakers, FM transmitters, and all manner of cases, car kits, cables, and cradles. There are places that sell iPhone accessories scattered all over the Web, but the following sites are faves with me:

- **Apple.** http://store.apple.com/us/browse/home/shop_iphone
- **Belkin.** www.belkin.com/ipod/iphone/
- **Griffin.** www.griffintechnology.com/devices/iphone/
- **NewEgg.** www.newegg.com/
- **EverythingiCafe.** http://store.everythingicafe.com/

Here are a few notes to remember when shopping for and using audio-related accessories for your iPhone:

- **Look for the logo.** Your iPhone may appear to be an iPod in fancy phone clothes, but it's a completely different device that doesn't fit or work with many iPod accessories. To be sure what you're buying is iPhone-friendly, look for the "Works with iPhone" logo.

- **Headsets, headphones, and earpieces.** The iPhone 4 like the 3G and iPhone 3GS before it uses standard headset jacks, which is good news if you're upgrading from the original iPhone, which had a jack that was recessed into the case. This means that just about any headset that uses a garden-variety stereo mini-plug will fit your iPhone 4 (or 3G or 3GS) without a hitch, and without requiring the purchase of an adapter.

- **External speakers.** There are legions of external speakers made for the iPod where you simply dock the iPod in the device and wail away. Unfortunately, the dimensions of the iPhone's bottom panel are different than any of the iPod models, so you won't be able to just plug-and-play your iPhone. Instead, you need an adapter — such as Apple's Universal Dock Adapter — to ensure a proper fit.

- **FM transmitters.** These are must-have accessories for car trips because they send the iPhone's output to an FM station, which you then play through your car stereo. The FM transmitters that work with the iPod don't generally work with iPhones, so look for one that's designed for the iPhone.

- **Electronic interference.** Because your iPhone is, after all, a phone, it generates a nice little field of electronic interference, which is why you need to switch it to Airplane mode when you're flying (see Chapter 2). That same interference can also wreak havoc on nearby external speakers and FM transmitters, so if you hear static when playing audio, switch to Airplane mode to get rid of it.

Getting More Out of Your iPhone's iPod App

Your iPhone is a living, breathing iPod thanks to its built-in iPod app, which you can fire up any time you want by tapping the iPod icon in the Home screen's menu bar. In the next few sections, you learn a few useful techniques that help you get more out of the iPod app.

Creating a custom iPod menu bar

Your iPhone doesn't come with the famous click-wheel found on physical iPods, so you need some other way of getting around. The iPod app's solution is to present a series of *browse buttons*, each one of which represents a collection of media files organized in some way. For example, tapping the Songs browse button displays a list of all the songs on your iPhone.

You see four browse buttons in the default menu bar — Playlists, Artists, Songs, and Videos — and a fifth button called More that displays a list of seven more browse buttons. Here's a summary of all eleven buttons:

- **Playlists.** Displays your playlists, which are collections of songs that you (or iTunes) have gathered together to play as a group. Your iPhone also enables you to create your own playlists, which I discuss later in this chapter. Tap any playlist to see the songs it holds.

- **Artists.** Displays an alphabetical list of the artists who perform all the songs in your iPhone's music collection. Tap the artist to see an album or songs.

- **Songs.** Offers an alphabetical list of every song on your iPhone. Tap a song to crank it up.

- **Videos.** Displays a list of the videos you have imported to your iPhone. They're organized by category: Movies, Movie Rentals, TV Shows, Music Videos, and Video Podcasts. Tap a video to start playing it.

- **Albums.** Gives you an alphabetical list of your iPhone's album collection, and with each album you see the title, artist, and album art. Tap the album to see the songs it holds.

- **Audiobooks.** Sends in a list of the audiobooks that you have imported to your iPhone. Tap a book to launch the story.

Genius
Sometimes iTunes goes a bit haywire and classifies a single-artist album as a compilation. If you see such an album in your iPhone's Compilations list, open iTunes on your computer, select all the tracks on that album, choose File ⇨ Get Info, choose No in the Compilation list, and then click OK. The next time you sync your iPhone, that album won't appear in Compilations.

- **Compilations.** Offers a list of your iPhone albums that contain multiple artists, such as soundtracks and collections of Christmas music. Tap an album to see its tracks.

- **Composers.** Displays an alphabetical list of the composers who wrote all the songs in your iPhone's music library. Tap the composer to see his or her albums or songs.

- **Genres.** Gives you a list of the genres represented by your iPhone's music (Pop, Rock, Classical, Jazz, and so on). Tap the genre to see its composers.

- **iTunes U.** Lists the lessons and other media that you've downloaded via the iTunes U portion of the iTunes store.

- **Podcasts.** Offers a list of all the podcasts that you have stored on your iPhone, organized alphabetically by publisher. A blue dot next to a publisher helpfully tells you that there are episodes of that podcast you haven't listened to. Tap the publisher to see the individual podcast episodes, sorted by date. Those episodes you haven't watched yet have a blue dot to their left.

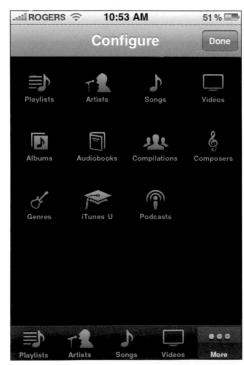

With eleven browse buttons available but only four menu bar slots, chances are there are one or more buttons that you use frequently but are exiled to the More list, thus requiring an extra tap to access. Extra taps are uncool! So if there's a browse button on the More list that you use all the time, you can move it to the menu bar for easier access. Here's how:

1. **On the Home screen, tap iPod to open the iPod app.**

2. **Tap More in the menu bar.**

3. **Tap Edit.** Your iPhone displays the Configure screen, which lists all ten browse buttons, as shown in Figure 7.1.

7.1 Use the Configure screen to create a custom iPod menu bar.

4. **Drag a browse button that you want to add to the menu bar and drop it on what-ever existing menu bar browse button you want it to replace.** For example, if you want to replace the Videos browse button with Podcasts, drag the Podcasts button and drop it on Videos. Your iPhone replaces the old browse button with the new one.

5. **Repeat step 4 to add any of your other preferred browse buttons to the menu bar.**

6. **Tap Done to save the new menu bar configuration.**

Genius If you use your iPhone's iPod app all the time, go ahead and customize the Home button to launch iPod. Tap Settings, tap General, tap Home Button to open the Home Button screen, and then tap iPod. Now you can switch to the iPod super-fast by double-clicking the Home button from any screen.

Rating a song

If you use song ratings to organize your tunes, you might come across some situations where you want to rate a song that's playing on your iPhone:

- You used your iPhone to download some music from the iTunes Store, and you want to rate that music.

- You're listening to a song on your iPhone and decide that you've given a rating that's either too high or too low and you want to change it.

In the first case, you could sync the music to your computer and rate it there; in the second case, you could modify the rating on your computer and then sync with your iPhone. However, these solutions are lame because you have to wait until you connect your iPhone to your computer. If you're out and about, you want to rate the song now, while it's fresh in your mind.

Yes, you can do that with your iPhone:

1. **Locate the song you want to rate and tap it to start the playback.** Your iPhone displays the album art and the name of the artist, song, and album at the top of the screen. To the right of these names, iPhone displays the Details icon.

2. **Tap the Details icon in the upper-right corner of the screen (just below the battery status).** Your iPhone "turns" the album art and displays a list of the songs on the album. Above that list are the five rating dots.

3. **Tap the dot that corresponds to the rating you want to give the song.** For example, to give the song a four-star rating, tap the fourth dot from the left, as shown in Figure 7.2.

4. **Tap the album art icon in the upper-right corner.** Your iPhone saves the rating and returns you to the album art view.

The next time you sync your iPhone with your computer, iTunes notes your new ratings and applies them to the same tracks in the iTunes library.

Browsing music with Cover Flow

Here in the second decade of the twenty-first century, physical CD collections are suffering the same fate that vinyl LP collections went through in the 1980s: they're disappearing. I'm not crying in my beer over this trend

7.2 Tap the dot that corresponds to the rating you want to give the currently playing track.

because a large anthology of CDs is an eyesore. However, there's one thing I do miss: flipping through CD covers looking for something that catches my eye. You may not be able to do this anymore, but your iPhone gives you the next best thing: Cover Flow. This feature displays all your album art as a kind of flip book. Only in this case I should call it a "flick" book because you can use your finger to flick back and forth through the album art, just like flipping through a CD collection.

Switching to Cover Flow mode takes a mere two steps:

1. **In the Home screen, tap the iPod icon to open the iPod app if it's not already open.**

2. **Rotate your iPhone into the landscape position.** Your iPhone switches to the Cover Flow view, and displays either the first album in your collection, or the album associated with whatever's currently playing (or most recently played), as shown in Figure 7.3.

7.3 Open iPod and rotate your iPhone into landscape mode to see the Cover Flow view.

You can flick to the right and left to navigate the albums. To see the tracks on an album, tap the album art (or the "i" icon in the bottom-right corner). To return to the regular iPod view, rotate your iPhone into the upright position.

Controlling music with voice commands

Controlling a computer with just voice commands has been a mainstream dream ever since the first Star Trek series. Mac OS X and Windows come with speech recognition features, but few people use them because they're difficult to configure and are more often than not frustrating to use. Third-party speech recognition programs are more powerful, but they tend to be expensive and still don't work all that well.

The dream of voice control remains unfulfilled on desktop machines, but on the iPhone 4 (and 3GS) Voice Control is a feature! You saw in Chapter 3 that you can use Voice Control to make calls just by talking to your iPhone. But Voice Control goes beyond phone calls and also lets you control the iPod app with voice commands. This is one of the slickest iPhone features, not just because you get a satisfyingly wide variety of commands to play with (as you'll soon see), but also because it just works. Unlike generic speech recognition programs that must support a wide variety of programs and commands, Voice Control only has to do two things — make calls and control the iPod — so it's optimized for those tasks.

Crank up Voice Control, by pressing and holding the Home button (or press and hold the center button on your earphones) until you hear a two-tone beep and you see the Voice Control screen.

159

The most basic iPod voice commands mimic the on-screen controls you see when you're playing a song. That is, while a song is playing, you can speak any of the following commands to control the playback:

- pause
- play
- next track (or next song)
- previous track (or previous song)

In each case, your iPhone repeats the command back to you so you know whether it heard you correctly. You can also get more sophisticated by speaking commands that use roughly the following format:

verb object subject

Here, *verb* is the action you want the iPod to take, which will most often be play; *object* is the type of iPod item you want to work with, such as song, album, or playlist; and *subject* is the particular item you want included in the action, such as the name of a song, album, playlist, or artist. Here are a few examples:

- play songs by the submarines
- play album blue horse
- play playlist my top rated

Again, your iPhone confirms the command by saying it back to you (for example, "playing songs by the submarines").

Here are a few more voice commands to play with:

- **turn on shuffle.** Use this command to activate the iPod's Shuffle mode.

- **what song is this.** Use this command to find out the name of the current song and artist. The iPhone responds with "now playing *song* by *artist*".

- **play more songs like this.** Use this command to create a playlist of songs that are similar to the current song. Your iPhone responds with "playing genius playlist based on *song* by *artist*". This is called a Genius playlist, which is explained in more detail later in this chapter.

Turning off the Shake to Shuffle feature

One of the nice little audio bonuses you get with your iPhone is the Shake to Shuffle feature, which lets you shuffle to a random song just by shaking your iPhone side to side. If you're playing songs by a particular artist, you get a random song from the same artist; if you're playing an album, you get a random song from that album.

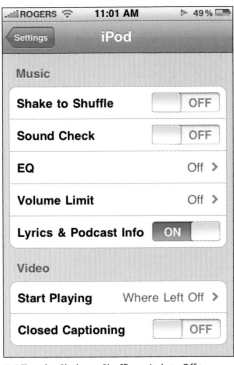

If you're not a fan of Shake to Shuffle (for example, you might find it shuffles when you don't want it to) or if you want to turn it off temporarily (for example, if you're taking the iPhone with you for a run or bull-riding session), here's how to disable it:

1. **On the Home screen tap Settings.** The Settings screen shows up.

2. **Tap iPod.** The iPod screen appears.

3. **Tap the Shake to Shuffle switch to the Off position, as shown in Figure 7.4.**

7.4 Tap the Shake to Shuffle switch to Off to disable this feature.

Answering an incoming call while listening to music on the headset

If you're listening to music on your iPhone and a call comes in, you obviously don't want the caller to be subjected to Blitzen Trapper at top volume. Fortunately, your iPhone smartphone is smart enough to know this, and it automatically pauses the music. If you have your iPhone headset on when the call arrives, use the following techniques to deal with it:

- **Answer the call.** Press and release the headset's mic button (it's the plastic button on one of the headset's cords).

- **Decline the call (send it directly to voicemail).** Press and hold the mic button for about two seconds, and then release. If you hear a couple of beeps, you successfully declined the call.

- **End the call.** Press and release the mic button.

Getting More Out of Your iPhone's iTunes App

If you have a fast Wi-Fi connection going (a 3G cellular connection will do in a pinch), you can use your iPhone to purchase music directly from the iTunes Store. To get there, tap the iTunes icon in the Home screen.

Creating a custom iTunes menu bar

Just like the iPod app, the iTunes app also presents you with a series of browse buttons, each one of which represents a section or feature of the mobile version of the iTunes Store (see Figure 7.5). For example, tapping the Ringtones browse button displays a list of ringtones that you can purchase.

You see four browse buttons in the default menu bar — Music, Videos, Ringtones, and Search — and a fifth button called More that displays a list of four more browse buttons. Here's a summary of all eight buttons:

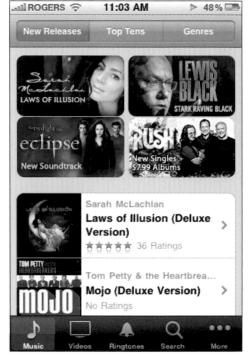

7.5 The iTunes app uses browse buttons to navigate the mobile iTunes Store.

- ⊚ **Music.** Enables you to browse and music on the iTunes Store using the New Releases, Top Tens, and Genres tabs.

- ⊚ **Videos.** Enables you to browse video content on the iTunes Store using the Movies, TV Shows, and Music Videos tabs.

- ⊚ **Ringtones.** Enables you to browse ringtones on the iTunes Store using the New Releases, Top Tens, and Genres tabs.

- ⊚ **Search.** Enables you to search the iTunes Store.

- ⊚ **Podcasts.** Enables you to browse podcasts on the iTunes Store using the What's Hot, Top Tens, and Categories tabs.

- ⊚ **Audiobooks.** Enables you to browse audiobooks on the iTunes Store using the Featured, Top Tens, and Categories tabs.

- **iTunes U.** Enables you to browse lessons on the iTunes Store using the What's Hot, Top Tens, and Categories tabs.

- **Downloads.** Lists the current downloads in progress.

If there's a browse button on the More list that you use all the time, you can move it to the menu bar for easier access. Here's how:

1. **On the Home screen, tap iTunes to open the iTunes app.**

2. **Tap More in the menu bar.**

3. **Tap Edit.** Your iPhone displays the Configure screen, which lists all eight browse buttons, as shown in Figure 7.6.

4. **Drag a browse button that you want to add to the menu bar and drop it on whatever existing menu bar browse button you want it to replace.** For example, if you want to replace the Ringtones browse button with Audiobooks, drag the Audiobooks button and drop it on Ringtones. Your iPhone replaces the old browse button with the new one.

5. **Repeat step 4 to add any of your other preferred browse buttons to the menu bar.**

6. **Tap Done to save the new menu bar configuration.**

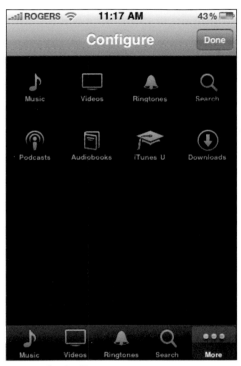

7.6 Use the Configure screen to create a custom iTunes menu bar.

Redeeming an iTunes gift card

If you've been lucky enough to receive an iTunes gift card or gift certificate for your birthday or some other special occasion (or just for the heck of it), you'd normally use the iTunes Store on your computer to redeem it. However, if you're not at your computer and the gift card is burning a hole in your pocket, don't fret: You can redeem the gift card right on your iPhone. Here's how:

1. **On the Home screen, tap iTunes to open the iTunes app.**

2. **Tap Music in the menu bar.**

3. **Scroll to the bottom of the Music screen and then tap Redeem.** iTunes then displays the Redeem screen shown in Figure 7.7.

4. **Use the Code box to type the code from the gift card or gift certificate.**

5. **Tap RedeemRepeat step 4 to add any of your other preferred browse buttons to the menu bar.** iTunes asks you to sign in to your account.

6. **Tap Continue.** iTunes prompts you for your account password.

7. **Type your iTunes password and then tap OK.** iTunes redeems the gift code and then displays your current account balance.

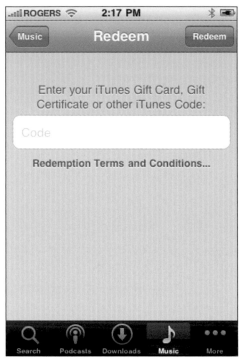

7.7 Use the Redeem screen to redeem an iTunes gift card or gift certificate.

Creating a Custom Ringtone for Your iPhone

Your iPhone comes stocked with 25 predefined ringtones. Although some of them are amazingly annoying, you ought to be able to find one you can live with. If you can't, or if you crave something unique, you can create a custom ringtone and use that.

The easiest way to cobble together a custom ringtone is to convert a song you purchase through iTunes:

1. **In iTunes, select the track you want to use.** If you're not sure which tracks in your library are ringtone-friendly, look for the bell icon in the Ringtone column (which itself shows a bell icon in the column header).

Note

No Ringtone column in sight? No problem. Right-click (or Control+click on your Mac) any column header, and then click Ringtone.

2. **Choose Store ⇨ Create Ringtone.** The Ringtone Editor appears. If you run the Create Ringtone command and an error message appears telling you that iTunes can't connect to the iTunes Store, it means your country's version of the iTunes Store can't handle ringtone purchases. That's a drag, but I show you a couple of ways to work around it in the next set of steps.

3. **Click and drag the highlighted area to specify which part of the song you want to use for your ringtone.** The maximum size of the ringtone snippet is 30 seconds.

4. **In the Looping pop-up menu, choose the interval you want between rings.** Click Preview any time you want to hear your ringtone in action.

5. **Click Buy.** iTunes rings up the purchase and adds the new ringtone to its Ringtones category.

The Create Ringtone feature is easy, for sure, but it only works on certain songs, and many international versions of the iTunes Store don't offer support for purchasing ringtones. Fortunately, you can get around both limitations using GarageBand, Apple's application for making homebrew music.

First, here are the steps to follow to create a ringtone out of any song in your iTunes library:

1. **Click the GarageBand icon in the Dock, click iPhone Ringtone, click Choose, type a name for the project, and then click Create.** GarageBand starts a new project for you.

2. **Choose Track ⇨ Delete Track to get rid of the default track.**

3. **Switch to iTunes, click and drag the song you want to use for your ringtone, and drop it inside GarageBand.** The program creates a new track for the song.

4. **Click and drag the Cycle Region to the approximate area of the song you want to use for the ringtone.** The Cycle Region, pointed out in Figure 7.8, defines the portion of the song that you would use for a ringtone. If you don't see the Cycle Region tool, click the Cycle Region button pointed out in Figure 7.8

5. **Click and drag the left edge of the Cycle Region to define the starting point of the ringtone.**

6. **Click and drag the right edge of the Cycle Region to define the starting point of the ringtone.**

7. **Choose Share ⇨ Send Ringtone to iTunes.** GarageBand converts the track to a ringtone, and then adds it to the Ringtones category in iTunes.

Cycle Region tool

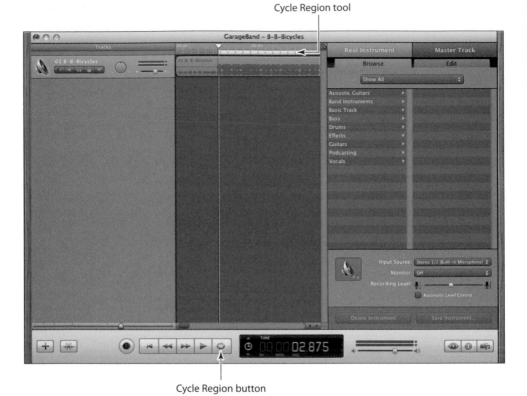

Cycle Region button

7.8 Use the Cycle Region to define what part of the song you want to use for the ringtone.

Genius

There's no reason you have to use commercial music for your ringtone. GarageBand makes it easy to create your own music from scratch. For example, choose File ⇨ New, click Magic GarageBand, click a music genre, and then click Choose. GarageBand creates a whole song for you, and you can even add your own instruments! (Click Audition, and then click Create Project when you're done.)

Note

The maximum length for a GarageBand ringtone is 40 seconds. To see how long the Cycle Region is, choose Control ⇨ Show Time in LCD.

The next time you sync your iPhone, click the Ringtones tab, select the Sync Ringtones check box, select the Selected ringtones option, select the check box beside your custom ringtone, and then click Apply. To apply the custom ringtone on your iPhone, tap Settings in the Home screen, tap

Sounds, and tap Ringtone. Your ringtone appears in the Custom section of the Ringtone screen. Tap it to use the snippet as your ringtone.

Working with Playlists

Although you can purchase and download songs directly from the iTunes Store on your iPhone, I'm going to assume that the vast majority of your music library is cooped up on your Mac or PC, and that you're going to want to transfer that music to your iPhone. Or perhaps I should say that you're going to want to transfer *some* of that music to the iPhone. Most of us now have multi-gigabyte music collections, so depending on the storage capacity of your iPhone (and the amount of other content you've stuffed into it, particularly videos and movies), it's likely that you only want to copy a subset of your music library.

If that's the case, then iTunes gives you three choices when it comes to selecting which tunes to transfer: artist, genre, and playlists. The first two are self-explanatory (and, in any case, I gave you the audio syncing details in Chapter 6), but it's the last of these three where you can take control of syncing music to your iPhone.

A *playlist* is a collection of songs that are related in some way, and using your iTunes library, you can create customized playlists that include only the songs that you want to hear. For example, you might want to create a playlist of upbeat or festive songs to play during a party or celebration. Similarly, you might want to create a playlist of your current favorite songs.

Playlists are the perfect way to control music syncing for the iPhone, so before you start transferring tunes, consider creating a playlist or three in iTunes.

Creating a favorite tunes playlist for your iPhone

Your iTunes library includes a Rating field that enables you to supply a rating for your tracks: one star for songs you don't like so much, up to five stars for your favorite tunes. You click the song you want to rate, and then click a dot in the Rating column (click the first dot for a one-star rating, the second dot for a two-star rating, and so on). Rating songs is useful because it enables you to organize your music. For example, the Playlists section includes a My Top Rated playlist that includes all your four- and five-star-rated tunes, ordered by the Rating value.

Rating tracks comes in particularly handy when deciding which music to use to populate your iPhone. If you have tens of gigabytes of tunes, only some of them will fit on your iPhone. How do you choose? One possibility would be to rate your songs, and then just sync the My Top Rated playlist to your iPhone.

The problem with the My Top Rated playlist is that it includes only your four- and five-star-rated tunes. You can fit thousands of tracks on your iPhone, but it's unlikely that you've got thousands of songs rated at four stars or better. To fill out your playlist, you should also include songs rated at three stars, a rating that should include lots of good, solid tunes.

To set this up, you have two choices:

- **Modify the My Top Rated playlist.** Right-click (or Control+click on a Mac) the My Top Rated playlist, and then click Edit Playlist. In the Smart Playlist dialog, click the second star, and then click OK.

- **Create a new playlist.** This is the way to go if you want to leave My Top Rated as your best music. Choose File ➪ New Smart Playlist to open the Smart Playlist dialog. Choose Rating in the Field list, Is Greater Than in the Operator list, and then click the second star. Figure 7.9 shows the configured dialog. Click OK, type a title for the playlist (such as Favorite Tunes), and then press Return (or Enter).

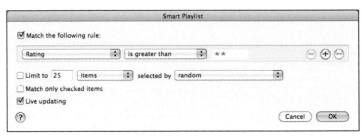

7.9 Use the Smart Playlist dialog to create a playlist that contains your tracks rated at three stars or more.

The next time you sync your iPhone, be sure to include either the My Top Rated playlist or the Smart Playlist you created.

Creating a playlist on your iPhone

iOS 4.0 The playlists on your iPhone are those you've synced via iTunes, and those playlists are either generated automatically by iTunes or they're ones you've cobbled together yourself. However, when you're out in the world and listening to music, you might come up with an idea for a different collection of songs. It might be girl groups, boy bands, or songs with animals in the title.

Whatever your inspiration, don't do it the hard way by picking out and listening to each song one at a time. Instead, you can use your iPhone to create a playlist on the fly.

To create a playlist using the iPod app, follow these steps:

1. **Open the iPod app.**

2. **Tap the Playlists icon.** This displays your playlists.

3. **Tap Add Playlist.** The iPod app displays the New Playlist dialog.

4. **Type the name of your playlist, and then tap Save.** The iPod app displays the Songs screen, which contains a list of all of your songs.

5. **Scroll through the list and tap the blue + key next to each song you want to add to your list.** Your iPhone turns a song gray when you add it, as shown in Figure 7.10.

6. **When you've added all the songs you want, tap Done.** The iPod app displays the playlist.

Your playlist isn't set in stone by any means. You can get rid of songs, change the song order, and add more songs. Follow these steps:

1. **In the iPod app, tap the Playlists icon to see your playlists.**

2. **Tap your playlist.** The iPod app displays the playlist settings and music.

3. **Tap Edit.** This changes the list to the editable version, as shown in Figure 7.11.

4. **To remove a song, tap the red Delete icon to the left of the song, and then tap the Delete button that appears.** If you change your mind, tap the red Delete icon again to cancel the deletion.

5. **To move a song within the playlist, slide the song's drag icon (it's on the right) up or down to the position you prefer.**

6. **To add more tracks, tap the + button in the upper-left corner, select another playlist, and then tap the blue + key next to each song you want to add.**

7. **When you finish editing, tap Done.** This sets the playlist.

Note

If your playlist is a bit of a mess, or if your mood suddenly changes, don't delete all the tracks one-by-one. Instead, open the playlist, tap Edit, and then tap Clear. When your iPhone asks you to confirm, tap Clear Playlist.

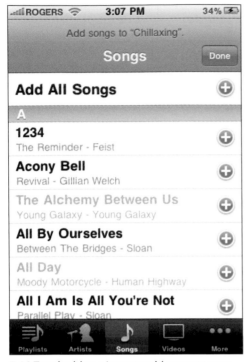

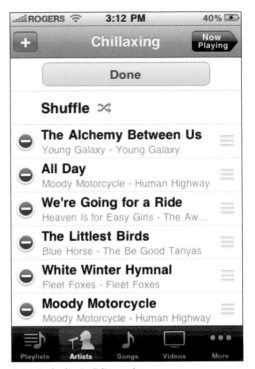

7.10 Tap the blue + icons to add songs to your playlist.

7.11 A playlist in Edit mode.

Creating a Genius playlist on your iPhone

You may be familiar with the iTunes Genius Sidebar, which shows you songs from the iTunes Store that are similar to a particular song in your library. It's a great way to find new music. Your iPhone's iPod app doesn't have a Genius Sidebar, but it has something sort of similar: a Genius playlist. The idea here is that you pick a song on your iPhone, and the iPod app creates a playlist of other songs on your iPhone that are similar. It's a ridiculously easy way to ride a particular sonic groove.

Here's how to create a Genius playlist:

1. **In the iPod app, tap Playlists.** The iPod app displays the Playlists screen.

2. **Tap Genius Playlist.** The iPod app displays a list of the songs on your iPhone.

Genius

An even easier way to create a Genius playlist is to play the song you want to use as the basis of the playlist, press and hold the Home button to bring up Voice Control, and then say "play more songs like this".

3. **Tap the song you want to use as the basis of the Genius playlist.** The iPod app gathers the similar tunes on your iPhone, briefly displays a list of them in the Genius Playlist screen, switches to the Now Playing window, and plays the song you chose.

4. **Tap the Back button.** The iPod app displays the Genius Playlist screen (see Figure 7.12), which holds the list of songs that are similar to the one you chose in step 3.

In the Genius Playlist screen, you can perform the following actions to mess around with your shiny, new playlist:

- Tap Refresh to recreate the playlist.
- Tap a song to play it.
- Tap Save to save the playlist to the Playlists screen.
- Tap New to crank out a new Genius playlist.

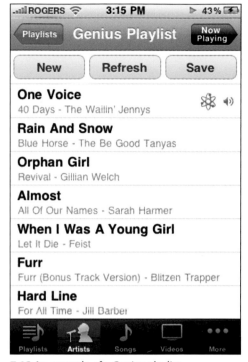

7.12 An example of a Genius playlist.

Customizing Your iPhone's Audio Settings

Audiophiles in the crowd don't get much to fiddle with in the iPhone, but there are a few audio settings to play with. Here's how to get at them:

1. **Press the Home button to get to the Home screen.**

2. **Tap the Settings icon.** The Settings screen opens.

3. **Tap the iPod icon.** Your iPhone displays the iPod settings screen, as shown in Figure 7.13.

Besides the Shake to Shuffle switch discussed earlier, you get three other settings to try out:

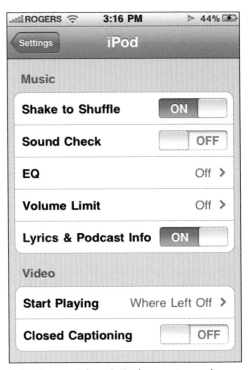

7.13 Use your iPhone's iPod screen to muck around with the audio settings.

- **Sound Check.** Every track is recorded at different audio levels, so invariably you get some tracks that are louder than others. With the Sound Check feature, you can set your iPhone to play all of your songs at the same level. This feature only affects the baseline level of the music and doesn't change any of the other levels, so you still get the highs and lows. If you use it, you don't need to worry about having to quickly turn down the volume when a really loud song comes on. To turn on Sound Check, in the iPod settings page, tap the Sound Check switch to the On position.

- **EQ.** This setting controls your iPhone's built-in equalizer, which is actually a long list of preset frequency levels that affect the audio output. Each preset is designed for a specific type of audio: vocals, talk radio, classical music, rock, hip-hop, and lots more. To set the equalizer, tap EQ and then tap the preset you want to use (or tap None to turn off the equalizer).

● **Volume Limit.** You use this setting to prevent the iPhone's volume from being turned up too high and damaging your (or someone else's) hearing. You know, of course, that pumping up the volume while you've got your earbuds on is an audio no-no, right? I thought so. However, I also know that when a great tune comes on, it's often a little *too* tempting to go for 11 on the volume scale. If you can't resist the temptation, use Volume Limit to limit the damage. Tap Volume Limit and then drag the Volume slider to maximum allowed volume.

● **Lyrics & Podcast Info.** Leave this setting On to see extra info about songs and podcasts when you click the Details button in the iPod app. For example, if you add lyrics for a song in iTunes (right-click the song, click Get Info, click the Lyrics tab), you see those lyrics in Details view.

Genius

If you're setting up an iPhone for a younger person, you should set the Volume Limit. However, what prevents the young whippersnapper from setting a higher limit? You can. In the Volume Limit screen, tap Lock Limit Volume. In the Set Code screen, tap out a four-digit code, and then tap the code again to confirm. This disables the Volume slider in the Volume Limit screen.

How Do I Max Out My iPhone's Photo and Video Features?

Your iPhone is a perk-filled device, to be sure, and one of the best of those perks is that the iPhone moonlights as a digital media player. Not only have you got the music, podcasts, and audiobooks that I talked about in Chapter 7, but you've also got movies, TV shows, videos, photos, and even YouTube right there in the palm of your hand. So when you're tired of calling, researching, e-mailing, scheduling, and other serious iPhone pursuits, you can kick back with a photo slideshow or a video to relax. However, your iPhone is capable of more than just playing and viewing media. It's actually loaded with cool features that enable you to create and manipulate photos and videos and use those files to enhance other parts of your digital life. This chapter is your guide to these features.

Getting More Out of Your iPhone's Photos

Your iPhone comes with a built-in digital camera so you can take pictures while you're running around town. Taking a picture is straightforward: on the Home screen, tap Camera, and then tap the Camera button. (If you have an iPhone 4 or 3GS, be sure to first flick the mode switch to Camera.)

While using the camera itself may be simple, what you can do with photos on your iPhone is pretty cool. You can e-mail photos to friends, take a photo and assign it to a contact, or make a slide show with music in the background. Your iPhone's large screen makes it the perfect portable photo album. No more whipping out wallet shots of your kids. Now you can show people your iPhone photo album!

To get to your photos, tap the Photos icon in your iPhone's Home screen to display the Photo Albums screen, which lists your photo albums. Tap an album to see its pictures, and then tap the picture you want to check out.

4.0 Taking advantage of the new iPhone 4 camera features

iOS 4.0   Before getting to the Photos app, I should take a second here to talk about the new camera in the iPhone 4. First, if you're moving up to the iPhone 4 from the iPhone 3G, you'll be pretty pleased at what you see. The camera on the iPhone 3G was pretty basic: a 2-megapixel camera with no scene modes, no zoom, and no video. It produces a decent image if you have plenty of available light and the subject isn't moving, but otherwise the photos it produces are on the mediocre side.

The camera hardware was a major source of disappointment with the iPhone 3G, so Apple decided to address at least some of the problems by adding four new camera features to the iPhone 3GS:

- **More megapixels.** The iPhone 3GS camera is 3 megapixels, which means 50 percent more pixels than the iPhone 3G.

- **Autofocus.** The iPhone 3GS camera automatically focuses on whatever subject is in the middle of the frame.

- **Tap to focus.** If the subject you want to focus on is not in the middle of the frame, you can tap the subject and the iPhone 3GS automatically moves the focus to that object, and it automatically adjusts the white balance and exposure.

Barbara "Yaeko" McCrum [Nakatani]

03/03/1931 ~ 09/30/2011

Born in Martinez, CA on March 3, 1931. Passed away at the age of 80 at Kaiser Hospital in S.S.F. with her family by her side. She was preceded in death by her husband of 54 years George and their son Raymond. She is survived by her eight children, Georgia Lynn [Chuck] Cox, George Jr. [Dolores], Georgeanna [Richard] Silveria, Georgette . Schiller, Donald [Patty], Georgina [Steve] Jackson, Georgialee McCrum, James [Jan], thirteen grandchildren, ten great-grandchildren and one great-great grandchild, and many other loving relatives. Funeral Service will be held on Wednesday October 5, 2011 at 11:00am at Nauman Lincoln Roos Mortuary, 322 Maple Ave., SSF, CA 94080.

Nauman Lincoln Roos Mortuary

322 Maple Avenue

So. San Francisco, CA 94080

650-583-8787

na
not
he
a
d
e
He
-
r
ct,"

A student leaves Oakl

Santana sent Ruby t
written response to the
report. In it, Oakland s
believes California Cap
owes the city some $36
Tagami said he would
ing to put that amount

on't get h

le
es
ear-
he
—
-
n
r-
es a
d
h.
ne

issue. Councilwoman
Brooks is pushing for
installation of technol
detects the location of
to increase safety.

Meanwhile, Mayor J
Quan is working on h
plan of action that has
released, said Sue Pip
mayor's spokeswoman

The city last week r
federal funding for 25
police officers who wi
assigned to patrol the
around some of the ci
lic middle schools.

But for all the conce
have been raised abou
of Oakland's 676-mem
police force, it doesn't

- **Automatic macro.** If you're taking a close-up of a flower or something similar, the iPhone 3GS has built-in macro capabilities to bring out the detail in such shots.

- **Geotagging.** The iPhone 3GS can use its built-in GPS sensor to add location data to each photo. When you first load the camera, it asks if it's okay to use your current location, so be sure to tap OK if you want your photos geotagged.

That's a good start, but Apple radically redesigned the camera system in iPhone 4, which now offers the following:

- **Front-facing camera.** The iPhone 4 comes with two cameras: One on the back for regular shots, and one on the front for taking self-portraits. In the Camera app, tap the Switch Camera icon (pointed out in Figure 8.1) to switch between the front and rear cameras.

- **Even more megapixels.** The iPhone 4's back camera is now 5 megapixels (the front camera is just 0.3 megapixels).

- **LED flash.** The iPhone 4 has a built-in LED flash, which sits right beside the rear camera, so now you can take pictures at night or in extremely low-light conditions. The LED flash is in Auto mode by default, which means it flashes automatically when the ambient light is low. To control this in the Camera app, tap the Flash icon (pointed out in Figure 8.1), and then tap On (to use the flash with every shot), Off (to never use the flash), or Auto.

- **Backside illumination sensor.** This rear sensor can tell when you're shooting in low-light conditions and adjust the camera settings to compensate.

- **5X digital zoom.** You can now zoom using the iPhone 4's back camera. Tap the screen to display the zoom slider, as shown in Figure 8.1, then tap-and-drag the slider right to zoom in, or left to zoom out.

8.1 Tap the screen and then drag the slider to zoom in and out.

Scrolling, rotating, zooming, and panning photos

You can do quite a lot with your photos once they are in your iPhone, and it isn't your normal photo browsing experience. You aren't just a passive viewer because you can actually take some control over what you see and how the pictures are presented.

You can use the following techniques to navigate and manipulate your photos:

- **Scroll.** You move forward or backward through your photos by flicking. Flick from the right to left to view the next photo; flick left to right to view the previous shot. Alternatively, tap the screen, and then tap the Previous and Next buttons to navigate your photos.

- **Rotate.** When a landscape shot shows up on your iPhone it gets letterboxed at the top (that is, you see black space above and below the image). To get a better view, rotate the screen into the landscape position and the photo rotates right along with it, filling the entire screen. When you come upon a photo with a portrait orientation, rotate the iPhone back to the upright position for best viewing.

- **Zoom.** Zooming magnifies the shot that's on the screen. There are two methods to do this.

  - **Double-tap the area of the photo that you want to zoom in on.** The iPhone doubles the size of the portion you tapped. Double-tap again to return the photo to its original size.

  - **Spread and pinch.** To zoom in, spread two fingers apart over the area you want magnified. To zoom back out, pinch two fingers together.

- **Pan.** After you zoom in on the photo, you may find that the iPhone didn't zoom in exactly where you wanted or you may just want to see another part of the photo. Drag your finger across the screen to move the photo along with your finger, an action known as *panning*.

Note You can scroll to another photo if you're zoomed in, but it takes a lot more work to get there because the iPhone thinks you're trying to pan. For faster scrolling, return the photo to its normal size, and then scroll.

Adding an existing photo to a contact

You can assign a photo from one of your albums to any of your contacts. This is one of our favorite iPhone features because it means that when the person calls you, his or her smiling mug appears on your screen. Now *that's* caller ID! There are two ways to assign a photo to a contact: You can assign the photo straight from a photo album, or you can go through the Contacts app.

First, here's how you assign a photo from a photo album:

1. **Tap Photos in the Home screen.** The Photos screen appears.

2. **Tap the photo album that has the image you want to use.**

3. **Tap the photo you want to use.** Your iPhone opens the photo.

4. **Tap the image to reveal the controls.**

5. **Tap the Action button.** The Action button is the button on the left side of the menu bar. (If you don't see the menu bar, tap the screen.) iPhone displays a list of actions you can perform.

6. **Tap Assign To Contact.** A list of all of your contacts appears.

7. **Tap the contact you want to associate with the photo.** The Move and Scale screen appears.

8. **Drag the image so that it's positioned on the screen the way you want.**

9. **Pinch or spread your fingers over the image to set the zoom level you want.**

10. **Tap Set Photo.** iPhone assigns the photo to the contact and returns you to your photo album.

To assign a photo using the Contacts app, follow these steps:

1. **On the Home screen, tap the Contacts icon to open the Contacts app.**

2. **Tap the contact that you want to add a photo to.** Your iPhone displays the contact's Info screen.

3. **Tap Edit to put the contact into Edit mode.**

4. **Tap Add Photo.** iPhone displays a list of photo options.

5. **Tap Choose Existing Photo.** Your iPhone displays the Photo Albums screen.

6. **Tap the album that contains the photo you want to use.**

7. **Tap the photo you want.** The Move and Scale screen appears.

8. **Drag the image so that it's positioned on the screen the way you want.**

9. **Pinch or spread your fingers over the image to set the zoom level you want.**

10. **Tap Choose.** iPhone assigns the photo to the contact and returns you to the Info screen.

11. **Tap Done.** Your iPhone exits Edit mode.

179

Taking a contact's photo with the iPhone camera

If you don't have a picture of a contact handy, that's not a problem because you can take advantage of your iPhone's camera to snap his or her image the next time you get together. You can do this either using the Camera app or via the Contacts list.

To assign a photo from the Camera app, follow these steps:

1. **In the Home screen, tap the Camera icon on the Home screen to enter the Camera app.** A shutter appears on the screen.

2. **Frame the person on your screen and say "Okay, say iPhooooone."**

3. **Tap the Camera button at the bottom of the screen to snap the picture.**

4. **Tap the Camera Roll icon in the bottom-left corner.** This opens the Camera Roll screen.

5. **Tap the photo you just took.** Your iPhone opens the photo and reveals the photo controls.

6. **Tap the Action button.** The Action button is the button on the left side of the menu bar. (If you don't see the menu bar, tap the screen.) iPhone displays a list of actions you can perform.

7. **Tap Assign To Contact.** A list of all of your contacts is displayed.

8. **Tap the contact you want to associate with the photo.** The Move and Scale screen appears.

9. **Drag the image so that it's positioned on the screen the way you want.**

10. **Pinch or spread your fingers over the image to set the zoom level you want.**

11. **Tap Set Photo.** iPhone assigns the photo to the contact and returns you to the photo.

To assign a photo using the Contacts app, follow these steps:

1. **On the Home screen, tap the Contacts icon to open the Contacts app.**

2. **Tap the contact that you want to add a photo to.** Your iPhone displays the contact's Info screen.

3. **Tap Edit to put the contact into Edit mode.**

4. **Tap Add Photo.** iPhone displays a list of photo options.

5. **Tap Take Photo.** This activates the camera on the iPhone.

6. **Frame the person on the screen, then tap the Camera button to take the photo.** The Move and Scale screen appears.

7. **Drag the image so that it's positioned on the screen the way you want.**

8. **Pinch or spread your fingers over the image to set the zoom level you want.**

9. **Tap Use Photo.** iPhone assigns the photo to the contact and returns you to the Info screen.

10. **Tap Done.** Your iPhone exits Edit mode.

Sending a photo via e-mail

More often than you'd think, it comes in really handy to be able to send photos from your iPhone to someone's e-mail. This is particularly true if it's a photo you've just taken with your iPhone camera, because then you can share the photo pronto, without having to trudge back to your computer. You also have the option of e-mailing an existing photo in one of your iPhone photo albums.

Caution

Having the technology to e-mail a photo at your fingertips is wonderful, but bear in mind that your recipient doesn't see the photo in its natural state. Instead, your iPhone shrinks the photo to 640 pixels wide by 480 pixels tall, a pale shadow of its original 2560-x-1920-pixel glory.

Here are the steps to follow to take a photo with the iPhone camera and then e-mail it:

1. **On the Home screen, tap Camera.** The Camera screen appears.

2. **Line up your subject and tap the Camera button to take the picture.**

3. **Tap the Camera Roll button.** The Camera Roll photo album appears.

4. **Tap the photo you just took.** A preview of the photo appears.

5. **Tap the Action icon.** The Action button is the button on the left side of the menu bar. (If you don't see the menu bar, tap the screen.) iPhone displays a list of actions you can perform.

6. **Tap Email Photo.** The New Message screen appears and iPhone embeds the photo in the body of the message.

7. **Choose your message recipient and enter a Subject line.**

8. **Tap Send.** If your photo is large, your iPhone asks whether you want to reduce the size by scaling the image to a smaller size.

9. **If you want to send the photo as is, tap Actual Size.** Otherwise, tap either Small or Medium to create a scaled-down version of the photo. Your iPhone sends the message and returns you to the photo.

If you have an existing image in one of your iPhone's photo albums that you'd prefer to e-mail, follow these steps:

1. **On the Home screen, tap Photos.** The Photo Albums screen appears.

2. **Tap the photo album that has the image you want to send.**

3. **Tap the photo you want to send.** Your iPhone opens the photo.

4. **Tap the Action button.** The Action button is the button on the left side of the menu bar. (If you don't see the menu bar, tap the screen.) iPhone displays a list of actions you can perform.

5. **Tap Email Photo.** In the New Message screen that is displayed, the photo appears in the body of the message.

6. **Choose your message recipient and enter a Subject line.**

7. **Tap Send.** If your photo is large, your iPhone asks whether you want to reduce the size by scaling the image to a smaller size.

8. **If you want to send the photo as is, tap Actual Size.** Otherwise, tap either Small or Medium to create a scaled-down version of the photo. Your iPhone sends the message and returns you to the photo.

Note

To send a photo via e-mail, you must have a default e-mail account set on your iPhone. See Chapter 5 for information about setting up a default e-mail account.

Sending a photo using MMS

If you want to send a photo in a text message using MMS, you can do it if your iPhone is running OS 3.0 or later and your cellular provider is MMS-friendly. Here are the steps to follow to take a photo with the iPhone camera and then send it via MMS:

1. **On the Home screen, tap Camera.** The Camera screen appears.

2. **Line up your subject and tap the Camera button to take the picture.**

3. **Tap the Camera Roll button.** The Camera Roll photo album appears.

4. **Tap the photo you just took.** A preview of the photo appears.

5. **Tap the Action icon.** The Action button is the button on the left side of the menu bar. (If you don't see the menu bar, tap the screen.) iPhone displays a list of actions you can perform.

6. **Tap MMS.** The New MMS screen appears, and iPhone embeds the photo in a new message as shown in Figure 8.2.

7. **Choose your message recipient.**

8. **Tap Send.** iPhone sends the message and returns you to the photo.

If you have an existing image in one of your iPhone's photo albums that you'd prefer to send using MMS, follow these steps:

1. **On the Home screen, tap Photos.** The Photo Albums screen appears.

2. **Tap the photo album that has the image you want to send.**

3. **Tap the photo you want to send.** Your iPhone opens the photo.

8.2 Oh what fun it is to send photos via MMS!

Sending a photo to your Flickr account

If you have a Flickr account, you can send photos from your iPhone by e-mail. Flickr gives you an e-mail address just for doing this. When you want to upload a photo to Flickr, all you do is attach it to an e-mail as described earlier in the chapter, and then enter the address given you by Flickr into the address field. You can find out the address to use this by going to the following page:

www.flickr.com/account/uploadbyemail

Saving a photo from an MMS message

If someone sends you a nice photo in an MMS message, you might want to save it to your iPhone so you can check it out whenever you want, assign it to a contact, sync it to your computer, and so on. Follow these steps to save a photo from a text message:

1. **On the Home screen, tap Messages.** The Messages screen appears,

2. **Tap the conversation that contains the photo message.** The Messages app opens the conversation screen.

3. **Tap the photo.** Your iPhone opens the photo for viewing.

4. **Tap the Action icon in the lower-left corner of the screen.** The Action options appear.

5. **Tap Save Image.** Your iPhone saves the image to the Camera Roll.

Starting a photo slide show

You can set up your own slide show on your iPhone including transition effects and even background music. That really impresses people.

You can get the standard slide show up and sliding by following these steps:

1. **On the Home screen, tap the Photos icon to open the Photos app.**

2. **Tap the album that you want to use in your slide show.** This opens the album to reveal its photos.

3. **Tap the Play icon.** The Play icon is the right-pointing arrow in the middle of the menu bar. (If you don't see the menu bar, tap the screen.) iPhone starts the slide show.

To pause the show, tap the screen, and then tap Play again to resume the festivities.

Creating a custom photo slide show

Okay, the basic slide show is pretty neat, with its nice dissolve transitions. However, your iPhone also offers a few settings for creating custom slide shows. Here's how to display them on your iPhone:

1. **On the Home screen, tap the Settings icon.** The Settings screen opens.

2. **Tap the Photos icon.** Your iPhone displays the Photos screen, as shown in Figure 8.3.

You get four settings to configure your custom slide show:

8.3 Use your iPhone's Photos screen to create a custom slide show.

- **Play Each Slide For.** You use this setting to set the amount of time that each photo appears on-screen. Tap Play Each Slide For, and then tap a time: 2 Seconds, 3 Seconds (this is the default), 5 Seconds, 10 Seconds, or 20 Seconds.

- **Transition.** You use this setting to specify the type of transition that your iPhone uses between each photo. Tap Transition and then tap the type of transition you prefer: Cube, Dissolve (the default), Ripple (*very* fun), Wipe Across, or Wipe Down.

- **Repeat.** This setting determines whether the slide show repeats from the beginning after the last photo is displayed. To turn on this setting, tap the Repeat switch to the On position.

- **Shuffle.** You use this setting to display the album photos in random order. To turn on this setting, tap the Shuffle switch to the On position.

Playing a slide show with background music

Here's is a little bonus that the iPhone throws your way. Yes, you can wow them back home by running a custom slide show, but you can positively make their jaws hit the floor when you add a music soundtrack to the show! They'll be cheering in the aisles.

Here's how you do it:

1. **Press the Home button to display the Home screen.**

2. **Tap the iPod icon to open the iPod app.**

Note

With the multitasking capabilities in iOS 4.0, you can open any music app (such as Pandora) and start a tune to use as the background music.

3. **Tap the playlist and then tap a song to get the playlist going.**

4. **Press the Home button to return to the Home screen.**

5. **Tap the Photos icon to open the Photo app.**

6. **Tap a photo album, and then tap Play to start the slide show.** Your iPhone runs the slide show, and all the while your music plays in the background.

Deleting a photo

If you mess up a photo using the camera, you should delete it before people think you have shoddy camera skills (because we all know it was the phone's fault, right?). Similarly, if your iPhone contains a synced photo you don't need any more, you can delete it to reduce clutter in the photo album that holds it. Happily, you don't have to worry about this being a permanent deletion, either. The syncing process only goes from your computer to your phone when it comes to photos that come from your computer. So even if you remove a photo from the iPhone, it remains safe on your computer.

To delete a photo, follow these steps:

1. **Tap Photos in the Home screen.**

2. **Tap the photo album that has the image you want to blow away.**

3. **Tap the doomed photo.** Your iPhone opens the photo.

4. **Tap the image to reveal the controls.**

5. **Tap the Trash icon.** The Trash icon is on the right side of the menu bar. (If you don't see the menu bar, tap the screen.) iPhone asks you to confirm the deletion.

6. **Tap Delete Photo.** iPhone tosses the photo into the trash, wipes its hands, and displays the previous photo in the album.

Getting More Out of Your iPhone's Video Features

The iPhone is a visual medium; it uses a touchscreen after all. The large screen makes it perfect as a portable media device. Its iPod app organizes and plays back videos that you import from your computer. Your commute (okay, your *nondriving* commute) doesn't have to be boring any more. Just put in your headphones and start an episode of your favorite show.

Playing videos, movies, and TV shows

In an ideal world, you'd watch all of your videos on a comfy couch in front of a flat-screen TV with a rockin' surround-sound system. Unfortunately, all that equipment isn't exactly portable. However, your iPhone is *very* portable and what's more, you probably carry it with you just about everywhere. Throw that nice large screen into the mix, and you've got yourself a great portable video player.

To watch a video on your iPhone, follow these steps:

1. **Tap the iPod icon on the Home screen.** This opens the iPod app.

2. **Tap the Videos browse button.** Your iPhone displays a list of your videos, organized by type: Movies, TV Shows, and Music Videos.

3. **Tap the video you want to watch.** The video opens on the screen and starts playing.

4. **Turn the screen to the landscape position to watch the video.**

When you first see an iPhone video, you might think you have no way to control the playback because there are no controls in sight. Fortunately for you, Apple realized that watching a movie with a bunch of buttons pasted on the screen wouldn't exactly enhance the movie-watching experience. I agree. The buttons are actually hidden, but you can force them out of hiding by tapping the screen, as you can see in Figure 8.4.

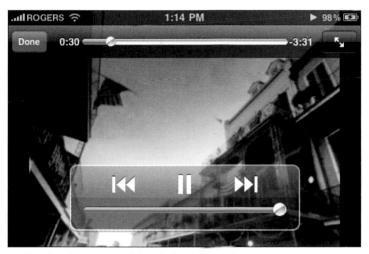

8.4 Tap the video to reveal the playback controls.

Here's what you see:

- **Progress Bar.** This bar shows you where you are in the video playback. The white ball shows you the current position, and you can drag the ball left (to rewind) or right (to fast forward). To the right is the time remaining in the video and on the left is the time elapsed.

- **Fill/Fit the Screen.** This button in the upper-right corner toggles the video between filling the entire screen (which may crop the outside edges of the video) and fitting the video to the screen width (which gives you letterboxed video with black bars above and below the video).

Note

You can also switch between filling the screen and fitting the screen by double-tapping the screen.

- **Previous.** Tap this button (the left-pointing arrows) to return to the beginning of the video or, if you're already at the beginning, to jump to the previous chapter (if the video has multiple chapters, as do most movies). Tap and hold this button to rewind the video.

- **Next.** Tap this button (the right-pointing arrows) to jump to the next chapter (if the video has multiple chapters). Tap and hold this button to fast-forward the video.

- **Pause/Play.** Tap this button to pause the playback, and then tap it again to resume.

Genius

You can use your iPhone headset to control video playback. Click the mic button once to play or pause. Click it twice to skip to the next chapter.

- **Chapter Guide.** Tap this button to see a list of chapters in the video. (You don't see this button if the video doesn't have multiple chapters).

- **Volume Bar.** This bar controls the video volume level. Drag the white ball to change the level. You can also use volume controls on the side of the phone.

- **Done.** Tap this button to stop the video and return to the list of videos on your iPhone. You can also press the Home button to stop the video and wind up on the Home screen.

Note

If you stop the video before the end, the next time you tap the video, it resumes the playback from the spot where you stopped it earlier. Nice!

Playing just the audio portion of a music video

When you play a music video, you get a two-for-one media deal: great music and (hopefully) a creative video. That's nice, but the only problem is you can't separate the two. For example, sometimes it might be nice to listen to just the audio portion of the music video. Why? Because you can't do anything else on your iPhone while a video is playing. If you press the Home button, for example, the video stops and the Home screen appears. That certainly makes sense, so it would be nice to be able to play just the audio portion, because your iPhone *does* let you perform some other tasks while playing audio.

Unfortunately, your iPhone doesn't give you any direct way to do this. You might think your only hope is to rip or purchase the song separately, but I've figured out a workaround. The secret is that if you add a music video to a regular music playlist, iPhone treats the music video like a regular song. When you play it on your iPhone using that playlist, you hear just the audio portion (and see just the first frame of the video as the album art).

To add a music video to a playlist in iTunes, follow these steps:

1. **Open iTunes on your computer.**

2. **It's best to use a custom playlist for this, so create your own playlist if you haven't done so already.**

3. **In Playlists, click Music Videos.** A list of all your music videos appears.

4. **Right-click (or Control+click on a Mac) the video you want to work with, click Add to Playlist, and then click a playlist.** iTunes adds the music video to the playlist.

5. **Repeat step 4 for any other music videos you want to just listen to.**

Sync your iPhone to download the updated playlist. Then tap iPod, Playlists, the playlist you used, and then the music video. Your iPhone plays the audio portion, and displays the first frame of the video. You're now free to move about the iPhone cabin while listening to the tune.

Playing iPhone videos on your TV

You can carry a bunch of videos with you on your iPhone so why shouldn't you be able to play them on a TV if you want? Well, you can. You have to buy another cord, but that's the only investment you have to make to watch iPhone videos right on your TV.

To hook your iPhone up to your TV, you have three choices:

- **Apple iPod AV cable.** This $19 cable has a stereo mini-plug on one end that connects to the iPhone's headset jack, and it has RCA connectors on the other end that connect to the AV inputs of your TV.

- **Apple Component AV cable.** This $49 cable has a dock connector on one end that plugs into the iPhone's dock connector, and it has component connectors on the other end that connect to the component inputs of your TV.

- **Apple Composite AV cable.** This $49 cable has a dock connector on one end that plugs into the iPhone's dock connector, and it has composite connectors on the other end that connect to the composite inputs of your TV.

The cable you choose depends on the type of TV you have. Older sets have AV inputs or possible composite inputs, while most newer flat-screen TVs have component inputs.

After setting up your cables, set your TV to the input and play your videos as you normally would.

Converting a video file to iPhone format

Your iPhone is happy to play video, but only certain formats are compatible with the iPhone. Here's the list:

- H.264 video, up to 720p, 30 frames per second, Main Profile level 3.1 with AAC-LC audio up to 160 Kbps, 48kHz, stereo audio in M4V, MP4, and MOV file formats

- H.264 video, up to 2.5 Mbps, 640 by 480 pixels, 30 frames per second, Baseline Profile up to Level 3.0 with AAC-LC audio up to 160 Kbps, 48 kHz, stereo audio in M4V, MP4, and MOV file formats

- MPEG-4 video, up to 2.5 Mbps, 640 by 480 pixels, 30 frames per second, Simple Profile with AAC-LC audio up to 160 Kbps, 48 kHz, stereo audio in M4V, MP4, and MOV file formats

If you have a video file that doesn't match any of these formats, you might think you're out of luck. Nope. You can use iTunes to convert that video to an MPEG-4 file that's iPhone-friendly. Here's how:

1. **If the video file isn't already in iTunes, choose File ⇨ Add to Library, or press ⌘+O.** The Add To Library dialog appears. If the file is already in iTunes, skip to step 3.

2. **Locate and choose your video file, and then click Open.** iTunes copies the file into the library, which may take a while depending on the size of the video file. In most cases, iTunes adds the video to the Movies section of the library.

3. **In iTunes, click your movie.**

4. **Choose Advanced ⇨ Create iPod or iPhone Version.** iTunes begins converting the video to the MPEG-4 format. This might take some time for even a relatively small video. When the conversion is complete, a copy of the original video appears in the iTunes library.

Recording video with the iPhone camera

If sometime in the first half of 2009 you polled people using the original iPhone or the iPhone 3G to find out the most important feature missing from their phone, I guarantee you the most popular choice would be video recording. Any smartphone worthy of the name should do all the things you need it to do during the course of your busy life, and one of the things you probably want to do is record events, happenings, moments, or just whatever's going on. Sure, a picture is worth the proverbial thousand words, but at 30 frames per second, a video is worth a lot more than that.

Caution The HD video recording capabilities of the iPhone 4 are so welcome that you might start shooting everything in sight. Be my guest! However, just be aware that your iPhone 4 churns through disk space at the rapid rate of 10 Mbps, which means each minute of video carves out nearly 80MB of disk real estate.

So it was applause all around when Apple announced that the iPhone 3GS would indeed come with video recording capabilities. Woo hoo! Apple upped the ante with the iPhone 4, which not only records in HD video, but also supports tap-to-focus and can use the LED flash in low-light situations.

And, this being an iPhone and all, it's no surprise that recording a video is almost criminally easy. Here's what you do:

1. **On the Home screen, tap the Camera button.** The Camera screen appears.

2. **Flick the mode switch in the lower-right corner from Camera to Video, as shown in Figure 8.5.**

3. **Tap the screen to focus the video, if necessary.**

4. **(iPhone 4 only) Tap the Flash icon, and then tap On, Off, or Auto.**

5. **(iPhone 4 only) Tap the Switch Camera icon if you want to use the front camera rather than the rear camera.**

8.5 Flick the Camera app's mode switch from Camera to Video.

6. **Tap the Record button.** Your iPhone starts recording video and displays the total recording time in the upper-right corner of the screen.

7. **When you're done, tap the Record button again to stop the recording.** Your iPhone saves the video to the Camera Roll.

Editing recorded video

Okay, being able to record video at the tap of a button is pretty cool, but your iPhone 4 or 3GS tops that by also letting you perform basic editing chores right on the phone. (Insert sound of jaw hitting floor here.) It's nothing fancy — basically, you can trim video from the beginning and end of the file — but it sure beats having to first sync the video to your computer and then firing up iMovie or some other video-editing software.

Here's how to edit a video right on your iPhone 4 (or 3GS):

1. **On the Home screen, tap the Camera button.** The Camera app loads.

2. **Click the Camera Roll button in the lower-left corner.** If you see a recent photo or video, tap Camera Roll again. The Camera Roll screen appears.

3. **Tap the video you want to edit.** Your iPhone starts playing the video.

4. **Tap anywhere to display the on-screen controls.** If the video is playing, tap Pause to stop the playback. You see a timeline of the video along the top of the screen.

5. **Tap and drag the left edge of the timeline to set the starting point of the video.**

6. **Tap and drag the right edge of the timeline to set the ending point of the video.** The trimmed timeline appears surrounded by orange, as shown in Figure 8.6.

8.6 Use the video timeline to set the start and end points of the video footage you want to keep.

Note Video thumbnails show a video camera icon in the lower-left corner and the duration of the video in the lower-right corner.

7. **Tap Play to ensure you've set the start and end points correctly.** If not, repeat steps 6 and 7 to adjust the timeline as needed.

8. **Tap Trim.** Your iPhone trims the video and then saves your work.

Sending a video via e-mail

If you want to share your newly shot and edited video with someone, you can e-mail it by following these steps:

1. **On the Home screen, tap the Camera button.** The Camera screen appears.

2. **Click the Camera Roll button in the lower-left corner to open the Camera Roll.**

3. **Tap the video you want to send.** If your iPhone 3GS starts playing the video, tap Pause.

4. **Tap the Action icon in the lower-left corner.** The Share options appear.

5. **Tap Email Video.** Your iPhone creates a new e-mail message that includes your video as an MPEG-4 Video file attachment.

6. **Fill in the rest of your message and send it.**

Note If your video is too long to send via e-mail, your iPhone lets you know and asks if you want to send a shorter version. If so, tap OK, use the trim control to shorten the clip and then tap Email.

Sending a video via MMS

To pass along your video in a text message using MMS, follow these steps:

1. **On the Home screen, tap the Camera button to launch the Camera app.**

2. **Click the Camera Roll button in the lower-left corner.** The Camera Roll screen appears.

3. **Tap the video you want to send.** If your iPhone starts playing the video, tap Pause.

Genius If you need more precision when trimming the timeline, tap and hold either the start trim control or the end trim control. Your iPhone expands the timeline to show more frames, which enables you to make more precise edits.

193

4. **Tap the Action icon in the lower-left corner.** The Share options pop up.

5. **Tap MMS.** Your iPhone displays the New MMS screen and includes your video as an MPEG-4 Video file.

6. **Select the recipient, and then tap Send.**

Note

If your video is too long to send via e-mail, your iPhone lets you know and asks if you want to send a shorter version. If so, tap OK, use the trim control to shorten the clip, and then tap Email.

Uploading recorded video to YouTube

Of course, the *real* reason you want to be able to instantly video something is because you want to upload that video to YouTube and share it with the world. Your iPhone is happy to help here, too, as shown by the following steps:

1. **On the Home screen, tap the Camera button.** The Camera screen appears.

2. **Click the Camera Roll button in the lower-left corner to open the Camera Roll.**

3. **Tap the video you want to share.** If your iPhone starts playing the video, tap Pause.

4. **Tap the Action icon in the lower-left corner.** The Share options appear.

5. **Tap Send to YouTube.** Your iPhone compresses the video and prompts you to log in to your YouTube account.

6. **Enter your YouTube username and password, and then tap Sign In.** The Publish Video screen appears.

7. **Tap a title, description, and tags for your video, and then choose a category.**

8. **Tap Publish.** Your iPhone publishes the video to your YouTube account. This may take several minutes, depending on the size of the video. When the video is published, you see a dialog with a few options.

9. **Tap one of the following options:**

   - **View on YouTube.** Tap this option to cue up the video on the YouTube site.

   - **Tell a Friend.** Tap this option to send an e-mail message that includes a link to the video on YouTube.

   - **Close.** Tab this option to return to the video.

Customizing your iPhone's video settings

Your iPhone offers a few video-related settings that you can try on for size. Follow these steps to get at them:

1. **Press the Home button to get to the Home screen.**

2. **Tap the Settings icon.** The Settings screen opens.

3. **Tap the iPod icon.** Your iPhone displays the iPod settings screen.

In the Video and TV Out sections, you get four settings to meddle with:

- **Start Playing.** This setting controls what your iPhone does when you stop and restart a video. You have two choices: Where Left Off (the default), which picks up the video from the same point where you stopped it; and From Beginning, which always restarts the video from scratch. Tap Start Playing, and then tap the setting you prefer.

- **Closed Captioning.** This setting toggles support for closed captioning on and off, when it's available. To turn on this feature, tap the Closed Captioning switch to the On position.

- **Widescreen.** This setting toggles support for widescreen TV output. If you have a widescreen TV and you want to play iPhone videos on the set, tap the Widescreen switch to the On position.

- **TV Signal.** This setting specifies the TV output signal. If you're going to play videos on a TV, tap TV Signal and then tap either NTSC or PAL.

4.0 Editing Video with iMovie for iPhone
iOS 4.0

Earlier I showed you the built-in editing feature that comes with the iPhone 4 (and 3GS), which essentially boils down to being able to trim video clips. That's pretty handy, but proper video editing requires features such as adding transitions and titles, changing the theme, adding a music track, and so on. Ah, you might be saying to yourself, all you have to do is sync your videos to your computer, and then use video editing software such as iMovie on the Mac to do all that.

Well, yes, you can certainly do that, but what if your computer is nowhere in sight? If it's just you, your iPhone, and some cool-but-not-ready-for-primetime video, you can go well beyond the iPhone's native video editing capabilities by purchasing the iMovie for iPhone app, which is available in the App Store for $4.99. With iMovie for iPhone, you can perform many of the same tasks that you can using the full-fledged iMovie application, including importing live and recorded videos and photos, trimming clips, adding transitions, applying a Ken Burns effect to a photo, adding titles and music tracks, applying themes, and much more.

Creating a new iMovie project

Assuming you've already purchased and installed the app, to get started with iMovie for iPhone (which, for efficiency's sake, I just call iMovie from here on), tap the iMovie icon. In the Projects screen that appears, follow these steps to get a new iMovie project off the ground:

1. **Tap the Add (+) icon.** iMovie displays the Add Project screen.

2. **Select a project theme.**

3. **If you want to include the theme's default music in your project, tap the Theme Music switch to On.**

4. **Tap Done.** iMovie saves your new project and adds it to the Projects list.

At this point iMovie prompts you to insert or record media. I show you how this works in the section on importing media into your project later in this chapter.

Opening a project for editing

For the rest of this chapter, you'll be working within a specific project, so go ahead and use the Projects list to tap the project you want to work with. You end up in iMovie's project editing environment. Figure 8.7 shows an example of the editing environment for a project that already has clips and other media imported.

There are three main elements in the iMovie editing environment:

- **Timeline.** This is the strip along the bottom of the screen, and it displays your video clips, photos, transitions, and music track.

- **Viewer.** This is the larger pane that takes up most of the top half of the window, and it shows your video when you play it and when you scroll through the timeline.

8.7 You see a screen similar to this when you open a video for editing in iMovie.

Note It's actually much easier to edit video in iMovie using landscape mode, rather than the portrait mode shown in Figure 8.7. However, the individual elements of the editing environment show up better in portrait mode, which is why I used that orientation for Figure 8.7.

● **Toolbars.** These appear above and below the Viewer. The upper toolbar has two buttons: Projects (on the left) which returns you to the Projects screen; and Play (on the right), which plays your movie; the lower toolbar also has two buttons: Import (on the left) which you use to import existing videos, photos, and music; and Record (on the right), which you use to import videos or photos shot with the iPhone camera.

Importing media into your project

With your new project on the go, your first task is to import media into the project. With iMovie, you can import three kinds of media: recorded video, existing video, and photos.

Importing a video from the camera

You can take whatever scene is currently happening around you and import it directly into your iMovie project using your iPhone's built-in camera. Here's how you do it:

1. **Open your iMovie project.**

2. **Scroll through the timeline to the location where you want the video to appear.**

3. **Tap the Record icon.** Your iPhone switches to the camera.

4. **Tap the screen to focus the video, if necessary.**

5. **Tap the red Record button.** Your iPhone starts recording video and displays the total recording time in the upper-right corner of the screen.

6. **When you're done, tap the Record button again to stop the recording.** iMovie displays a preview of the recorded video.

7. **If the video looks good, tap Use to add it to the timeline.** Otherwise, tap Retake and then reshoot the video.

Importing existing video

If you've already recorded your video, or if you've synced some video from your computer, you can add the existing video into your project timeline. Here are the steps to follow:

1. **Open your iMovie project.**

2. **Scroll through the timeline to the location where you want the video to appear.**

3. **Tap the Import icon. iMovie displays the importing screen.**

4. **Tap Video.** iMovie displays the Video screen, which includes thumbnails of the available videos on your iPhone.

5. **Scroll through the videos until you find the one you want to import.**

6. **Tap the video.** iMovie adds the video to the timeline.

Importing a photo from the camera

You can take a still image and import it directly into your iMovie project using your iPhone's built-in camera. Here's how you do it:

1. **Open your iMovie project.**

2. **Scroll through the timeline to the location where you want the video to appear.**

3. **Tap the Record icon.** Your iPhone switches to the camera.

4. **Flick the mode switch in the lower-right corner from Video to Camera.**

5. **Tap the screen to focus the photo, if necessary.**

6. **Tap the Shutter button.** Your iPhone takes the photo and displays a preview of the result.

7. **If the photo looks good, tap Use to add it to the timeline.** Otherwise, tap Retake and then reshoot the photo.

Importing an existing photo

You can also import a photo to your project, which iMovie automatically animates by applying a Ken Burns effect (which is an automatic pan-and-zoom effect popularized by filmmaker Ken Burns). Follow these steps to add a photo to your project.

1. **Open your iMovie project.**

2. **Scroll through the timeline to the location where you want the photo to appear.**

3. **Tap the Import icon.** iMovie displays the importing screen.

4. **Tap Photos.** iMovie displays the Photos screen.

5. **Tap the album that contains the photo you want to import.** iMovie displays thumbnails of the album's photos.

6. **Tap the photo.** iMovie adds the photo to the timeline.

Working with video clips

iMovie gives you a surprisingly complete collection of video editing tools that enable you to move and trim clips, change the transitions, work with a photo's Ken Burns effect, and add clip titles.

Moving a clip

If a clip doesn't appear where you want it, follow these steps to move it to the position you prefer:

1. **Tap and hold the middle of the clip you want to move.**

2. **Drag the clip left or right through the timeline.**

3. **Drop the clip when you reach the location you want.** iMovie moves the clip.

Trimming a clip

If an imported video clip includes footage at the beginning or end (or both) that you don't want to include in your movie, you can trim those unwanted scenes. Here are the steps to follow:

1. **Tap the clip you want to trim.** iMovie displays the trim controls, as shown in Figure 8.8.

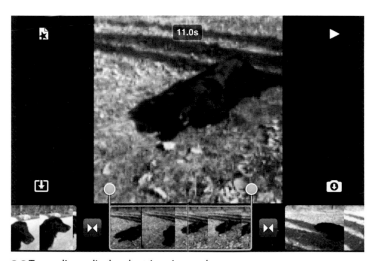

8.8 Tap a clip to display the trimming tools.

Genius

For more precise trimming, spread your fingers on the clip to expand it in the timeline. If you go too far, pinch the clip to shrink it.

2. **Tap and drag the left trim control to set the starting point of the clip.**

3. **Tap and drag the right trim control to set the ending point of the clip.**

Changing the transition between two clips

iMovie makes transitions a no-brainer because it adds them automatically between any two clips when you add videos or photos to the timeline. It also defines different transitions for each theme applied to a project. (I show you how to change themes a bit later.) If you don't like the theme transitions, you can switch to a cross dissolve transition (where the end of one clips dissolves into the beginning of the next clip), or you can turn off the transition altogether. You can also vary the length of the transition.

Here are the steps to follow:

1. **Double-tap the transition you want to work with.** iMovie displays the Transition Settings window, shown in Figure 8.9.

2. **Tap the transition you want: Theme, Cross Dissolve, or None.**

3. **Tap the length of the transition, in seconds.**

4. **Tap Done.** iMovie saves the transition settings.

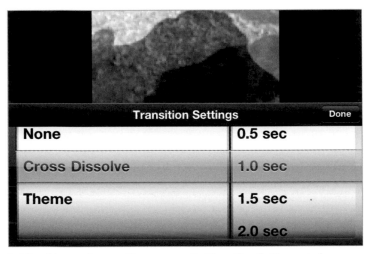

8.9 Double-tap the transition to open the Transition Settings window.

Adjusting a photo's Ken Burns effect

I mentioned earlier that when you import a photo, iMovie automatically applies a Ken Burns effect, which pans and zooms the photo. You can control the panning and zooming by following these steps:

1. **Tap the photo you want to edit.** iMovie selects the photos and displays the Ken Burns effect tools, as shown in Figure 8.10.

2. **Set the start of the pan by dragging the photo to the starting position you prefer.**

3. **Set the opening zoom level by pinching or spreading on the photo.**

4. **Tap Start.**

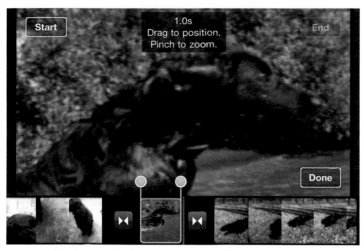

8.10 Tap the photo to display the Ken Burns effect tools.

5. **Set the end of the pan by dragging the photo to the ending position you prefer.**

6. **Set the closing zoom level by pinching or spreading on the photo.**

7. **If you want to return to the start settings, tap End and repeat steps 2 and 3.**

8. **Tap Done.** iMovie saves the settings.

Adding a title to a clip

You can get your movie off to a proper start by adding a title to your opening clip. iMovie offers a number of title styles that you can choose from, and it automatically adds the video location (picked up from the geolocation data supplied by the iPhone camera) as the subtitle.

Follow these steps to add a title to any clip:

1. **Double-tap the clip you want to work with.** iMovie displays the Clip Settings screen.

2. **Tap Title Style.** iMovie opens the Title Style screen.

3. **Tap the title style you're adding: Opening, Middle, or Ending.**

4. **Tap inside the Title Text Here text box.** iMovie displays the Edit Title screen.

5. **Type the title and tap Done to return to the Title Style screen.**

6. **Tap Done.** iMovie adds the title to the clip.

Removing a clip

If you add a clip accidentally, or if you decide a clip is no longer needed, you can use either of the following techniques to remove it from your project:

201

● Double-tap the clip to open the Clip Settings screen, and then tap Delete.

● Tap and drag the clip up and off the timeline. When you release the clip, iMovie deletes it.

Working with your project

Your iMovie project is coming along nicely, thank you, with its trimmed clips, transitions, Ken Burns effects, and titles. What else can iMovie do? Three things, actually: add music, change the theme, and export your project to a movie file.

Adding a music track

What would a video be without a music track playing in the background? Boring, that's what! Fortunately, iMovie lets you add either a song from your iTunes music library, or an audio track from the project's current theme. Here's how it works:

1. **Tap the Import icon.** iMovie displays the importing screen.

2. **Tap Audio.** iMovie displays the Audio screen.

3. **Tap the music category you want to use.** To use an audio track from the project's theme, tap Theme Music; otherwise, tap an iTunes music category such as Playlists, Albums, or Artists.

4. **Navigate the music until you locate the track you want to add.** For example, if you selected the Artists category, you'd need to select an artist, and then select an album.

5. **Tap the track.** iMovie adds the track to the bottom of the timeline, as shown in Figure 8.11.

8.11 After you select song or audio track, iMovie displays the track as a green strip at the bottom of the timeline.

Changing the project theme

The secret of iMovie's easy movie-making is the project theme which, as you've seen, you can take advantage of to automatically apply clip transitions, title styles, and music tracks to give your movie a cohesive and consistent feel. iMovie ships with five built-in themes, so you can pick the one that best complements your movie subject.

Follow these steps to change the project theme:

1. **Open your iMovie project.**

2. **Tap Settings (the gear icon that appears to the left of the timeline).** iMovie displays the Select Theme screen.

3. **Tap the theme you want to use.** iMovie displays a preview of the theme, as shown in Figure 8.12.

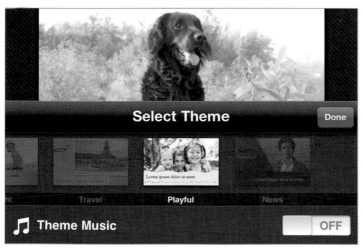

8.12 In the Select Theme screen, tap a theme to see a preview of the theme's look.

4. **If you want to use the music tracks that come with the theme, tap the Theme Music switch to On.**

5. **Tap Done.** iMovie saves your settings and updates the project with the new theme.

Exporting your project

With your clips imported and trimmed, your transitions and titles in place, your music added and your theme applied, your movie is finally ready for primetime. Although you can play the movie within the editing environment (by tapping the Play button in the upper toolbar), you won't really be able to show off your movie until you export it to a movie file. iMovie gives you three choices: HD (720p), Large (540p), or Medium (360p).

Follow these steps to export you project:

1. **If you have your project open in the editing environment, tap Projects to return to the Projects screen.**

2. **Select the project you want to export.**

3. **Tap the Export icon in the lower left corner of the screen.** iMovie asks you to select an export size, as shown in Figure 8.13.

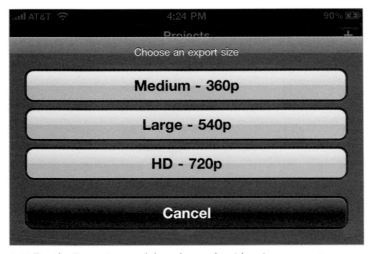

8.13 Tap the Export icon and then choose the video size you want.

4. **Tap the size you want.** iMovie exports the project to a movie file, which it stores in your iPhone's Camera Roll.

Can I Use My iPhone to Manage Contacts and Appointments?

The iPhone has never been about just the technology. Yes, it looks stylish, has enough bells and whistles to cause deafness, and it just works, but iPhone users don't know or care about things like antennas and flash drives and memory chips and whatever else Apple somehow managed to cram into that tiny case. These things don't matter because the iPhone has always been about helping you get things done and helping you make your life better, more creative, and more efficient. And as you see in this chapter, your iPhone can also go a long way toward making your life — particularly your contacts and your calendar — more organized.

Managing Your Contacts

One of the paradoxes of modern life is that as your contact information becomes more important, you store less and less of that information in the easiest database system of them all — your memory. That is, instead of memorizing phone numbers like you used to, you now store your contact info electronically. When you think about it, this isn't exactly surprising because it's not just a landline number that you have to remember for each person; it might also be a cell number, an instant messaging handle, an e-mail address, a Web site address, a physical address, and more. That's a lot to remember, so it makes sense to go the electronic route. And for the iPhone, "electronic" means the Contacts app, which seems basic enough, but it's actually loaded with useful features that can help you organize and get the most out of the contact management side of your life.

Creating a new contact

I showed you how to sync your computer's contacts program (such as Address Book on the Mac or Windows, or Outlook's Contacts folder) in Chapter 6. That's by far the easiest way to populate your iPhone Contacts app with a crowd of people, but it might not include everyone in your posse. If someone's missing and you're not around your computer, you can add that person directly to your iPhone Contacts.

Begin by creating a contact with just the basic info: first name, last name, and company name. In subsequent sections, I show you how to add data such as phone numbers and e-mail addresses. Here are the steps to follow:

1. **In the Home screen, tap the Contacts icon.** Your iPhone opens the All Contacts screen. If you are in the Phone app, you can also tap the Contacts icon.

2. **Tap the + button at the top right of the screen.** The New Contact screen appears, as shown in Figure 9.1.

9.1 Use the New Contact screen to enter the person's name and company name.

3. **Tap the First box, and then enter the person's first name.** If you're jotting down the contact data for a company or some other inanimate object, skip to step 6.

4. **Tap the Last box and then enter the person's surname.**

5. **If you want to note where the person works (or if you're adding a business to your Contacts app), tap the Company box and enter the company name.**

6. **Tap Done.** Your iPhone saves the new contact and returns you to the All Contacts screen.

Editing an existing contact

Now that your new contact is off to a flying start, you can go ahead and fill in details such as phone numbers, addresses (e-mail, Web, and real world), and anything else you can think of (or have the patience to enter into your iPhone; it can be a lot of tapping!). The next few sections take you through the steps for each type of data. When you're done, be sure to tap Done to preserve all your hard work.

Note There are a couple of techniques that I don't go into here because I already covered them elsewhere. See Chapter 3 to learn how to assign a ringtone to your contact; see Chapter 8 to get the scoop on sprucing up your contact with a photo.

However, the steps I show also apply to any contact that's already residing in your iPhone. Here, then, are the steps required to open an existing contact for editing:

1. **In the Home screen, tap the Contacts icon to open the All Contacts screen.**

2. **Tap the contact you want to edit.**

3. **Tap Edit.** Your iPhone displays the contact's data in the Info screen.

4. **Make your changes, as described in the next few sections.**

5. **Tap Done.** Your iPhone saves your work and returns you to the All Contacts screen.

Assigning phone numbers to a contact

Your iPhone is, of course, a phone, so it's only right and natural to use it to call your contact. Sure, but which number? Work? Home? Cell? Pager? Fortunately, there's no need to choose just one, because your iPhone is happy to store all these numbers, plus a few more if need be.

Here are the steps to follow to add one or more phone numbers for a contact:

1. **With the contact's data open for editing, tap inside the Phone field.** Your iPhone displays a numeric keypad, as shown in Figure 9.2.

2. **Enter the phone number with area code first.** Your iPhone helpfully adds extra stuff like parentheses around the area code and the dash.

3. **Examine the label box to see if the default label is the one you want.** If it is, skip to step 5; if it's not, tap the label box to open the Label screen.

4. **Tap the label that best applies to the phone number you're adding (your iPhone automatically sends you back to the Info screen after you tap), such as mobile, iPhone, home, or work.**

5. **Repeat steps 1 to 4 to add any other numbers you want to store for this contact.** Note that each time you add a number, Contacts creates a new phone field below the current field, and you tap inside the new field to add the new number.

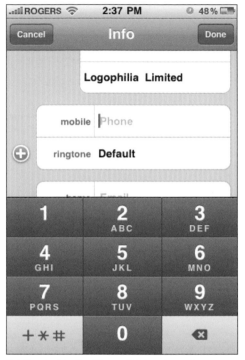

9.2 Tap inside the Phone field and use the numeric keypad to assign a phone number to your contact.

Genius

Some numbers — such as those used by long-distance calling cards — require a pause in mid-dial to wait for the system to do something. To tell your iPhone to pause for two seconds while dialing, tap the +*# key, and then tap the Pause key. The iPhone inserts a comma (,) to indicate the pause location.

Assigning e-mail addresses to a contact

It makes sense that you might want to add a phone number or three for a contact, but would you ever need to enter multiple e-mail addresses? Well, sure you would! Most people have at least a couple of addresses — usually home and work addresses — and some Type A e-mailers have a dozen or more. Life is too short to enter that many e-mail addresses, but you need at least the important ones if you want to use your iPhone's Mail app to send a note to your contacts.

Follow these steps to add one or more e-mail addresses for a contact:

1. **With the contact's data open for editing, tap inside the Email field.** Your iPhone displays the keyboard, as shown in Figure 9.3.

2. **Type the person's e-mail address.**

3. **Check out the label box to see if the default label is the one you want.** If it is, skip to step 5; if it's not, tap the label box to open the Label screen.

4. **Tap the label that best applies to the e-mail address you're inserting (your iPhone automatically sends you back to the Info screen after you tap), such as home or work.**

5. **Repeat steps 1 to 4 to add other e-mail addresses for this contact, as you see fit.** Note that each time you add an E-mail address, Contacts creates a new E-mail field below the current field. You tap inside the new field to add the new address.

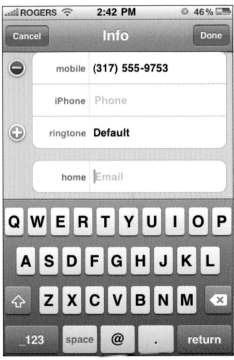

9.3 Tap inside the Email field and enter an e-mail address for your contact.

Assigning Web addresses to a contact

Who on Earth doesn't have a Web site these days? It could be a humble home page, a blog, a home business site, or it could be someone's corporate Web site. Some busy Web beavers may even have all four! Whatever Web home a person has, it's a good idea to toss the address into his or her contact data because later on you can simply tap the address and your iPhone (assuming it can see the Internet from here) immediately fires up Safari and takes you to the site. Does your pal have multiple Web sites? No sweat: Your iPhone is happy to take you to them all.

Genius

To save some wear and tear on your tapping finger, don't bother adding the http:// stuff at the beginning of the address. Your iPhone adds those characters automatically anytime you tap the address to visit the site. Same with the www. prefix. So if the full address is http://www.wordspy.com, you need only enter wordspy.com.

211

You can add one or more Web addresses for a contact by making your way through these steps:

1. **With the contact's data open for editing, tap inside the URL field.** Your iPhone displays the keyboard, as shown in Figure 9.4. Note the . (period) and .com keys in the on-screen keyboard, which come in very handy.

2. **Enter the person's Web address.**

3. **Examine the label box to see if the default label is the one you want.** If it is, skip to step 5; if it's not, tap the label box to open the Label screen.

4. **Tap the label that best applies to the Web address you're inserting (your iPhone automatically sends you back to the Info screen after you tap), such as home page or work.**

5. **Repeat steps 1 to 4 to add other Web addresses for this contact.** Note that each time you add a Web address, Contacts creates a new URL field below the current field, and you tap inside the new field to add the new URL.

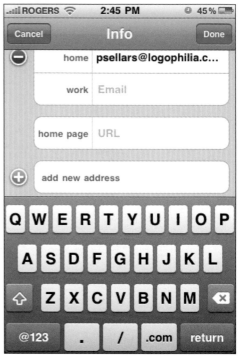

9.4 Tap inside the URL field and enter a Web address for your contact.

Assigning physical addresses to a contact

With all this talk about cell numbers, e-mail addresses, and Web addresses, it's easy to forget that people actually live and work somewhere. You may have plenty of contacts where the location of that somewhere doesn't much matter, but if you ever need to get from here to there, taking the time to insert a contact's physical address really pays off. Why? Because you need only tap the address and your iPhone displays a Google map that shows you the precise location. From there you can get directions, see a satellite map of the area, and more. (I talk about all this great map stuff in Chapter 8.)

Tapping out a full address is a bit of work, but as the following steps show, it's not exactly root-canalishly painful:

1. **With the contact's data open for editing, tap inside the Add New Address field.** Your iPhone displays the address-fields, as shown in Figure 9.5.

2. **Tap the first Street field and then enter the person's street address.**

3. **If necessary, tap the second Street field, and then enter even more of the person's street address.**

4. **Tap the City field, and then enter the person's city.**

5. **Tap the State field, and then enter the person's state.** Depending on what you later select for the country, this field might have a different name, such as Province.

6. **Tap the ZIP field, and then enter the ZIP code.** Again, depending on what you later select for the country, this field might have a different name, such as Postal Code.

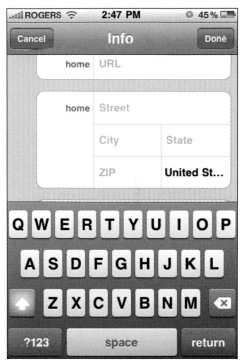

9.5 Tap Add New Address to display the fields shown here so you can tap out your contact's physical coordinates.

7. **Tap the Country to open the Country screen, and then tap the contact's country.**

8. **Examine the label box to see if the default label is the one you want.** If it is, skip to step 10; if it's not, tap the label box to open the Label screen.

9. **Tap the label that best applies to the physical address you're inserting (your iPhone automatically sends you back to the Info screen after you tap), such as home or work.**

10. **Repeat steps 1 to 9 to add other addresses for this contact.**

Creating a custom label

When you fill out your contact data, your iPhone insists that you apply a label to each tidbit: home, work, mobile, and so on. If none of the predefined labels fits, you can always just slap on the generic label: other. You could do that, but it seems so, well, dull. If you've got a phone number or address that you can't shoehorn into any of your iPhone's prefab labels, get creative and make up a label. Here's how:

1. **With the contact's data open for editing, tap the label beside the field you want to work with.** The Label screen appears.

2. **Tap Add Custom Label.** Scroll to the bottom of the screen to see this command. The Custom Label screen appears, as shown in Figure 9.6.

3. **Type the custom label.**

4. **Tap Save.** Your iPhone returns you to the screen for the field you were editing, and applies the new label.

5. **Edit the field data, if necessary.**

6. **Tap Done.** Your iPhone saves the contact data as well as your custom label.

9.6 Use the Custom label screen to forge your very own custom label for your contacts.

Conveniently, you can apply your custom label to any type of contact data. For example, if you create a label named college, you can apply that label to a phone number, e-mail address, Web address, or physical address.

If a custom label wears out its welcome, follow these steps to delete it:

1. **With the contact's data open for editing, tap any label.** The Label screen appears.

2. **Tap Edit.** Your iPhone puts the Label screen into Edit mode.

3. **Tap the Delete icon to the left of the custom label you want to remove.** Your iPhone displays a Delete button to the right of the label.

4. **Tap Delete.** Your iPhone deletes the custom label.

5. **Tap Done.** Your iPhone exits edit mode.

6. **Tap Cancel.** Your iPhone returns you to the Info screen.

Adding extra fields to a contact

The New Contact screen (which appears when you add a contact) and the Info screen (which appears when you edit an existing contact) display just the fields you need for basic contact info. However, these screens lack quite a few common fields. For example, you might need to specify a contact's prefix (such as Dr. or Professor), suffix (such as Jr., Sr., or III), or job title.

Thankfully, your iPhone is merely hiding these and other useful fields where you can't see them. There are 11 hidden fields that you can add to any contact:

- Prefix
- Phonetic First Name
- Phonetic Last Name
- Middle
- Suffix
- Nickname
- Job Title
- Department
- Birthday
- Date
- Notes

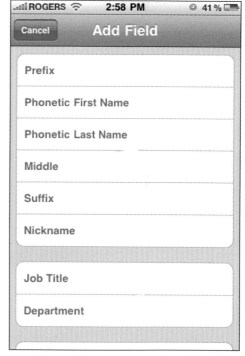

The iPhone is only too happy to let you add as many of these extra fields as you want. Here are the steps involved:

1. **With the contact's data open for editing, tap Add Field.** The Add Field screen appears, as shown in Figure 9.7.

9.7 The Add Field screen shows the hidden fields that you can add to any contact.

2. **Tap the field that you want to add.** Your iPhone adds the field to the contact's data.

3. **Enter the field data.**

4. **Tap Done.** Your iPhone saves the new info.

Keeping track of birthdays and anniversaries

Do you have trouble remembering birthdays? If so, then I feel your pain because I, too, used to be pathetically bad at keeping birthdays straight. And no wonder: These days you not only have to keep track of birthdays for your family and friends, but increasingly often you have to remember birthdays for staff, colleagues, and clients, too. It's too much! My secret is that I simply gave up and outsourced the job to my iPhone's Contacts app, which has a hidden field that you can use to store birth dates.

To add the Birthday field to a contact, follow these steps:

1. **With the contact's data open for editing, tap Add Field.** Your iPhone opens the Add Field screen.

2. **Tap Birthday.** The Contact's app adds the Birthday field to the contact's data, and its nifty scroll wheels appear, as shown in Figure 9.8.

3. **Scroll the left wheel to set the day of the month for the birth date.**

4. **Scroll the middle wheel to set the month for the birth date.**

5. **Scroll the right wheel to set the year of the birth date.**

6. **Tap Done.** Your iPhone saves the birthday info and displays it on the contact's Info screen.

9.8 Use the fun scroll wheels in the Add Birthday screen to set the contact's birth date.

Everyone has a birthday, naturally, but lots of people have anniversaries, too. It could be a wedding date, a quit-smoking date, or the date that someone started working at the company. Whatever the occasion, you can add it to the contact info so that it's staring you in the face as a friendly reminder each time you open that contact.

Follow these steps to include an anniversary with a contact:

1. **With the contact's data open for editing, tap Add Field.** The Add Field screen appears.

2. **Tap Date.** The Contacts app adds an anniversary field to the contact and displays the scroll wheels, as shown in Figure 9.9.

3. **Scroll the left wheel to set the day of the month for the anniversary.**

4. **Scroll the middle wheel to set the month for the anniversary.**

5. **Scroll the right wheel to set the year of the anniversary.**

6. **The label box should already show the anniversary label, but if not, tap the label box, and then tap anniversary.**

7. **Tap Done.** The iPhone saves the anniversary and displays it on the contact's Info screen.

9.9 Use the scroll wheels to add an anniversary to a contact's info.

Note

Although you can only add one birthday to a contact (not surprisingly), you are free to add multiple anniversaries. Open the contact's data for editing and tap the empty Date field that appears below the most recent date you entered.

Add notes to a contact

The standard contact fields all are designed to hold specific data: a name, an address, a date, and so on. Sometimes, however, you might need to enter more free-form data:

- The highlights of a recent client meeting
- A list of things to do for the contact
- How you met the contact or why you added the person to your Contacts app
- Contact data that doesn't have a proper field: spouse's or partner's name, kids' names, account numbers, gender, hobbies, and on and on

Whatever it is, your iPhone offers a Note field that you can add to a contact and then scribble away in as needed. To add the Note field to a contact, follow these steps:

1. **With the contact's data open for editing, tap Add Field.** Your iPhone opens the Add Field screen.

2. **Tap Notes.** Contacts app adds a notes field to the contact and displays the keyboard, as shown in Figure 9.10.

3. **Tap your notes into the large text box.**

4. **Tap Done.** Your iPhone saves the note text and displays it on the contact's Info screen.

Creating a new contact from an electronic business card

Entering a person's contact data by hand is a tedious bit of business at the best of times, so it helps if you can find a faster way to do it. If you can cajole a contact into sending his or her contact data electronically, then you can add that data with just a couple of taps. What do I mean when I talk about sending contact data electronically? The world's contact management gurus long ago came up with a standard file format for contact data: the vCard. It's a kind of digital business card that exists as a separate file. People can pass this data along by attaching their (or someone else's) card to an e-mail message.

If you get a message with contact data, you see an icon for the VCF file, as shown in Figure 9.11.

To get this data into your Contacts app, follow these steps:

1. **In the Home screen, tap Mail to open the Mail app.**

2. **Tap the message that contains the vCard attachment.**

3. **Tap the icon for the vCard file.** Your iPhone opens the vCard.

4. **Tap Create New Contact.** If the person is already in your Contacts app, but the vCard contains new data, tap Add to Existing Contact, and then tap the contact.

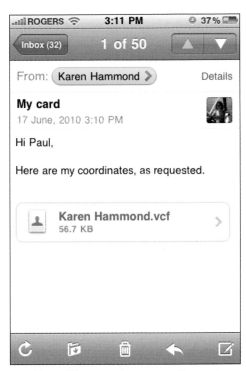

9.10 Use the Add Note screen to tap out notes related to the contact.

9.11 If your iPhone receives an e-mail message with an attached vCard, an icon for the file appears in the message body.

Delete a contact field

People change, and so does their contact info. Most of the time these changes require you to edit an existing field, but sometimes people actually shed information. For example, they might get rid of their pager or fax machine, or they might shutter a Web site. Whatever the reason, you should delete that data from the contact to keep the Info screen tidy and easier to navigate.

To delete a contact field, follow these steps:

1. **In the Contacts app, tap the contact you want to work with.**

2. **Tap Edit.** The Info screen appears.

3. **Tap the red Delete icon to the left of the field you want to trash.** Your iPhone displays a Delete button to the right of the field.

4. **Tap Delete.** Your iPhone removes the field.

5. **Tap Done.** Your iPhone returns you to the contact's Info screen.

Delete a contact

It feels good to add new contacts but, life being what it is, you don't get a lifetime guarantee with these things: friends fall out or fade away; colleagues decide to make a new start at another firm; clients take their business elsewhere; and some of your acquaintances simply wear out their welcome after a while. You move on, and so does your Contacts app, and the best way to do that is to delete the contact to help keep the list trim and tidy.

Follow these steps to delete a contact:

1. **In the Contacts app, tap the contact you want to get rid of.**
2. **Tap Edit.** The Info screen appears.
3. **Tap the Delete Contact button at the bottom of the screen.** Your iPhone asks you to confirm the deletion.
4. **Tap Delete Contact.** Your iPhone removes the contact and returns you to the All Contacts screen.

Tracking Your Appointments

When you meet someone and ask "How are you?," the most common reply these days is a short one: "Busy!" We're all as busy as can be these days, and that places-to-go, people-to-see feeling is everywhere. All the more reason to keep your affairs in order, and that includes your appointments. Your iPhone comes with a Calendar app that you can use to create items, called events, which represent your appointments. Calendar acts as a kind of electronic personal assistant, leaving your brain free to concentrate on more important things.

Adding an appointment to your calendar

I showed you how to sync your computer's calendar application (such as iCal on the Mac, or Outlook's Calendar folder) in Chapter 6, and that's the easiest way to fill your iPhone with your appointments. However, something always comes up when you're running around, so you need to know how to add an appointment directly to your iPhone Calendar.

Here are the steps to follow to add a basic appointment:

1. **In the Home screen, tap the Calendar icon.** Your iPhone opens the Calendar app.
2. **Tap Month, and then tap the date on which the appointment occurs.** If the appointment happens in a different month, use the arrow keys to the right and left of the month and year to navigate to the month you want.

3. **Tap the + button at the top right of the screen.** The Add Event screen appears, as shown in Figure 9.12.

4. **Tap the Title/Location box.** You see the Title & Location screen.

5. **The cursor starts off in the Title box, so enter a title for the appointment.** You can also tap the Location box and then enter the location of the appointment.

6. **Tap Done.** The Calendar app saves the data and returns you to the Add Event screen.

7. **Tap the Starts/Ends box.** The Start & End screen appears, as shown in Figure 9.13.

8. **Tap Starts, and then use the scroll wheels to set the date and time that your appointment begins.**

9. **Tap Ends, and then use the scroll wheels to set the date and time that your appointment finishes.**

10. **If you have multiple calendars, tap Calendar, and then tap the calendar in which you want this appointment to appear.**

11. **Tap Done.** The Calendar app saves your info and returns you to the Add Event screen.

12. **Tap Done.** The Calendar app adds the event to the calendar.

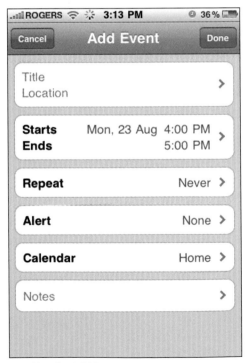

9.12 Use the Add Event screen to create your appointment.

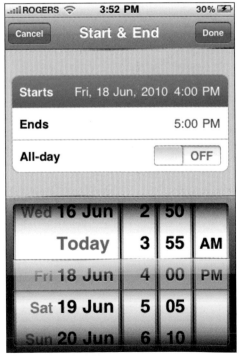

9.13 Use the Start & End screen to set your appointment times.

221

When you add an appointment, Calendar displays a dot underneath the day as a visual reminder that you've got something going on that day. Tap the day and Calendar displays a list of all the events you've scheduled, as shown in Figure 9.14. (If you have multiple calendars and you want to see all your appointments, tap Calendars and then tap All to open the All Calendars screen.)

If you want to see the duration of each appointment, tap the date and then tap Day. Calendar switches to Day view and shows your appointments as blocks, as you can see in Figure 9.15.

9.14 Tap a date in Calendar to see all the events you've scheduled on that day.

9.15 Tap Day to switch to Day view and see your events as blocks of time.

Editing an existing appointment

Whether you've scheduled an appointment by hand or synced the appointment from your computer, the event details might change: a new time, a new location, and so on. Whatever the change, you need to edit the appointment to keep your schedule accurate.

Here are the steps to follow to edit an existing appointment:

1. **In the Home screen, tap the Calendar icon to open the Calendar.**

2. **Tap the date that contains the appointment you want to edit.**

3. **Tap the appointment.** You can do this either in Month view or in Day view. Calendar displays the event info.

4. **Tap Edit.** Your iPhone displays the appointment data in the Edit screen.

5. **Make your changes to the appointment.**

6. **Tap Done.** Your iPhone saves your work and returns you to the event details.

Setting up a repeating event

One of Calendar's truly great timesavers is the repeat feature, which enables you to set up a single event, and then get Calendar to automatically repeat the same event at a regular interval. For example, if you set up an event for a Friday, you can repeat the event every week, which means that Calendar automatically sets up the same event to occur on subsequent Fridays. You can continue the events indefinitely or end them on a specific date.

Follow these steps to configure an existing event to repeat:

1. **In Calendar, tap the date that contains the appointment you want to edit.**

2. **Tap the appointment.** Calendar opens the event info.

3. **Tap Edit.** Calendar displays the event data in the Edit screen.

4. **Tap Repeat.** The Repeat Event screen appears, as shown in Figure 9.16.

5. **Tap the repeat interval you want to use.**

6. **Tap Done to return to the Edit screen.**

7. **Tap End Repeat.** The End Repeat screen appears, as shown in Figure 9.17.

8. **You have two choices here:**

   - **Have the event repeats stop on a particular day.** Use the scroll wheels to set the day, month, and year that you want the final event to occur, and then tap Done to return to the Edit screen.

   - **Have the event repeat indefinitely.** Tap Repeat Forever. Calendar returns you to the Edit screen.

9. **Tap Done.** Calendar saves the repeat data and returns you to the event details.

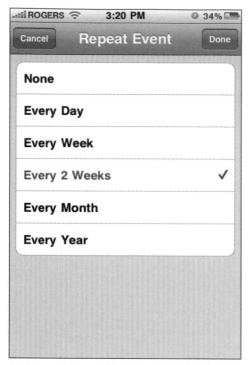

9.16 Use the Repeat Event screen to decide how often you want your event to recur.

9.17 Use the End Repeat screen to decide how long you want the even to repeat.

Converting an event to an all-day event

Some events don't really have specific times that you can pin down. These include birthdays, anniversaries, sales meetings, trade shows, conferences, and vacations. What all these types of events have in common is that they last all day: in the case of birthdays and anniversaries, literally so; in the case of trade shows and the like, "all day" refers to the entire work day.

Why is this important? Well, suppose you schedule a trade show as a regular appointment that lasts from 9AM to 5PM. When you examine that day in Calendar, you see a big fat block that covers the entire day. If you also want to schedule meetings that occur at the trade show, Calendar lets you do that, but it shows these new appointments "on top" of this existing trade show event. This makes the schedule hard to read, so you might miss an appointment.

To solve this problem, configure the trade show (or whatever) as an all-day event. Calendar clears it from the regular schedule and displays the event separately, near the top of the Day view. Here are the steps to follow:

1. **In Calendar, tap the date that contains the appointment you want to edit.**

2. **Tap the appointment.** Calendar opens the event info.

3. **Tap Edit.** Calendar switches to the Edit screen.

4. **Tap Starts/Ends.** The Start & End screen appears.

5. **Tap the All-day switch to the On position.**

6. **Tap Done to return to the Edit screen.**

7. **Tap Done.** Calendar saves the event and returns you to the event details.

Figure 9.18 shows Calendar in Day view with an all-day event added.

9.18 All-day events appear in the all-day section near the top of the Day view screen.

Adding an alert to an event

One of the truly useful secrets of stress-free productivity in the modern world is what I call the set-it-and-forget-it school of appointments. That is, you set up an appointment electronically, and then get the same technology to remind you when the appointment occurs. That way, your mind doesn't have to waste energy fretting about missing the appointment because you know your technology has your back.

With your iPhone, the technology of choice for doing this is Calendar and its alert feature. When you add an alert to an event, Calendar automatically displays a reminder of the event, which is a dialog that pops up on the screen. Your iPhone also vibrates and sounds a few beeps to get your attention. You also get to choose when the alert triggers (such as a specified number of minutes, hours, or days before the event), and you can even set up a second alert just to be on the safe side.

Follow these steps to set an alert for an event:

1. **In Calendar, tap the date that contains the appointment you want to edit.**

2. **Tap the appointment.** Calendar opens the event info.

3. **Tap Edit.** Calendar displays the event data in the Edit screen.

4. **Tap Alert.** The Event Alert screen appears, as shown in Figure 9.19.

5. **Tap the number of minutes, hours, or days before the event you want to see the alert.**

6. **Tap Done to return to the Edit screen.**

7. **To set up a backup alert, tap Second Alert, tap the number of minutes, hours, or days before the event you want to see the second alert, and then tap Done.**

8. **Tap Done.** Calendar saves your alert choices and returns you to the event details.

Figure 9.20 shows an example of an alert. Tap View Event to see the details, or tap OK to dismiss the alert.

Caution If you flick the Ring/Silent switch on the side of the iPhone to the Silent setting, remember that you won't hear the Calendar alert chirps. When the alert runs, your iPhone still vibrates, and you still see the alert message on-screen.

Genius You can disable the alert chirps if you find them annoying. On the Home screen, tap Settings, tap Sounds, and then tap the Calendar Alerts switch to the Off position.

Setting a birthday or anniversary reminder

If someone you know has a birthday coming up, you certainly don't want to forget! You can use your iPhone's Contacts app to add a Birthday field for that person, and that works great if you actually look at the contact. If you don't, you're toast. The best way to remember is to get your iPhone to do the remembering for you.

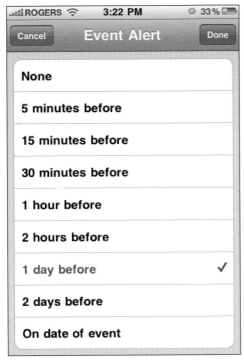

9.19 Use the Event Alert screen to tell Calendar when to remind you about your event.

9.20 Your iPhone displays an alert similar to this when it's time to remind you of an upcoming event.

Follow these steps to set up a reminder about a birthday (or anniversary or some other important date):

1. **In Calendar, tap the date on which the birthday occurs.**

2. **Tap the + button at the top right of the screen.** The Add Event screen appears.

3. **Tap the Title/Location box, type a title for the event ("Karen's Birthday," for example), and then tap Done.** Calendar saves the data and returns you to the Add Event screen.

4. **Tap Starts/Ends, tap the All-day switch to the On position, use the scroll wheels to choose the birthday, and then tap Done.**

5. **Tap Repeat, tap Every Year, and then tap Done.**

6. **Tap Alert, tap the On date of event option, and then tap Done.**

7. **Tap Second Alert, tap the 2 days before option, and then tap Done.** This gives you a couple of days' notice, so you can go out and shop for a card and a present!

8. **Tap Done.** Calendar saves the event, and you have another load off your mind.

Displaying a list of your upcoming events

Calendar's Month view indicates dates that have scheduled events by displaying a teensy dot under the day number. So now you know you have something scheduled on those days, but the dots don't convey any more information than that. To see the scheduled events, you have to tap each day. Way too much work! A better way to is have Calendar do the work for you by displaying a list of what's scheduled over the next few days. Here's how:

1. **In the Home screen, tap the Calendar icon.** Your iPhone opens the Calendar.

2. **Tap the List button.** Calendar displays a list of your upcoming events, as shown in Figure 9.21. Tap an event to see its details.

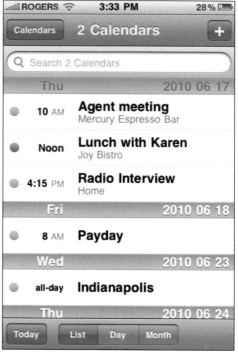

9.21 Tap Calendar's List button to see what's ahead on your schedule.

Handling Microsoft Exchange meeting requests

If you've set up a Microsoft Exchange account in your iPhone, there's a good chance you're using its push features, where the Exchange Server automatically sends incoming e-mail messages to your iPhone, as well as new and changed contacts and calendar data. If someone back at headquarters adds your name to a scheduled meeting, Exchange generates an automatic meeting request, which is an e-mail message that tells you about the meeting and asks if you want to attend.

How will you know? Tap Calendar in the Home screen and then examine the bottom right of the screen. The menu bar icon that looks like an inbox tray will have a red dot with a number inside telling you how many meeting requests you have waiting for you (see Figure 9.22).

Note

If you don't see the inbox tray icon, then you need to turn on syncing for your Exchange calendar. I show you how to do this in Chapter 5.

228

Note Meeting requests show up as events in your calendar, and you can recognize them thanks to their gray background. So another way to open the meeting details is to tap the meeting request in your calendar.

It's best to handle such requests as soon as you can, so here's what you do:

1. **Tap the inbox-like icon in the bottom-right corner of the screen.** Calendar displays your pending meeting requests.

2. **Tap the meeting request you want to respond to.** Calendar displays the meeting details, as shown in Figure 9.23.

3. **Tap your response:**

   - **Accept.** Tap this button to confirm that you can attend the meeting.

   - **Maybe.** Tap this button if you're not sure and will decide later.

   - **Decline.** Tap this button to confirm that you can't attend the meeting.

9.22 Calendar's meeting requests icon shows you how many Exchange meeting requests you have.

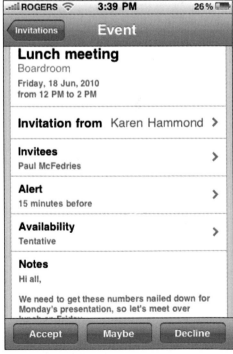

9.23 The details screen for an Exchange meeting request.

Subscribing to a calendar

If you know of someone who has published a calendar, you might want to keep track of that calendar within your iPhone's Calendar app. You can do that by subscribing to the published calendar. iPhone sets up the published calendar as a separate item in the Calendar app, so you can easily switch between your own calendars and the published calendar.

To pull this off, you need to know the address of the published calendar. This address usually takes the following form: *server*.com/*calendar*.ics.

Here, *server*.com is the address of the calendar server, and *calendar*.ics is the name of the iCalendar file (almost always preceded by a folder location). For calendars published to MobileMe, the address always looks like this: ical.me.com/*member*/*calendar*.ics.

Here, *member* is the MobileMe member name of the person who published the calendar. Here's an example address:

ical.me.com/aardvarksorenstam/aardvark.ics

Follow these steps to subscribe to a published calendar:

1. **On the Home screen, tap Settings.** Your iPhone opens the Settings screen.
2. **Tap Mail, Contacts, Calendars.** The Mail, Contacts, Calendars screen appears.
3. **Tap Add Account.** The Add Account screen opens.
4. **Tap Other.** Your iPhone displays the Other screen.
5. **Tap Add Subscribed Calendar.** You see the Subscription screen, as shown in Figure 9.24.
6. **Use the Server text box to enter the calendar address.**
7. **Tap Next.** Your iPhone connects to the calendar.
8. **Tap Save.** Your iPhone adds an account for the subscribed calendar.

To view the subscribed calendar, tap Calendar on the Home screen to open the Calendar app, and then click Calendars to open the Calendars screen. Your new calendar appears in the Subscribed section, as shown in Figure 9.25. Tap the calendar to view its appointments.

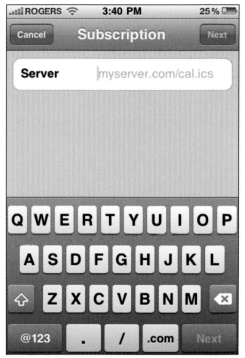

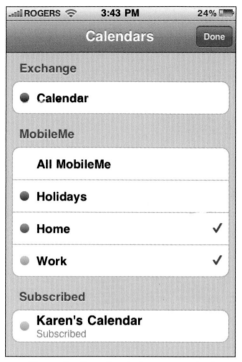

9.24 Use the Subscription screen to specify the address of the calendar you want to subscribe to.

9.25 Your calendar subscriptions appear in the Subscribed section of the Calendars screen.

How Do I Use My iPhone to Navigate My World?

You'd be well within your rights to describe your iPhone as a "Swiss Army phone" because it's positively bristling with tools: a phone, a Web browser, a media player, and a PDA (personal digital assistant). But your iPhone also includes a broad range of features that help you organize and make sense of your life (some parts of it, anyway). I'm talking here about even more tools: an alarm clock, a stopwatch, a map, a GPS device, a weather forecast, a voice recorder, even a stock ticker! In this chapter, I explain these tools and show you how each one can help make small slices of your life easier and more productive.

Finding Your Way with Maps and GPS

When you're out in the real world trying to navigate your way between the proverbial points A and B, the questions often come thick and fast. "Where am I now?" "Which turn do I take?" "What's the traffic like on the highway?" "Can I even get there from here?" Fortunately, the answers to those and similar questions are now just a few finger taps away. That's because your iPhone comes loaded not only with a way-cool Maps app brought to you by the good folks at Google, but it also has a global positioning system (GPS) receiver. Now your iPhone knows exactly where it is (and so, by extension, you know where you are, too), and it can help you get where you want to go.

To get the Maps app on the job, tap the Maps icon in your iPhone's Home screen. Figure 10.1 shows the Maps screen.

Viewing your destination

When you want to locate a destination using Maps, the most straightforward method is to search for it:

1. **Tap inside the Search box in the upper-right corner of the screen.**

2. **Type the name, address, or a keyword or phrase that describes your destination.**

3. **In the on-screen keyboard, tap Search.** The Maps app locates the destination, moves the map to that area, and drops a pin on the destination, as shown in Figure 10.2.

Now that you have your destination pinpointed (literally!), you can read the map to find your way — by looking for street names, local landmarks, nearby major intersections, and so on. (You also can use the Maps app to get specific directions, and I show you how that works later in this chapter.) However, it's always hard to transfer the abstractions of a map to the real-world vista you see outside your car window (or whatever) when you're close to the destination.

Fortunately, Maps can bridge that gap. If Google Street View is available in that area, you see a red icon on the left side of the destination pushpin. Tap that icon, and Maps immediately shows you the destination in all its Street View glory, as shown in Figure 10.3. To get your bearings, flick the screen left or right to get a full 360-degree view of the area surrounding your destination.

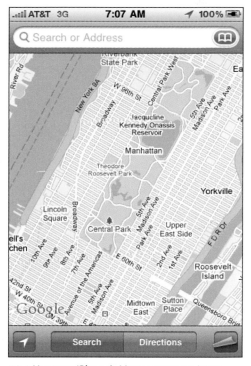

10.1 Use your iPhone's Maps app to navigate your world.

10.2 When you search for a destination, Maps displays a pin to mark its location on the map.

10.3 Tap the Google Street View icon to see a real-world representation of your destination.

Displaying your current location

When you arrive at an unfamiliar shopping mall and you need to get your bearings, your first instinct might be to seek out the nearest mall map and look for the inevitable "You Are Here" marker. This gives you a sense of your current location with respect to the rest of the mall, so locating The Gap shouldn't be all that hard.

When you arrive at an unfamiliar part of town or a new city, have you ever wished you had something that could provide you with that same "You Are Here" reference point? If so, you're in luck because you have exactly that waiting for you right in your iPhone. Tap the Tracking button in the Maps app menu bar, as pointed out in Figure 10.4 That's it! Your iPhone examines GPS coordinates, Wi-Fi hot spots, and nearby cellular towers to plot your current position. When it completes the necessary processing and triangulating, your iPhone displays a map of your current city, zooms in on your current area, and then adds a blue dot to the map to pinpoint your current location, as shown in Figure 10.4. Amazingly, if you happen to be in a car, taxi, or other moving vehicle, the blue dot moves in real time.

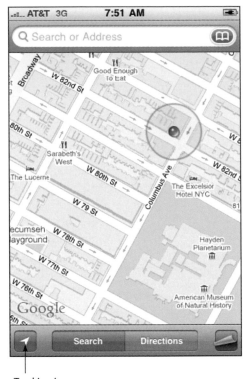

Tracking icon

10.4 Tap the Tracking button to see your precise location as a blue dot on a map.

Genius

Knowing where you are is a good thing, but it's even better to know what's nearby. For example, suppose you're in a new city and you're dying for a cup of coffee. Tap Search in the menu bar, tap the Search box, type **coffee** (or perhaps **café** or **espresso**, depending on what you're looking for), and then tap Search. The Maps app drops a bunch of pins that correspond to nearby locations that match your search. Tap a pin to see the name, and tap the blue More Info icon to see the location's phone number, address, and Web site.

Displaying a map of a contact's location

In the old days (a few years ago!), if you had a contact located in an unfamiliar part of town or even in another city altogether, visiting that person required a phone call or e-mail asking for directions. You'd then write down the instructions, get written directions via e-mail, or perhaps even get a crudely drawn map faxed to you. Those days, fortunately, are long gone thanks to a myriad of online resources that can show you where a particular address is located and even give you driving directions to get there from here (wherever "here" may be).

Even better, your iPhone takes it one step further and integrates with Google Maps to generate a map of a contact's location based on the person's contact address. So as long as you've tapped in (or synced) a contact's physical address, you can see where he or she is located on the map.

To display a map of a contact's location, follow these steps:

1. **In the Home screen, tap the Contacts icon to open the Contacts app.**

2. **Tap the contact you want to work with.** Your iPhone displays the contact's data.

3. **Tap the address you want to map.** Your iPhone switches to the Maps app and drops a push pin on the contact's location.

Note You can also display a map of a contact's location by using the Maps app itself. In the menu bar, tap the Bookmarks icon (it's on the right side of the Search box). Tap Contacts, and then tap the contact you want to map. The Maps app maps the contact's address.

Saving a location as a bookmark for easier access

If you know the address of the location you want to map, you can add a pushpin for that location by opening the Maps app and running a search on the address. That is, you tap Search in the menu bar, tap the Search box, type the address, and then tap the Search button.

That's no big deal for one-time-only searches, but what about a location you refer to frequently? Typing that address over and over gets old in a hurry, I assure you. You can save time and tapping by telling the Maps app to save that location on its Bookmarks list, which means you can access the location usually with just a few taps.

Follow these steps to add a location to the Maps app's Bookmarks list:

1. **Search for the location you want to save.** The Maps app marks the location with a pushpin and displays the name or address of the location in a banner above the pushpin.

2. **Tap the blue More Info icon in the banner.** The Maps app displays the Info screen with details about the location:

   - If the location is in your Contacts list, you see the contact's data.

   - If the location is a business or institution, you see the address as well as other data such as the organization's phone number and Web address.

   - For all other locations, you see just the address.

3. **Tap Add to Bookmarks.** The Maps app displays the Add Bookmarks screen.

4. **Edit the name of the bookmark, if you want to, and then Tap Save.** The Maps app adds the location to the Bookmarks list.

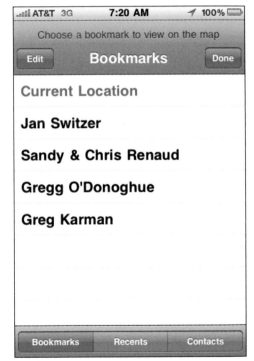

To map a bookmarked location, follow these steps:

1. **Tap the Bookmark icon in the menu bar.** The Maps app opens the Bookmarks screen.

2. **Tap Bookmarks in the menu bar.** The Maps app displays your list of bookmarked locations, as shown in Figure 10.5.

3. **Tap the location you want to map.** The Maps app displays the appropriate map and adds a pushpin for the location.

10.5 You can access frequently used locations with just a few taps by saving them as bookmarks.

Genius

The Bookmarks screen also comes with a Recents button in the menu bar. Tap this button to see your last few searches, locations entered, and driving directions requested. To get the Maps app to run any item again, just tap it.

Specifying a location when you don't know the exact address

Sometimes you have only a vague notion of where you want to go. In a new city, for example, you might decide to head downtown and then see if there are any good coffee shops or restaurants. That's fine, but how do you get downtown from your hotel in the suburbs? Your iPhone can give you directions, but it needs to know the endpoint of your journey, and that's precisely the information you don't have. Sounds like a conundrum, for sure, but there's a way to work around it. You can drop a pin on the map in the approximate area where you want to go. The Maps app can then give you directions to the dropped pin.

Here are the steps to follow to drop a pin on a map:

1. **In the Maps app, display a map of the city you want to work with:**

    - If you're in the city now, tap the Tracking icon in the lower-left corner of the screen.

    - If you're not in the city, tap Search, tap the Search box, enter the name of the city (and perhaps also the name of the state or province), and then tap the Search button.

2. **Use finger flicks to pan the map to the approximate location you want to use as your destination.**

3. **Tap the Action button in the lower-right corner of the screen.** The Maps app displays a list of actions.

4. **Tap Drop Pin.** The Maps app drops a purple pin in the middle of the current map.

5. **Drag the purple pin to the location you want.** The Maps app creates a temporary bookmark called Dropped Pin that you can use when you ask the iPhone for directions (as described next).

Getting directions to a location

One possible navigation scenario with your iPhone's Maps app is to specify a destination (using a contact, an address search, a dropped pin, or a bookmark), then tap the Tracking button. This gives you a map that shows both your destination and your current location. (Depending on how far away the destination is, you may need to zoom out — by pinching the screen or by tapping the screen with two fingers — to see both locations on the map.) You can then eyeball the streets to see how to get from here to there.

Genius

Instead of getting directions to the destination, you might need directions *from* the destination. No sweat. When you map the destination, tap the blue More Info icon, and then tap Directions From Here. If you're already in the Directions screen, tap the Swap button to the left of the Start and End boxes. The Maps app swaps the locations.

Note

Instead of seeing the directions one step at a time, you might prefer to see them all at once. Tap the Action icon in the lower-right corner of the screen, and then tap List.

"Eyeball the streets"? Hah, how primitive! Your iPhone's Maps app can bring you into the 21st century by not only showing you a route to the destination, but also by providing you with the distance and time it should take, *and* giving you street-by-street, turn-by-turn instructions. It's one of your iPhone's sweetest features, and it works like so:

1. **Use the Maps app to add a pushpin for your journey's destination.** Use whatever method works best for you: the Contacts list, an address search, a dropped pin, or a bookmark.

2. **Tap Directions in the menu bar.** The Maps app opens the Directions screen. As shown in Figure 10.6, you should see Current Location in the Start box, and your destination address in the End box.

3. **If you want to use a starting point other than your current location, tap the Start box and then type the address of the location you want to use.**

4. **Tap Route.** The Maps app figures out the best route and then displays it on the map in the Overview screen, which also shows the trip distance and approximate time.

Swap icon

10.6 Use the Directions screen to specify the starting and ending points of your trip.

5. **Tap the icon for the type of directions you want: Car, Transit, or Walking.** The Maps app adjusts the route accordingly.

6. **Tap Start.** The Maps app displays the directions for the first leg of the journey.

7. **Tap the Next (right arrow) key.** You see the directions for the next leg of the journey. Repeat to see the directions for each leg. You can also tap the Previous (left arrow) key to go back.

Getting live traffic information

Okay, it's pretty darn amazing that your iPhone can tell you precisely where you are and precisely how to get somewhere else. However, in most cities it's the getting somewhere else part that's the problem. Why? One word: traffic. The Maps app might tell you the trip should take 10 minutes, but that could easily turn into a half hour or more if you run into a traffic jam.

That's life in the big city, right? Maybe not. If you're on a highway in a major U.S. city, the Maps app can most likely supply you with — wait for it — real-time traffic conditions! This is really an amazing tool that can help you avoid traffic messes and find alternative routes to your destination.

To see the traffic data, tap the Action icon in the lower-right corner of the screen, and then tap Show Traffic. As you can see in Figure 10.7, the Maps app uses four colors to illustrate the traffic flow:

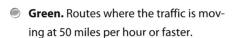

10.7 For most U.S. metropolitan highways, the color of the route tells you the current speed of the traffic.

-  **Green.** Routes where the traffic is moving at 50 miles per hour or faster.

- **Yellow.** Routes where the traffic is moving between 25 and 50 mph.

- **Red.** Routes where the traffic is moving at 25 mph or slower.

- **Gray.** Routes that currently have no traffic data.

Now you don't have to worry about finding a news radio station and waiting for the traffic report. You can get real-time traffic information whenever you need it.

241

4.0 Controlling app access to GPS

iOS 4.0 When you open an app that comes with a GPS component, the app displays a dialog like the one shown in Figure 10.8 to ask you permission to use the iPhone's GPS hardware to determine you current location. Tap OK if that's just fine with you; tap Don't Allow if you think that your current location is none of the app's business.

However, after you make your decision, you might change your mind. For example, if you deny your location to an app, that app might lack some crucial functionality. Similarly, if you allow an app to use your location, you might have second thoughts about compromising your privacy.

Whatever the reason, you can control an app's access to GPS by following these steps:

1. **In your iPhone's Home screen, tap Settings.** The Settings app appears.
2. **Tap General.** The General screen appears.
3. **Tap Location Services.** The Location Services screen appears, as shown in Figure 10.9.

10.8 When you first launch a GPS-aware app, it asks your permission to use your current location.

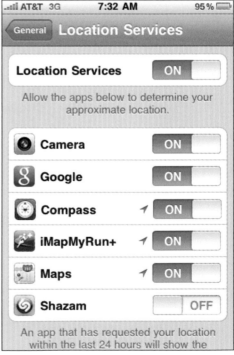

10.9 Use the Location Services screen to control which apps have access to your location.

4. **Configure app access to GPS as follows:**

- If you want to deny your current location to all apps, tap the Location Services switch to Off.

- If you want to deny your current location to specific apps, for each app tap the On/Off switch to Off.

Sharing Map Data

If you want to show someone where you live, where you work, or where you want to meet, you could just send the address, but that's *so* last century. The more modern way is to send your friend a digital map that shows the location. Your iPhone makes this a snap, as the following sections show.

E-mailing a map location

Practically everyone has an e-mail address (everyone online, that is), so sending someone a map attached to an email message makes sense. Here are the steps to follow:

1. **Use the Maps app to add a pushpin for the location you want to send.** Use whatever method works best for you: the Contacts list, an address search, a dropped pin, or a bookmark. If you want to send you current location, display it, and then tap the beacon.

2. **Tap the blue More Info icon.** Maps displays the Info screen for the location.

3. **Tap Share Location.** Maps displays the Share Location Using options.

4. **Tap Email.** Your iPhone creates a new e-mail message that includes a Google Maps link to the location.

5. **Fill in the rest of your message and send it.**

Sending a map location using MMS

If you want to send someone a map, but you're not sure whether that person will check his or her e-mail in time, your iPhone lets you send the map in a text message instead. If your cellular provider supports Multimedia Messaging Service (MMS), follow these steps to text a map to someone:

1. **Add a pushpin for the location you want to send.** Use the Contacts list, an address search, a dropped pin, or a bookmark. To send your current location, display it and then tap the beacon to display the banner.

2. **Tap the More Info icon.** The location's Info screen appears.

3. **Tap Share Location.** The Share Location Using options appear.

4. **Tap MMS.** Your iPhone displays the New MMS screen and includes the map location in the Send box.

5. **Select the recipient.**

6. **Tap Send.**

Getting your bearings with the Compass

Your iPhone is loaded with fancy equipment, perhaps the most famous of which is the accelerometer, which enables the iPhone to sense when its orientation changes. (It's the accelerometer that makes so many of the iPhone games so addictive.) The iPhone 3GS comes with a new internal gadget: a magnetometer, which is a device that measures the direction and intensity of a magnetic field. That sounds a bit esoteric, but having data about the magnetic field means that the iPhone 3GS can orient itself with respect to direction. It is, in short, a compass!

With the iPhone acting as a compass, you can do two things:

- **Orient a map.** In Maps, tap the Tracking button to see your current location, and then tap the Tracking button a second time. Your iPhone orients the map so that it matches the direction you're facing. Nice!

- **Get your bearings.** On the Home screen, tap the Utilities Folder, tap Compass and, if your iPhone asks whether Compass can use you current location, tap OK. This launches the new Compass app which, as you can see in Figure 10.10, bears an uncanny resemblance to a real compass. And, like a real compass, the Compass app always points to north (true north or magnetic north; tap the "i" button in the bottom right corner to choose), so you always know which way you're going.

10.10 The iPhone 4 comes with a Compass app that uses the phone's built-in magnetometer to show you which way you're going.

How Do I Manage My eBook Library on My iPhone?

Chances are good that you're holding a physical book in your hands right now as you read these words. Physical books are an awesome invention: They're portable, easy-to-use, and fully "show-off-able," whether being read on the subway or sitting on a bookshelf at home. Physical books aren't going away anytime soon, but the age of electronic books — eBooks — is upon us. Amazon's Kindle lit a fire under the eBook category, but it's clunky to use and tied to Amazon; Apple filled in these gaps by offering iBooks for the iPad, an app that's easy to use and supports an open eBook format, and the iPhone now has its own version of iBooks. The iPhone screen is a bit on the small side, but the new Retina display in the iPhone 4 renders text sharply and clearly, so reading books on the iPhone shouldn't be a chore. This chapter introduces you to eBooks on the iPhone.

Installing the iBooks App

In this chapter, I concentrate on iBooks, which is Apple's eReader app. However, it's important to stress right off the bat that you're not restricted to using iBooks for reading eBooks on your iPhone. Tons of great eBook apps are available (I mention a few of them at the end of this chapter; see the section on reading other eBooks on your iPhone), so feel free to use any or all of them in addition to (or even instead of) iBooks.

Unlike most of the other apps I've talked about in this book, iBooks isn't part of the default iPhone app collection. Instead, you have to install it (it's free) from the App Store:

1. **On the Home screen, tap App Store.** Your iPhone opens the App Store.

2. **Tap search to open the Search page.**

3. **Tap inside the Search box to display the keyboard, type iBooks, and then tap Search.** The search results appear.

4. **Tap the iBooks app.** The app's Info screen appears.

5. **Tap the FREE icon.** The Free icon changes to the Install icon.

6. **Tap Install.** The App Store asks for your iTunes account password.

7. **Type your password, and tap OK.** The App Store downloads and installs the app, and an iBooks icon appears on the Home screen.

8. **When the installation is complete, tap the iBooks icon to launch the app.** iBooks asks if you want to sync your eBook bookmarks and notes with your iTunes account, as shown in Figure 11.1. Syncing is a good idea if you plan on using iBooks on other devices, such as an iPad or iPod touch.

11.1 When you first launch iBooks, the app asks whether you want to turn on syncing got bookmarks and notes.

9. **Tap Sync.** Alternatively, tap Don't Sync if you don't need this functionality. Figure 11.2 shows the iBooks Bookshelf, which looks like a bookcase.

Getting Your Head around eBook Formats

If there's one reason why eBooks haven't taken off (in the same way that, say, digital music now rules the planet), it's because the eBook world is hopelessly, head-achingly confusing. As I write this, at least two dozen (yes, two *dozen*!) different eBook formats are available, with new formats jumping on the eBook bandwagon with distressing frequency. That's bad enough, but it gets worse when you consider that some of these formats require a specific eReading device or program. For example, the Kindle eBook format requires either the Kindle eReader or the Kindle app; similarly, the Microsoft LIT format requires the Microsoft Reader program. Finally, things turn positively chaotic when you realize that some formats come with built-in restrictions that prevent you from reading eBooks in other devices or programs, or sharing eBooks with other people.

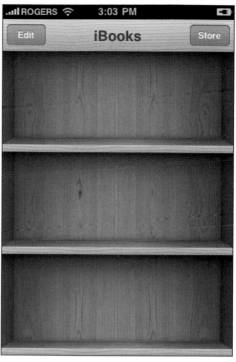

11.2 The iBooks Bookshelf is designed to mimic a real bookcase.

We're a long way from the simplicity and clarity that comes with having a near-universal eBook format (such as the MP3 format in music), but there are signs of hope because one format seems to be slowly emerging from the fray: EPUB. This is a free and open eBook standard created by the International Digital Publishing Forum (IDPF; see www.idpf.org). EPUB files, which use the .epub extension, are supported by most eReader programs and by most eReader devices (with the Amazon Kindle being the very noticeable exception). EPUB is leading the way not only because it's free and non-proprietary, but also because it offers quite a few cool features:

- Text is resizable, so you can select the size that's most comfortable for you.

- The layout and formatting of the text is handled by cascading style sheets (CSS), which is an open and well-known standard that makes it easy to alter the look of the text, including changing the font.

- Text is "re-flowable," which means that when you change the text size or the font, the text wraps naturally on the screen to accommodate the new character sizes. (This is opposed to some eBook formats that simply zoom in or out of the text.)

- A single eBook can have alternative versions of the book in the same file.

- eBooks can include high-resolution images right on the page.

- Publishers can protect book content by adding *digital rights management* (DRM) support. DRM refers to any technology that restricts the usage of content to prevent piracy. (Depending on where you fall in the "information wants to be free" spectrum, DRM may not be "cool" and may not even be considered a "feature.")

So the first bit of good news is that the iBooks app supports the EPUB format, so all the features listed here are available in the iBooks app.

Note For the record, I should also mention that you can use the iBooks app to read books in three other formats: plain text, HTML, and PDF.

The next bit of good news is iBooks' support for EPUB means that a vast universe of public domain books is available to you. On its own, Google Books (http://books.google.com/) offers over a *million* public domain eBooks. Several other excellent EPUB sites exist on the Web, and I tell you about them, as well as tell you how to get them onto your iPhone, a bit later (see the section on adding other EPUB eBooks).

By definition, public-domain eBooks are DRM-free, and you can use them in any way you see fit. However, lots of the EPUB books you'll find come with DRM restrictions. In the case of iBooks, the DRM scheme-of-choice is called FairPlay. This is the DRM technology that Apple used on iTunes for many years. Apple phased out DRM on music a while ago, but still uses it for other content, such as movies, TV shows, and audiobooks.

FairPlay means that many of the eBooks you download through iBooks face the following restrictions:

- You can access your books on a maximum of five computers, each of which must be authorized with your iTunes Store account info.

- You can read your eBooks only on your iPhone, iPad, iPod touch, or on a computer that has iTunes installed.

It's crucial to note here two restrictions you'll trip over with DRM-encrusted eBooks:

- FairPlay eBooks do *not* work on other eReader devices that support the EPUB format, including the Sony Reader and the Barnes & Noble Nook.

- EPUB format books that come wrapped in some other DRM scheme do *not* work on your iPhone.

However, remember that DRM is an optional add-on to the EPUB format. Although it's expected that most publishers will bolt FairPlay DRM onto books they sell in the iBookstore, it's not required, so you should be able to find DRM-free eBooks in the iBookstore (and elsewhere).

Note   If you have an Amazon Kindle, I'm afraid you won't be able to transfer any of your Kindle eBooks directly to your iPhone, or vice versa. The Kindle doesn't support EPUB, so it can't load even your DRM-free EPUB books. The Kindle uses a proprietary eBook format, so Kindle eBooks won't transfer to the iPhone (or any other eReader). However, Amazon does offer a Kindle app for the iPhone, so you can use that app to read your Kindle books.

Managing Your iBooks Library

The iBooks app comes with a virtual wood bookcase, which is a nice bit of eye candy, for sure, but is certainly no more than that because the real point is to fill that bookcase with your favorite digital reading material. So your first task is to add a few titles to the bookcase, and the next few sections show you how to do just that.

Browsing books in the iBookstore

You'll see a bit later that you can grab eBooks via the iTunes Store, but what if you're out and about with your iPhone, you've got a bit of time to kill, and you decide to start a book? That's no problem, because iBooks has a direct link to Apple's new book marketplace, the iBookstore. Your iPhone can establish a wireless connection to the App Store anywhere you have Wi-Fi access or a cellular signal (ideally 3G for faster downloads). You can browse and search the books, read reviews, and purchase any book you want (or grab a title from the large collection of free books). The eBook downloads to your iPhone and adds itself to the iBooks bookcase. You can start reading within seconds!

What about the selection? When Apple announced the iPad and the iBooks app, they also announced that five major publishers would be stocking the iBookstore: Hachette, HarperCollins, Macmillan, Penguin, and Simon & Schuster. Since then, a number of other publishers have been added; so along with all those free eBooks, you can rest assured the iBookstore will eventually have an impressive selection.

To access the iBookstore, follow these steps:

1. **Display the iBooks Bookshelf.**
   - If you haven't loaded the app yet, tap the iBooks icon to open the iBooks app.
   - If you're in the iBooks app and reading a book, tap the screen to display the controls and then tap Bookshelf.

2. **Tap the Store icon.**

As you can see in Figure 11.3, your iPhone organizes the iBookstore similar to the App Store. That is, you get five browse buttons in the menu bar — Featured, Charts, Browse, Search, and Purchases. You use these buttons to navigate the iBookstore.

Here's a summary of what each browse button does for you:

- **Featured.** Tap this button to display a list of books picked by the iBookstore editors. The list shows each book's cover, title, author, category, star rating, number of reviews, and price. Tap New to see the latest apps, and tap What's Hot to see the most popular items.
- **Charts.** Tap this button to see a collection of charts, including the Top Paid books, the Top Free books, and the New York Times bestseller lists.

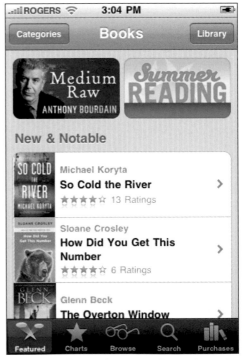

11.3 Use the browse buttons in the iBookstore's menu bar to locate and manage apps for your iPhone.

- **Browse.** Tap this button to browse through the bookstore using an alphabetical list of author names, also divided into the Top Paid and the Top Free lists. You can also tap Categories to browse the iBookstore by subject.

- **Search.** Tap this button to run a search on the iBookstore.

- **Purchases.** Tap this button to see a list of the books you've downloaded.

Note Tap a book to get more detailed information about it. The Info screen that appears (see Figure 11.4, a bit later in this chapter) is divided into two sections: The top section shows standard book data, such as the title, author, cover, publisher, and number of pages; the bottom section gives you a description of the book, lists related books, and offers user reviews of the book.

Downloading a free eBook

Thousands upon thousands of books are in the public domain, meaning that the rights of those books are no longer owned by any publisher or author. This means anyone can publish such books, and the digital versions tend to be free for the taking. You might think these would be ancient, obscure tomes of little interest to anybody, but you'd be surprised. The iBookstore has a Classics category that offers some of the best books in history, from Bram Stoker's *Dracula* to Lewis Carroll's *Alice's Adventures in Wonderland* (a personal fave).

Note In the iBookstore, the free books say FREE on the right side of the book link. If you're looking for a good place to quickly populate your iBooks Bookshelf, tap Charts and then tap the Top Free tab.

Follow these steps to download and install a free eBook:

1. **Locate the eBook you want to read, and tap it.** The book's Info screen appears.

2. **Tap the Free icon.** The Free icon changes to the Get Book icon.

3. **Tap Get Book.** The iBookstore might ask for your iTunes Store account password.

4. **Tap the Password box, type your password, and tap OK.** The iBooks app switches back to the Bookshelf bookcase, places your book on the top shelf, and displays a progress bar that tracks the download (most eBooks download in just a few seconds).

5. **When the download is complete, tap the eBook's cover to start reading.**

If the app is quite big and you're surfing the Internet over a cellular connection — particularly an EDGE connection — your iPhone may abort the installation and tell you that you need to connect to a Wi-Fi network to download the app.

Sampling an eBook

You'll see in the next section that paid books set you back anywhere from $4.99 to $14.99 on average. (Textbooks and specialized technical books can easily run you well over $100!) Before forking over that kind of cash, you may want to make sure you really want the book. Checking out other readers' ratings and reviews can help, but there's nothing like checking out the book itself. In an offline bookstore, you can just leaf through the pages; in the online iBookstore, you can do the next best thing: read a sample of the book. Here's how:

1. **In the iBooks app, locate the eBook you want to purchase.** Browse the categories or charts, or use the Search box to track down the book.

2. **Tap the eBook.** The eBook's Info screen appears.

3. **Tap the Get Sample icon.** The iBookstore might ask for your iTunes Store account password.

4. **Tap the Password box, type your password, and tap OK.** The iBooks app switches back to the bookcase and adds the sample.

5. **When the download is complete, tap the sample to start reading.**

Purchasing an eBook

If you're sure you want to purchase a paid eBook — that is, you've read the book's description, checked out the rating, read the reviews, and perhaps even read a sample of the book — then you're ready to follow these steps to purchase and download the book:

1. **In the iBooks app, locate the eBook you want to purchase and tap it.** The eBook's Info screen appears. Figure 11.4 shows an example.

2. **Tap the price icon.** The price changes to the Buy Book icon.

3. **Tap the Buy Book icon.** The iBookstore might ask for your iTunes Store account password.

4. **Tap the Password box, type your password, and tap OK.** The iBooks app returns you to the Bookshelf, adds your book to the top shelf of the bookcase, and displays a progress bar that tracks the download process (which should take just a few seconds).

5. **When the download is complete, tap the book and start reading.**

Adding other EPUB eBooks to your library

With the apparent ascendance of the EPUB format, publishers and book packagers are tripping over each other to make their titles EPUB-friendly. As a result, the Web is awash in EPUB books, so you don't have to get all your iPhone's eBook content from the iBookstore. Here's a short list of some sites where you can download .epub files to your computer:

11.4 The Info screen of a book in the iBookstore.

- **BooksOnBoard.** This site offers a variety of eBooks, although most aren't compatible with iBooks, thanks to DRM. To find non-DRM titles, go to the Advanced Search page and select the Adobe EPUB check box. www.booksonboard.com.

- **epubBooks.** This is a terrific site for all things related to the EPUB format, and it offers a wide selection of public domain EPUB books. www.epubbooks.com.

- **eBooks.com.** This site has a variety of books in various eBook formats, although most won't work in the iBooks app because most of the EPUB books use the DRM scheme from Adobe. However, you can go to the Search Options page and search for the "Unencrypted EPUB" file format to see the iBooks-friendly titles they offer. http://ebooks.com.

- **Feedbooks.** This site offers public domain titles in several formats, including EPUB. www.feedbooks.com.

- **ManyBooks.** This site offers a nice collection of free eBooks in a huge variety of formats. When you download a book, be sure to choose the EPUB (.epub) format in the Select Format drop-down list. http://manybooks.net/.

- **Smashwords.** This intriguing site offers titles by independent and self-published authors. All eBooks are DRM-free, and each book is available in the EPUB format. www.smashwords.com.

- **Snee.** This site offers lots of children's picture books in the EPUB format. www.snee.com/epubkidsbooks/.

After you've downloaded an EPUB title to your computer, follow these steps to import the book into iTunes:

1. **In iTunes for the Mac, choose File ⇨ Add to Library or press ⌘+O.** In iTunes for Windows, choose File ⇨ Add File to Library or press Ctrl+O. The Add to Library dialog box appears.

2. **Locate and click the EPUB file you downloaded.**

3. **In iTunes for the Mac, click Choose.** In iTunes for Windows, click Open. iTunes adds the eBook to the Books section of the library.

Editing the iBooks Library

When you add a book to the iBooks Bookshelf, the app clears a space for the new title on the left side of the top shelf of the bookcase. The rest of the books get shuffled to the right and down.

This is a sensible way to go about things if you read each book as you download it because it means the iBooks Bookshelf displays your books in the order you read them. Of course, life isn't always that orderly, and you might end up reading your eBooks more haphazardly, which means the order the book appears in the Bookshelf won't reflect the order you read them.

Similarly, you may have one or more books in your iBooks Bookshelf that you refer to frequently for reference, or because you're reading them piecemeal (such as a book of poetry, for example, or a collection of short stories). In that case, it would be better to have such books near the top of the bookcase where they're slightly easier to find and open.

For these and similar Bookshelf maintenance chores, iBooks lets you shuffle the books around to get them into the order you prefer. Here's how it works:

1. **Display the iBooks Bookshelf.**
   - If you haven't loaded the app yet, tap the iBooks icon to open the iBooks app.
   - If you're in the iBooks app and reading a book, tap the screen to display the controls, and then tap Bookshelf.

You can also organize your books by list. In the bookshelf screen, tap the Lists icon, which is the icon with three horizontal lines to the right of the Search box. You can then tap the buttons on the bottom of the screen to organize your books by Titles, Authors, or Categories. Tap Bookshelf to view your books in the order they appear on the bookshelf. Tap the Bookshelf icon (the four squares to the right of the Search box) when you're ready to return to the Bookshelf view.

2. **Tap Edit.** iBooks opens the Bookshelf for editing, as shown in Figure 11.5.

3. **Tap and drag the book covers to the bookcase positions you prefer.**

4. **If you want to remove a book from your library, tap the X icon in the upper-left corner of the book's cover, and then click Delete when iBooks asks you to confirm.**

5. **Tap Done.** iBooks closes the Bookshelf for editing.

Syncing Your iBooks Library

If you've used your computer to grab an eBook from the iBookstore or add a downloaded eBook to the iTunes library, you'll want to get that book onto your iPhone as soon as possible. Similarly, if you've downloaded a few eBooks on your iPhone, it's a good idea to back them up to your computer.

11.5 With the bookshelf open for editing, you can move and remove books.

Running the Sync

You can do both by syncing eBooks between your computer and your iPhone:

1. **Connect your iPhone to your computer.** iTunes opens and accesses the iPhone. If you added eBooks to your iPhone, be sure to wait until iTunes syncs them to your computer.

2. **In iTunes, click your iPhone in the Devices list.**

3. **Click the Books tab.**

4. **Select the Sync Books check box.**

5. **To sync only some of your books, select the Selected Books option.**

6. **In the book list, select the check box beside each book that you want to sync, as shown in Figure 11.6.**

11.6 You can sync selected books with your iPhone.

7. **Click Apply.** iTunes syncs the iPhone using your new book's settings.

Creating a custom eBook cover

If you've obtained any free books from the iBookstore, or if you've downloaded public domain books to iTunes, you'll no doubt have noticed that many (or, really, most) of these books use generic covers. That's no big deal for a book or two, but it can get monotonous if you have many such books in your iBooks library (as well as making it hard to find the book you want). To work around this, you can create custom book covers from your own photos.

Your first task is to convert a photo (or any image) to something that's usable as a book cover. This involves loading the image into your favorite image-editing program and then doing three things:

- Crop the image so that it's 420 pixels wide and 600 pixels tall.

- Use the image editing program's text tool to add the book's title to the image.

- Save the image as a JPEG file. (If the image is already JPEG, be sure to save it under a different name so you don't overwrite the original image.)

Now you're ready to use the new image as a book cover, which you do by importing the cover image into iTunes:

1. **In iTunes, click the Books category.** iTunes displays your eBooks.

2. **Right-click (or Control-click on a Mac) the book you want to customize, and then click Get Info.** iTunes displays the book's Info dialog.

3. **Click the Artwork tab.** This tab includes a large box for the book cover image.

4. **Use Finder (on a Mac) or Explorer (on a Windows PC) to locate the new cover image.** On a Mac, you can also locate the image in iPhoto.

5. **Click the new image and drop it inside the large box in the Artwork tab.**

6. **Click OK.** iTunes applies the new image as the book's cover.

Reading eBooks with the iBooks App

If you're a book-lover like me, when you have your iBooks Bookshelf bookcase groaning under the weight of all your eBooks, you may want to spend some time just looking at all the covers sitting prettily in that beautiful bookcase. Or not. If it's the latter, then it's time to get some reading done. The next few sections show you how to control eBooks and modify the display for the best reading experience.

Controlling eBooks on the reading screen

When you're ready to start reading a book using iBooks, getting started couldn't be simpler:

1. **Display the iBooks Bookshelf.**
   - If you haven't loaded the app yet, tap the iBooks icon to open the iBooks app.
   - If you're in the iBooks app and reading a book, tap the screen to display the controls and then tap Bookshelf.

2. **Tap the book you want to read.** iBooks opens the book.

Here's a list of techniques you can use to control an eBook while reading it:

- **To flip to the next page, tap the right side of the screen.**
- **To flip to the previous page, tap the left side of the screen.**
- **To "manually" turn a page, flick the page with your finger.** Flick left to turn to the next page; flick right to turn to the previous page.

- **To access the iBooks controls, tap the middle of the screen.** To hide the controls, tap the middle of the screen again.

- **To access the book's Table of Contents, display the controls and tap the Contents icon, pointed out in Figure 11.7.** You can then tap an item in the Table of Contents to jump to that section of the book.

- **To go to a different page in the book, display the controls and tap a dot at the bottom of the screen.**

- **To search the book, display the controls, tap the Search icon in the upper-right corner, type your search text, and tap Search.** In the search results that appear, tap a result to display that part of the book.

- **To return to the iBooks Bookshelf, display the controls and tap Bookshelf in the upper-left corner.**

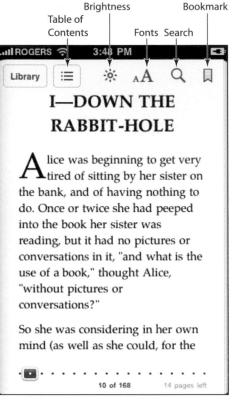

11.7 Tap the middle of the screen to display the controls, and then tap the Contents icon to display the book's Table of Contents.

Formatting eBook text

I mentioned near the top of the show that the EPUB format supports multiple text sizes and multiple fonts, and that the text "reflows" seamlessly to accommodate the new text size. The iBooks app takes advantage of these EPUB features, as shown here:

1. **While reading an eBook, tap the middle of the screen to display the controls.**

2. **Tap the Font icon, pointed out earlier in Figure 11.7.** iBooks displays the Font options.

3. **Tap the larger "A" to increase the text size.** Tap the smaller "A" to reduce the font size.

4. **Tap Fonts.** iBooks displays a list of typefaces, as shown in Figure 11.8.

5. **Tap the typeface you want to use.** iBooks reformats the eBook for the new typeface.

6. **Tap the middle of the screen to hide the controls.**

Saving your spot with a bookmark

Reading an eBook with the iBooks app is so pleasurable you may not want to stop! You have to eat sometime, however, so when it's time to set aside the book, mark your location with a bookmark:

1. **Display the page where you want to set your bookmark.**

2. **Tap the page.** iBooks displays its controls.

3. **Tap the Bookmark icon, pointed out earlier in Figure 11.7.** iBooks saves your spot by creating a bookmark at the location you chose.

To return to your place, follow these steps:

1. **Tap the page.** iBooks displays the reading controls.

2. **Tap the Contents icon.** iBooks displays the reading controls.

3. **Tap the Bookmarks tab.** iBooks offers up a list of the saved bookmarks.

4. **Tap the bookmark.** iBooks returns you to the bookmarked page.

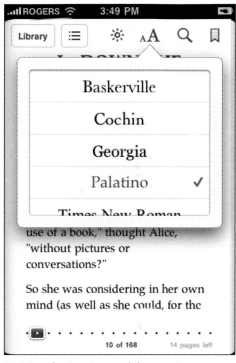

11.8 Tap the Font icon and then tap Fonts to see a list of typefaces.

Looking up a word in the dictionary

While you're perusing an eBook, you may come across an unfamiliar word. You can look it up using any of the umpteen online dictionaries, but there's no need for that with iBooks:

1. **Tap and hold the word you're furrowing your brow over.** iBooks displays a set of options.

2. **Tap Dictionary.** The first time you do this, iBooks tells you that it needs to download a dictionary.

3. **Tap Download.** iBooks loads the dictionary, looks up the word, and then displays its definition.

4. **Tap Done to close the definition.**

Highlighting text

If you come across a pithy bit of prose or some useful tidbit of information, you can use the iBooks equivalent of a yellow marker to highlight the text:

1. **Tap and hold any part of the text you want to highlight.** iBooks displays a set of options as well as selection handles around the text.

2. **Use the selection handles to select the full text you want to highlight.**

3. **Tap Highlight.** iBooks displays the selected text with a yellow background.

Adding a note to an eBook

While you're reading an eBook, you might get the urge to annotate some text, or write down a thought or question that comes to mind. You may not be able to write in the margins of an eBook, but you can use iBooks to add notes to the book:

1. **Tap and hold any part of the text where you want your note to appear.** iBooks displays a set of options as well as selection handles around the text.

2. **Use the selection handles to select the full text to which you want your note to apply.**

3. **Tap Note.** iBooks displays a large text area and the keyboard.

4. **Type your note and then tap.** iBooks highlights the selected text and displays the Note icon to the right of the text, as shown in Figure 11.9.

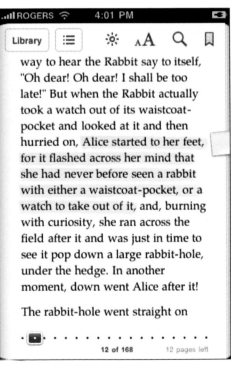

11.9 You can add notes to your eBooks.

Reading Other eBooks on Your iPhone

In this chapter, I focused on the iBooks app, mostly because it's an excellent app that's optimized for the iPhone and integrates seamlessly with iTunes. But the iPhone is arguably the best eReader available today, so it seems a shame to ignore the massive universe of eBooks that aren't iBooks-compatible. If you want to turn your iPhone into the ultimate eReader that's capable of reading practically *any* eBook in practically *any* format, then just head for the App Store and install the appropriate eReader apps.

A complete list of eReader apps would extend for pages, so I'll just hit the highlights here:

- **Barnes & Noble eReader.** If you don't have the Nook, Barnes & Noble's eReading device, you can still read Barnes & Noble eBooks by installing the company's eReader app, which supports the EPUB format protected by Adobe's DRM scheme.

- **eReader.** This app supports the eReader format.

- **iSilo.** This app supports the iSilo and Palm Doc formats.

- **Kindle.** Amazon's Kindle app is the way to go if you want to read Kindle eBooks on your iPhone.

- **Stanza.** This powerful app supports an amazing variety of eBook formats, including EPUB (protected by Adobe DRM), eReader, and Mobipocket.

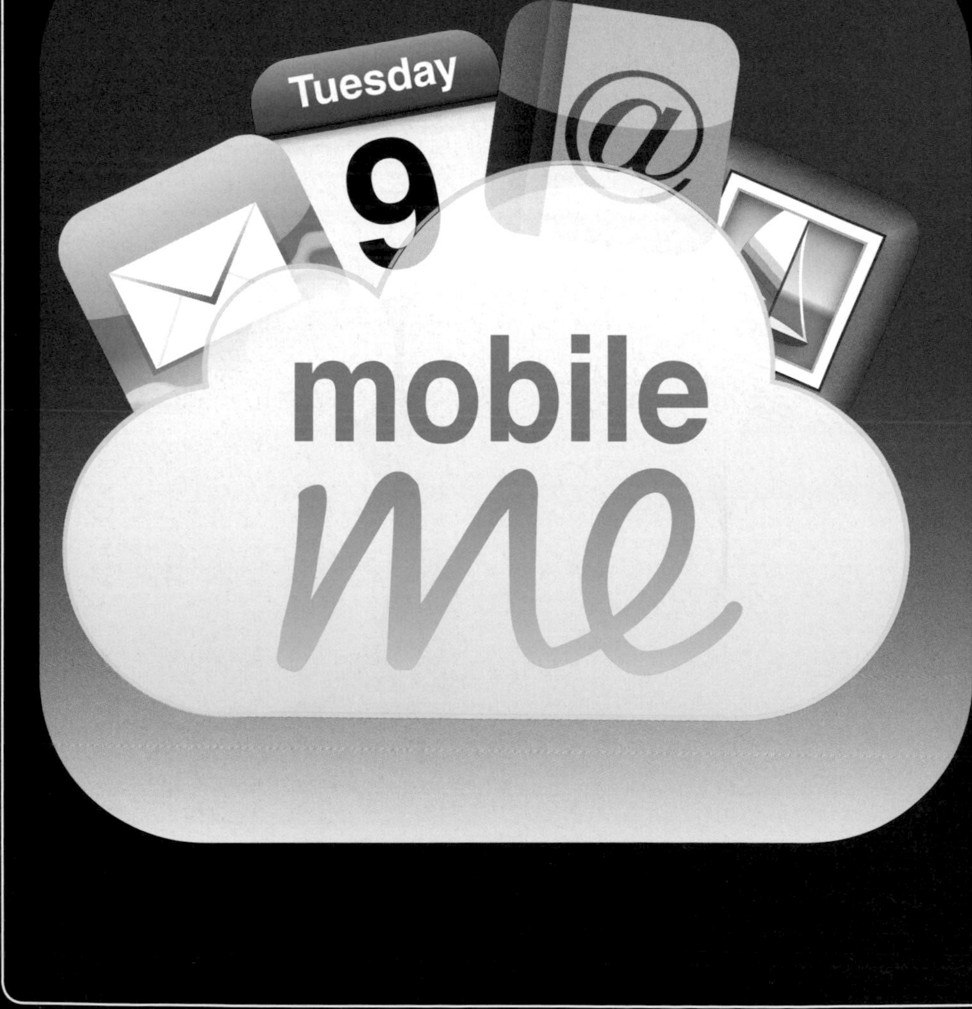
Tuesday
9
mobile
me

When you go online, you take your life along with you, of course, so your online world becomes a natural extension of your real world. However, just because it's online doesn't mean the digital version of your life is any less busy, chaotic, or complex than the rest of your life. Apple's MobileMe service is designed to ease some of that chaos and complexity by automatically syncing your most important data — your e-mail, contacts, calendars, and bookmarks. Although the syncing itself may be automatic, setting up is not, unfortunately. This chapter shows you what to do.

Understanding MobileMe

These days, the primary source of online chaos and confusion is the ongoing proliferation of services and sites that demand your time and attention. What started with Web-based e-mail has grown to a Web site, a blog, a photo-sharing site, online bookmarks, and perhaps a few social networking sites, just to consume those last few precious moments of leisure time. You might be sitting in a chair, but you're getting run ragged anyway!

A great way to simplify your online life is to get a MobileMe account. For a Basic Membership fee ($99 per year currently), or a Family Pack membership, which consists of one main account plus four subaccounts ($149 per year currently), you get a one-stop Web shop that includes e-mail, an address book, a calendar, a Web Gallery for sharing photos, and a generous 20GB of online file storage (40GB with the Family Pack). The price is, admittedly, a bit steep, but it really is convenient to have so much of your online life in one place.

Note If you don't want to commit any bucks before taking the MobileMe plunge, you can sign up for a 60-day trial that's free and offers most of the features of a regular account. Go to www.apple.com/mobileme/ and click Free Trial.

The Web applications that make up MobileMe — Mail, Contacts, Calendar, Gallery, and iDisk — are certainly useful and are surprisingly functional for online applications. That's the "Me" side of MobileMe (because the Web applications are housed on Apple's me.com site), but that's not the big news with MobileMe. The real headline generator is the "Mobile" side of MobileMe. What's *mobile* is simply your data, particularly your e-mail accounts, contacts, calendars, and bookmarks. That data is stored on a bunch of me.com networked servers, which collectively Apple calls the *cloud*. When you log in to your MobileMe account at me.com, you use the Web applications to interact with that data.

That's pretty mundane stuff, right? What's revolutionary here is that you can let the cloud know about all the other devices in your life: your Mac, your home computer, your work PC, your notebook, and, of course, your iPhone. If you log in to your MobileMe account and, say, add a new appointment, the cloud takes that appointment and immediately sends the data to all your devices. Fire up your Mac, open iCal, and the appointment's there; switch to your Windows PC, click Outlook's Calendar folder, and the appointment's there; tap Calendar on your iPhone's Home screen and, yup, the appointment's there, too.

This works if you change data on any of your devices. Move an e-mail message to another folder on your Mac, and the same message is moved to the same folder on the other devices and on your MobileMe account; modify a contact on your Windows PC, and the changes also propagate everywhere else. In each case, the new or changed data is sent to the cloud, which then sends the data to each device, usually in a matter of seconds. This is called *pushing* the data, and the new MobileMe applications are described as *push e-mail*, *push contacts*, and *push calendars*.

Note

If you've used e-mail, contacts, and calendars in a company that runs Microsoft Exchange Server, then you're no doubt used to push technology because Exchange has done that for a while through its ActiveSync feature (a feature that your iPhone supports, by the way). MobileMe push is a step up, however, because you don't need a behemoth corporate server to make it happen. Apple calls MobileMe "Exchange for the rest of us."

With MobileMe, you never have to worry about entering the same information into all of your devices. With MobileMe, you won't miss an important meeting because you forgot to enter it into the calendar on your work computer. With MobileMe, you can never forget data when you're traveling because you have up-to-moment data with you at all times. MobileMe practically organizes your life for you; all you have to do is show up.

Understanding MobileMe Device Support

MobileMe promises to simplify your online life, but the first step to that simpler existence is to configure MobileMe on all the devices that you want to keep in sync. The next few sections show you how to configure MobileMe on various devices, but it's important to understand exactly which devices can do the MobileMe thing. Here's a summary:

- **iPhone.** MobileMe works with any iPhone that's running version 2.0 or later of the iPhone OS.

- **Mac.** You must be running OS X 10.4.11 or later. To access the MobileMe Web applications, you need either Safari 3 or later, or Firefox 2 or later.

- **Windows XP.** You must be running Windows XP Service Pack 2 or later. To access the MobileMe Web applications, you need Internet Explorer 7 or later, Safari 3 or later, or Firefox 2 or later. For push e-mail you need either Outlook Express or Outlook 2003 or later; for push contacts, you need either Windows Address Book or Outlook 2003 or later; for push calendar, you need Outlook 2003 or later.

- **Windows Vista.** Any Vista version works with MobileMe. To access the MobileMe Web applications, you need Internet Explorer 7 or later, Safari 3 or later, or Firefox 2 or later. For push e-mail you need either Windows Mail or Outlook 2003 or later; for push contacts, you need either Windows Contacts or Outlook 2003 or later; for push calendar, you need Outlook 2003 or later.

● **Windows 7.** Any Windows 7 version works with MobileMe. To access the MobileMe Web applications, you need Internet Explorer 8 or later, Safari 3 or later, or Firefox 2 or later. For push e-mail you need either Windows Live Mail or Outlook 2003 or later; for push contacts, you need either Windows Live Contacts or Outlook 2003 or later; for push calendar, you need Outlook 2003 or later.

Configuring MobileMe on Your iPhone

MobileMe is designed particularly with the iPhone in mind, because it's when you're on the town or on the road when you need data pushed to you. To ensure your iPhone works seamlessly with your MobileMe data, you need to add your MobileMe account and configure the iPhone's MobileMe sync settings.

Setting up your MobileMe account on your iPhone

Start by setting up your MobileMe account on your iPhone:

1. **On the Home screen, tap Settings.** Your iPhone opens the Settings screen.

2. **Tap Mail, Contacts, Calendars.** The Mail, Contacts, Calendars screen appears.

3. **Tap Add Account.** The Add Account screen appears.

4. **Tap the MobileMe logo.** Your iPhone displays the MobileMe screen, as shown in Figure 12.1.

5. **Tap the Name text box and enter your name.**

6. **Tap the Address text box and enter your MobileMe e-mail address.**

7. **Tap the Password text box and enter your MobileMe password.** You can also tap the Description text box and enter a short description of the account.

12.1 Use the MobileMe screen to configure your MobileMe account on your iPhone.

8. **Tap Next.** Your iPhone verifies the account info and displays the MobileMe screen, as shown in Figure 12.2.

9. **If you want to use push e-mail, leave the Mail switch set to On.**

10. **If you want to use push contacts, tap the Contacts switch to On.**

11. **If you want to use push calendars, tap the Calendars switch to On.**

12. **If you want to use push bookmarks, tap the Bookmarks switch to On.**

13. **If you want to use push notes, tap the Notes switch to On.**

14. **Tap Save.** Your iPhone returns you to the Mail settings screen with your MobileMe account added to the Accounts list.

12.2 Use this MobileMe screen to activate push e-mail, contacts, calendars, bookmarks, and notes.

Setting up MobileMe synchronization on your iPhone

The "mobile" part of MobileMe means that no matter where you are, your e-mail messages, contacts, and calendars get pushed to your iPhone and remain fully synced with all your other devices. Your iPhone comes with this push feature turned on, but if you want to double-check this, or if you want to turn off push in order to concentrate on something else, you can configure the setting by following these steps:

1. **In the Home Screen, tap Settings.** The Settings screen appears.

2. **Tap Mail, Contacts, Calendars.** The Mail, Contacts, Calendars screen appears.

3. **Tap Fetch New Data.** Your iPhone displays the Fetch New Data screen, as shown in Figure 12.3.

4. **If you want MobileMe data sent to you automatically, tap the Push switch to the On position.** Otherwise, tap Push to the Off position.

5. **If you turned push off, tap the frequency with which your iPhone should fetch new data: Every 15 Minutes, Every 30 Minutes, Hourly, or Manually.**

Configuring MobileMe on Your Mac

If you want to keep your Mac in sync with MobileMe's push services, you need to add your MobileMe account to the Mail application and configure your Mac's MobileMe synchronization feature.

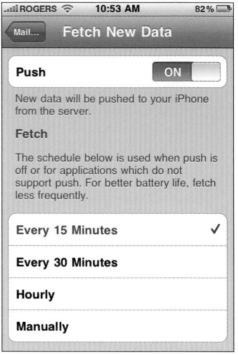

12.3 You use the Fetch New Data screen to configure MobileMe synchronization on your iPhone.

Setting up your MobileMe account on your Mac

Here are the steps to follow to get your MobileMe account into the Mail application:

1. **In the Dock, click the Mail icon.** The Mail application appears.

2. **Choose Mail ⇨ Preferences to open the Mail preferences.**

3. **Click the Accounts tab.**

4. **Click +.** Mail displays the Add Account dialog.

5. **Type your name in the Full Name text box.**

6. **Type your MobileMe e-mail address in the Email Address text box.**

7. **Type your MobileMe password in the Password text box.**

8. **Click Create.** Mail verifies the account info and then returns you to the Accounts tab with the MobileMe account added to Accounts list.

Setting up MobileMe synchronization on your Mac

Macs were made to sync with .Mac, so syncing with MobileMe should be a no-brainer. To ensure that's the case, you need to configure your Mac to make sure MobileMe sync is activated and that your e-mail accounts, contacts, and calendars are part of the sync process. Follow these steps to set your preferences:

1. **Click the System Preferences icon in the Dock.** Your Mac opens the System Preferences window.

2. **In the Internet & Wireless section, click the MobileMe icon.** The MobileMe preferences appear.

3. **Click the Sync tab.**

4. **Select the Synchronize with MobileMe check box.** Your Mac enables the check boxes beside the various items you can sync, as shown in Figure 12.4.

12.4 Select the Synchronize with MobileMe check box and then select the items you want to sync.

5. **In the Synchronize with MobileMe list, choose Automatically.**

6. **Select the check box beside each data item you want to sync with your MobileMe account, particularly the following push-related items:**

- **Bookmarks**
- **Calendars**
- **Contacts**
- **Mail Accounts**
- **Notes**

7. **Click the Close button.** Your Mac is now ready for MobileMe syncing.

Configuring MobileMe on Your Windows PC

MobileMe is happy to push data to your Windows PC. However, unlike with a Mac, your Windows machine wouldn't know MobileMe if it tripped over it. To get Windows hip to the MobileMe thing, you need to do two things:

- **Download and install the latest version of iTunes (at least 9.2).**
- **Download and install the MobileMe Control Panel for Windows, which you can find here:** http://support.apple.com/downloads/MobileMe_Control_Panel_for_Windows.

With that done, you now configure MobileMe to work with your Windows PC by following these steps:

1. **On the Windows PC that you want to configure to work with MobileMe, choose Start ⇨ Control Panel to open the Control Panel window.**
2. **Double-click the MobileMe icon.** If you don't see this icon, first open the Network and Internet category. The MobileMe Preferences window appears.
3. **Use the Member Name text box to type your MobileMe member name.**
4. **Use the Password text box to type your MobileMe password.**
5. **Click Sign In.** Windows signs in to your account.
6. **Click the Sync tab.**
7. **Select the Sync with MobileMe check box and then choose Automatically in the Sync with MobileMe list, as shown in Figure 12.5.**
8. **Select the Contacts check box, and then use the Contacts list to select the address book you want to sync.**

9. **Select the Calendars check box, and then use the Calendars list to select the calendar you want to sync.**

10. **Select the Bookmarks check box, and then use the Bookmarks list to select the Web browser you want to sync.**

11. **If you want to run a sync immediately, click Sync Now.**

12. **If you see the First Sync Alert dialog box, choose Merge Data, and then click Allow.**

13. **Click OK.**

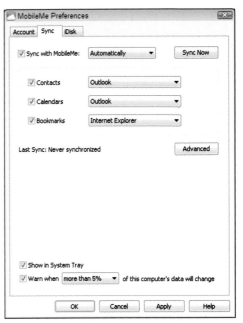

12.5 Use the MobileMe Preferences dialog box to set up your Windows PC to work with MobileMe.

Using Your iPhone to Work with MobileMe Photos and Videos

Push e-mail, push contacts, and push calendars are the stars of the MobileMe show, and rightly so. However, the MobileMe interface at me.com also includes another Web application that shouldn't be left out of the limelight: the Gallery. You use this application to create online photo albums that you can share with other people, and even allow those folks to download your photos and upload their own.

You'll generally work with the Gallery either within the MobileMe interface on me.com, or by using compatible applications on your computer, such as iPhoto on your Mac. However, your iPhone can also work with the Gallery, as you see in the next few sections.

Using your iPhone to send photos to the MobileMe gallery

Your MobileMe account includes a Gallery application that you can use to create and share photo albums. You can upload photos to an album directly from the me.com site, or you can use iPhoto on your Mac to handle the upload chores.

However, what if you're cruising around town and use your iPhone to snap a great photo of something? Do you really want to wait until you get back to your computer, sync the iPhone, and then upload the photo? Of course not! Fortunately, you don't have to because you can send photos directly to your MobileMe Gallery right from your iPhone.

Configuring an album to allow e-mail uploads

Before you can send those photos to your MobileMe Gallery, you have to configure the MobileMe album to allow e-mail photo uploads. Follow these steps:

1. **Use a Web browser to navigate to me.com and log in to your MobileMe account.**

2. **Click the Switch Apps icon (the cloud), and then click the Gallery icon to access the MobileMe Gallery.**

3. **Display the Album Settings dialog:**
   - If you're creating a new photo album, click +.
   - If you want to use an existing album, click the album, and then click Adjust Settings.

4. **Select the Adding of photos via email or iPhone check box, as shown in Figure 12.6.**

5. **If you want Gallery visitors to see the e-mail address used for sending photos to this album, select the Show: Email address for uploading photos check box.**

6. **If you're creating a new album, type a name and configure the other settings as needed.**

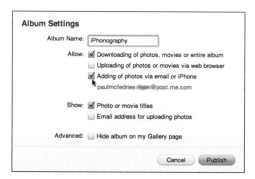

12.6 In the Album Settings dialog, select the Adding of photos via email or iPhone check box.

7. **Click Publish.** If you're creating a new album, click Create, instead.

Sending a photo to your own MobileMe Gallery

Now you're ready to send photos from your iPhone directly to your MobileMe Gallery. Here's how it works:

1. **On the Home screen, tap Photos to open the Photos app.**

2. **Tap the photo album that contains the photo you want to upload.**

3. **Tap the photo.**

4. **Tap the Action icon in the lower-left corner.** Your iPhone displays a list of actions.

Caution If you configure your album so that anyone can see it, be careful about showing the e-mail address, otherwise your gallery could be invaded by irrelevant or even improper photos.

Note If you selected the Email address for uploading photos check box, album visitors can see the upload address by clicking the Send to Album icon in your Web Gallery page.

5. **Tap Send to MobileMe.** Your iPhone displays the Publish Photo screen, as shown in Figure 12.7.

6. **Tap a title for the photo as well as an optional description.**

7. **Tap the album you want to use for the photo.**

8. **Tap Publish.** Your iPhone blasts the photo to your MobileMe Gallery and then displays a list of options.

9. **Tap one of the following options:**

   - **View on MobileMe.** Tap this option to open the MobileMe Gallery and view the photo on your iPhone.

   - **Tell a Friend.** Tap this option to create a new e-mail message that includes a link to the photo that you just published.

   - **Close.** Tap this option to return to your photo album.

12.7 Use the Publish Photo screen to ship a photo to your MobileMe Gallery.

Sending a photo to someone else's MobileMe Gallery

If you want to send a photo to another person's MobileMe Gallery, first check to make sure that e-mail uploads are allowed. Open the other person's Web gallery in any desktop browser (this won't work in your iPhone's Safari browser), and then click Send to Album. If you see the Send to Album dialog, note the e-mail address, and then click OK. (If nothing happens when you click Send to Album, it means the person doesn't want to share the address with the likes of you.)

Assuming you have the album upload address in your mitts, you can send a photo from your iPhone to that person's MobileMe Gallery by following these steps:

1. **On the Home screen, tap Photos to open the Photos app.**

2. **Tap the photo album that contains the photo you want to upload.**

3. **Tap the photo.**

4. **Tap the Action icon in the lower-left corner.** Your iPhone displays a list of actions.

5. **Tap Email Photo.** Your iPhone displays the New Message screen.

6. **Tap the To field, and then enter the other person's MobileMe Gallery upload e-mail address.**

7. **Tap the Subject field, and then edit the subject text.** This is the title that appears under the photo in the MobileMe Gallery.

8. **Tap Send.** Your iPhone fires off the photo to the other person's Gallery.

Sending a video to your MobileMe Gallery

If you've used your iPhone to record video footage, you can send that video to your MobileMe Gallery. Here's how:

1. **On the Home screen, tap the Photos button to launch the Photos app.**

2. **Click the Camera Roll album.** The Camera Roll screen appears.

3. **Tap the video you want to send.** If your iPhone 3GS starts playing the video, tap Pause.

4. **Tap Share.** The Share options appear.

5. **Tap Send to MobileMe.** Your iPhone compresses the video and then displays the Publish Video screen.

6. **Tap a title for the video as well as an optional description.**

7. **Tap the album you want to use for the video.**

8. **Tap Publish.** Your iPhone sends the video to your MobileMe Gallery (this may take several minutes, depending on the size of the video) and then displays a list of options.

9. **Tap one of the following options:**

   - **View on MobileMe.** Tap this option to open the MobileMe Gallery, where you can then click the video to view it on your iPhone.

   - **Tell a Friend.** Tap this option to create a new e-mail message that includes a link to the video that you just published.

   - **Close.** Tap this option to return to your Camera Roll.

Viewing your MobileMe Gallery in your iPhone

Once you have an album or two lurking in your MobileMe Gallery, others can view your albums by using your special Gallery Web address, which takes the following form:

http://gallery.me.com/*username*

Here, *username* is your MobileMe username. For a specific album, the address looks like this:

http://gallery.me.com/*username*/#*nnnnnn*

Here, *nnnnnn* is a number that MobileMe assigns to you.

Naturally, because your Gallery is really just a fancy Web site, you can access it using your iPhone's Safari browser, which also provides you with tools for navigating an album.

Here are the steps to follow to use your iPhone to access and navigate a photo album in your MobileMe Gallery:

1. **On the Home screen, tap Safari.** Your iPhone opens the Safari screen.

2. **Tap the address bar to open it for editing.**

3. **Enter your MobileMe Gallery address, and then tap Go.** The My Gallery page appears.

4. **Tap the album you want to view.** Safari displays thumbnail images for each photo.

5. **Tap the first photos you want to view.** Safari displays the photos as well as the controls for navigating the album, as shown in Figure 12.8. If you don't see the controls, tap the photo.

12.8 Safari showing a photo from a MobileMe Gallery album.

6. **Tap the Next and Previous buttons to navigate the photos.** If you prefer a slide show, tap the Play button instead.

How Do I Fix My iPhone?

The good news about iPhone problems — whether they're problems with iPhone software or with the iPhone itself — is that they're relatively rare. On the hardware side, although the iPhone is a sophisticated device that's really a small computer (not just a fancy phone), it's far less complex than a full-blown computer, and so far less likely to go south on you. On the software side (and to a lesser extent on the accessories side), application developers (and accessory manufacturers) only have to build their products to work with a single device made by a single company. This really simplifies things, and the result is fewer problems. Not, however, *no* problems. Even the iPhone sometimes behaves strangely or not at all. This chapter gives you some general troubleshooting techniques for iPhone woes and also tackles a few specific problems.

General Techniques for Troubleshooting Your iPhone

If your iPhone is behaving oddly or erratically, it's possible that a specific component inside the phone is the cause, and in that case you don't have much choice but to ship your iPhone back to Apple for repairs. Fortunately, however, most glitches are temporary and can often be fixed by using one or more of the following techniques:

- **Restart your iPhone.** By far the most common solution to an iPhone problem is to shut down and then restart the phone. By rebooting the iPhone, you reload the entire system, which is often enough to solve many problems. You restart your iPhone by pressing and holding the Sleep/Wake button for a few seconds, until you see the Slide to Power Off screen (at which point you can release the button). Drag the Slide to Power Off slider to the right to start the shutdown. When the screen goes completely black, your iPhone is off. To restart, press and hold the Sleep/Wake button until you see the Apple logo, and then release the button.

- **Reboot your iPhone's hardware.** When you restart your iPhone by pressing and holding Sleep/Wake for a while, what you're really doing is rebooting the system software. If that still doesn't solve the problem, you might need to reboot the iPhone's hardware, as well. To do that, press and hold down the Sleep/Wake button and the Home button. Keep them pressed until you see the Apple logo (it takes about eight seconds or so), which indicates a successful restart.

Genius

The hardware reboot is also the way to go if your iPhone is *really* stuck and holding down just the Sleep/Wake button doesn't do anything.

- **Recharge your iPhone.** It's possible that your iPhone just has a battery that's completely discharged. Connect your iPhone to your computer or to the dock. If it powers up and you see the battery logo (this might take a few seconds), then it's charging just fine and will be back on its feet in a while.

- **Shut down a stuck app.** If your iPhone is frozen because an app has gone haywire, you can usually get it back in the saddle by forcing the app to quit. Press and hold the Home button for about six seconds. Your iPhone shuts down the app and returns you to the Home screen.

- **Check for iPhone software updates.** If Apple knows about the problem you're having, it will fix it and then make the patch available in a software update. I tell you how to update your iPhone a bit later in this chapter.

● **Check for app updates.** It's possible that a bug in an app is causing your woes. On the Home screen, tap App Store, and then tap Updates to see if any updates are available. If so, tap each app, and tap the Free button (or, in the unlikely event that the update costs money, tap the Buy button) to make it so.

● **Erase and restore your content and settings.** This may seem like drastic advice, but it's possible to use iTunes to perform a complete backup of everything on your iPhone. You can then reset the iPhone to its original, pristine state, and then restore the backup. I showed you how to back up your iPhone in Chapter 1, and I explain the rather lengthy restore process later in this chapter.

● **Reset your settings.** Sometimes your iPhone goes down for the count because its settings have become corrupted. In that case, you can restore the iPhone by restoring its original settings. If iTunes doesn't recognize your iPhone, then the restore option is out. However, you can still reset the settings on the iPhone itself. Tap Settings in the Home screen, tap General, tap Reset, and then tap Reset All Settings. When your iPhone asks you to confirm, tap Reset All Settings.

Genius

If resetting the settings doesn't get the job done, it could be some recalcitrant bit of content that's causing the problem. In that case, tap Settings in the Home screen, tap General, tap Reset, and then tap Erase All Content and Settings. When your iPhone asks you to confirm, tap Erase iPhone.

Troubleshooting connected devices

There are only a few ways that you can connect devices to your iPhone: using the headset jack, using the Dock connector, and using Bluetooth. So although the number of devices you can connect is relatively limited, that doesn't mean you might never have problems with those devices.

If you're having trouble with a device attached to your iPhone, the good news is that a fair chunk of those problems have a relatively limited set of causes, so you may be able to get the device back on its feet by attempting a few tried-and-true remedies that work quite often for many devices. If it's not immediately obvious what the problem is, then your hardware troubleshooting routine should always start with these very basic techniques:

● **Check connections, power switches, and so on.** Some of the most common (and some of the most embarrassing) causes of hardware problems are the simple physical things: making sure that a device is turned on and checking that cable connections are secure. For example, if you can't access the Internet through your iPhone's Wi-Fi connection, make sure your network's router and wireless access point are turned on, and make sure that the cable between your router and the ISP's modem is properly connected.

- **Replace the batteries.** Wireless devices such as headsets really chew through batteries, so if such a device is working intermittently or not at all, always try replacing the batteries to see if that solves the problem.

- **Turn the device off and then on again.** You *power cycle* a device by turning it off, waiting a few seconds for its innards to stop spinning, and then turning it back on again. You'd be amazed how often this simple procedure can get a device back up and running. For a device that doesn't have an on/off switch, try either unplugging the device from the power outlet, or try removing and replacing the batteries.

- **Reset the device's default settings.** If you can configure a device, then perhaps some new setting is causing the problem. If you recently made a change, try returning the setting back to its original value. If that doesn't do the trick, most configurable devices have some kind of Restore Default Settings option that enables you to quickly return the device to its factory settings.

- **Upgrade the device's firmware.** Some devices come with *firmware*, a small program that runs inside the device and controls its internal functions. For example, all routers have firmware. Check with the manufacturer to see if a new version exists. If it does, download the new version and then see the device's manual to learn how to upgrade the firmware.

Updating the iPhone software

The iPhone's software should update itself from time to time when you connect it to your computer, provided the computer has an Internet connection. This is another good reason to sync your iPhone regularly. The problem is, you might hear about an important update that adds a feature you're really looking forward to or perhaps fixes a gaping security hole. What do you do if iTunes isn't scheduled to check for an update for a few days?

In that case, you take matters into your own hands and check for updates yourself:

1. **Connect your iPhone to your computer.** iTunes opens and connects to your iPhone.

2. **Click your iPhone in the Devices list.**

3. **Click the Summary tab.**

4. **Click Check for Update.** iTunes connects to the Apple servers to see if any iPhone updates are available. If an update exists, you see the iPhone Software Update dialog, which offers a description of the update.

5. **Click Next.** iTunes displays the Software License Agreement.

6. **Click Agree.** iTunes downloads the software update and installs it.

Restoring the iPhone's data and settings

Sometimes your iPhone goes down for the count because its settings have become corrupted. In that case, you can restore the iPhone by restoring its original settings. The best way to go about this is to use the Restore feature in iTunes, because that enables you to make a backup of your settings. However, it does mean that your iPhone must be able to connect to your computer and be visible in iTunes.

If that's not the case, see the instructions for resetting in Chapter 1. Otherwise, follow these steps restore your iPhone:

1. **Connect your iPhone to your computer.**

2. **In iTunes, click your iPhone in the Devices list.**

3. **Click Sync.** This ensures that iTunes has copies of all the data from your iPhone.

4. **Click the Summary tab.**

5. **Click Restore.** iTunes asks if you want to back up your settings.

 Caution If you have confidential or sensitive data on your iPhone, that data becomes part of the backup files and could be viewed by some snoop. To prevent this, select the Summary tab's Encrypt iPhone backup check box, and then use the Set password dialog to specify your decryption password.

6. **Click Back Up.** iTunes asks you to confirm you want to restore.

7. **Click Restore.**

8. **If the iPhone Software Update dialog appears, click Next, and then click Agree.** iTunes downloads the software, backs up your iPhone, and then restores the original software and settings. When your iPhone restarts, iTunes connects to it and displays the Set Up Your iPhone screen, as shown in Figure 13.1.

9. **Select the Restore from the backup of option.**

10. **If you happen to have more than one iPhone backed up, use the list to choose yours.**

11. **Click Continue.** iTunes restores your backed-up data, restarts your iPhone, and then syncs the iPhone.

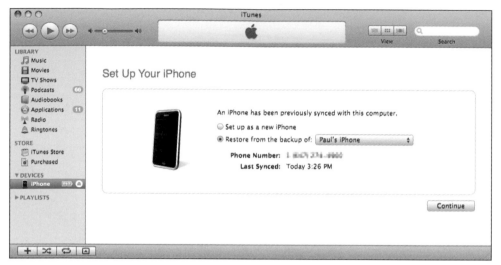

13.1 When your factory-fresh iPhone restarts, use iTunes to restore your settings and data.

12. **Go through the tabs and check the sync settings to make sure they're set up the way you want.**

13. **If you made any changes to the settings, click Sync.** This ensures that your iPhone has all of its data restored.

Putting your iPhone in Device Firmware Upgrade mode

In some rare cases, your iPhone goes utterly haywire, where not only does iTunes not recognize the device, but even completely resetting the iPhone doesn't solve the problem. (This sort of scenario occurs most often if you've tried something naughty, such as jailbreaking your iPhone.) If this happens, you can still recover everything, but you have to do it using a special hardware mode called Device Firmware Upgrade (DFU) mode. This mode essentially bypasses the current OS installed on the phone (which is good because in this scenario your current OS is toast), and tells iTunes to install a factory-fresh version of the OS. You can then restore your stuff as described in the previous section.

Follow these steps to put your iPhone into DFU mode:

1. **Turn off your iPhone.**

2. **Connect your iPhone to your Mac or Windows PC.**

3. **Launch iTunes.**

4. **Press and hold down the Sleep/Wake button and the Home button for exactly ten seconds.**

5. **After ten seconds, release the Sleep/Wake button, but continue to hold down the Home button for another ten seconds.**

6. **After ten seconds, release the Home button.** iTunes now recognizes your iPhone and displays the dialog shown in Figure 13.2.

7. **Click OK.** iTunes asks you to confirm, as shown in Figure 13.3.

8. **Click Restore and Update.** iTunes restores your iPhone's factory state.

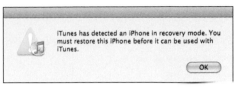

13.2 When you bot your iPhone in DFU mode, iTunes recognizes the phone and displays this dialog to remind you to restore the phone.

13.3 iTunes asks you to confirm that you want to revert to your iPhone's factory settings.

Genius

If you need to exit DFU mode before restoring your iPhone, hold down the Sleep/Wake and Home buttons for ten seconds. If that doesn't work for some reason, or if you find your iPhone is stuck in DFU mode, then you need to download and install a program called QuickPwn from blog.iphone-dev.org. Disconnect your iPhone, run QuickPwn, and wait until it prompts you to connect. Connect your phone and then follow the instructions that QuickPwn provides.

Taking Care of the iPhone Battery

Your iPhone comes with a large lithium-ion battery, and Apple claims the new iPhone 4 gives you up to 300 hours of standby time; 7 hours of talk time (on a 3G network; 14 hours on an EDGE network); 6 hours of Internet use (on a 3G connection; 10 hours using Wi-Fi); 40 hours of audio playback; and 10 hours of video playback. Those are all impressive times, although count on getting less in the real world.

The biggest downside to the iPhone battery is that it's not, in Apple parlance, a *user-installable* feature. If your battery dies, you have no choice but to return it to Apple to get it replaced. Which is all the more reason to take care of your battery and try to maximize battery life.

Tracking battery use

Your iPhone doesn't give a ton of battery data, but you can monitor both the total usage time (this includes all activities: calling, surfing, playing media, and so on) and standby time (time when your iPhone was in Sleep mode). Here's how:

1. **On the Home screen, tap Settings.** The Settings screen appears.

2. **Tap General.** Your iPhone displays the General options screen.

3. **Tap Usage.** Your iPhone displays the Usage screen.

4. **Tap the Battery Percentage On/Off switch to the On position.** Your iPhone shows you the percentage of battery life left in the status bar beside the battery icon, as shown in Figure 13.4.

13.4 In the iPhone Usage screen, turn on the Battery Percentage option to monitor battery life in the iPhone status bar.

Note If you don't want to clutter the status bar with the battery percentage, you can instead examine the Usage value and the Standby value that appear in the Usage screen. As your battery runs down, check the Usage screen periodically to get a sense of your iPhone's battery use.

Tips for extending your battery life

Reducing battery consumption as much as possible on the iPhone not only extends the time between charges, but it also extends the overall life of your battery. Here are a few suggestions:

- **Dim the screen.** The touch screen drains a lot of battery power, so dimming it reduces that power. On the Home screen, tap Settings, tap Brightness, and then drag the slider to the left to dim the screen.

Note
Paradoxically, the *less* you use your iPhone, the *more* often you should cycle its battery. If you often go several days or even a week or two without using your iPhone (I can't imagine!), then you should cycle its battery at least once a month.

- **Cycle the battery.** All lithium-based batteries slowly lose their charging capacity over time. If you can run your iPhone on batteries for 4 hours today, later on you'll only be able to run it for 3 hours on a full charge. You can't stop this process, but you can delay it significantly by periodically *cycling* the iPhone battery. Cycling — also called reconditioning or recalibrating — a battery means letting it completely discharge and then fully recharging it again. To maintain optimal performance, you should cycle your iPhone's battery every one or two months.

- **Slow the auto-check on your e-mail.** Having your e-mail poll the server for new messages eats up your battery. Don't set it to check every 15 minutes if possible. Ideally, set it to Manual check if you can. See Chapter 5 for information on how to do this.

- **Turn off push.** If you have a MobileMe account, consider turning off the push feature to save battery power. Tap Settings, Mail, Contacts, Calendars, tap Fetch New Data. In the Fetch New Data screen, tap the Push setting to Off and tap Manually in the Fetch section (see Figure 13.5).

- **Minimize your tasks.** If you won't be able to charge your iPhone for a while, avoid background chores such as playing music or secondary chores such as organizing your contacts. If your only goal is to read all your e-mail, stick to that until it's done because you don't know how much time you have.

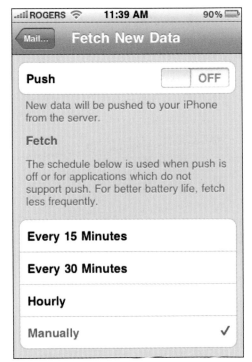

13.5 You can save battery power by turning off your iPhone's push features.

Sending Your iPhone in for Repairs

To get your iPhone repaired, you could take your phone to an Apple store or send it in. Visit www.apple.com/support and follow the prompts to find out how to send your iPhone in for repairs. Remember that the memory comes back wiped, so be sure to sync with iTunes, if you can. Also, don't forget to remove your SIM card before you send it in.

- **Put your iPhone into Sleep mode by hand, if necessary.** If you are interrupted — for example, the pizza delivery guy shows up on time — don't wait for your iPhone to put itself to sleep because those few minutes use up precious battery time. Instead, put your iPhone to sleep manually right away by pressing the Sleep/Wake button.

- **Avoid temperature extremes.** Exposing your iPhone to extremely hot or cold temperatures reduces the long-term effectiveness of the battery. Try to keep your iPhone at a reasonable temperature.

- **Turn off Wi-Fi if you don't need it.** When Wi-Fi is on, it regularly checks for available wireless networks, which drains the battery. If you don't need to connect to a wireless network, turn off Wi-Fi to conserve energy. Tap Settings, tap Wi-Fi, and then tap the Wi-Fi setting to Off.

- **Turn off GPS if you don't need it.** When GPS is on, the receiver exchanges data with the GPS system regularly, which uses up battery power. If you don't need the GPS feature for the time being, turn off the GPS antenna. Tap Settings, tap General, tap Location Services, and then tap the Location Services setting to Off.

- **Turn off Bluetooth if you don't need it.** When Bluetooth is running, it constantly checks for nearby Bluetooth devices, and this drains the battery. If you aren't using any Bluetooth devices, turn off Bluetooth to save energy. Tap Settings, tap General, tap Bluetooth, and then tap the Bluetooth setting to Off.

Genius

If you don't need all three of your iPhone's antennas for a while, a faster way to turn them off is to switch your iPhone to Airplane mode. Tap Settings, and then tap the Airplane Mode switch to the On position.

Solving Specific Problems

The generic troubleshooting and repair techniques that you've seen so far can solve all kinds of problems. However, there are always specific problems that require specific solutions. The rest of this chapter takes you through a few of the most common of these problems.

Your battery won't charge

If you find that your battery won't charge, here are some solutions:

- **If the iPhone is plugged into a computer to charge via the USB port, it may be that the computer has gone into standby.** Waking the computer should solve the problem.

- **The USB port might not be transferring enough power.** For example, the USB ports on most keyboards don't offer much in the way of power. If you have your iPhone plugged into a keyboard USB port, plug it into a USB port on the computer itself.

- **Attach the USB cable to the USB power adapter, and then plug the adapter into an AC outlet.**

- **Double-check all connections to make sure everything is plugged in properly.**

- **Try an iPod cord if you have one.**

If you can't seem to locate the problem after these steps, you may need to send your iPhone in for service.

You have trouble accessing a Wi-Fi network

Wireless networking adds a whole new set of potential snags to your troubleshooting chores because of problems such as interference and device ranges. Here's a list of a few troubleshooting items that you should check to solve any wireless connectivity problems you're having with your iPhone:

- **Make sure the Wi-Fi antenna is on.** Tap Settings, tap Wi-Fi, and then tap the Wi-Fi switch to the On position.

- **Make sure the iPhone isn't in Airplane mode.** Tap Settings and then tap the Airplane Mode switch to the Off position.

- **Check the connection.** The iPhone has a tendency to disconnect from a nearby Wi-Fi network for no apparent reason. Tap Settings. If the Wi-Fi setting shows as Not Connected, tap Wi-Fi, then tap your network in the list.

289

- **Renew the lease.** When you connect to a Wi-Fi network, the access point gives your iPhone a Dynamic Host Control Protocol (DHCP) lease that allows it to access the network. You can often solve connectivity problems by renewing that lease. Tap Settings, tap Wi-Fi, and then tap the blue More Info icon to the right of the connected Wi-Fi network. Tap the DHCP tab, and then tap the Renew Lease button, as shown in Figure 13.6.

- **Reconnect to the network.** You can often solve Wi-Fi network woes by disconnecting from the network and then reconnecting. Tap Settings, tap Wi-Fi, and then tap the blue More Info icon to the right of the connected Wi-Fi network. Tap the Forget This Network button to disconnect, and then reconnect to the same network.

13.6 Open the connected Wi-Fi network's settings, and then tap Renew Lease to get a fresh lease on your Wi-Fi life.

- **Reset your iPhone's network settings.** This removes all stored network data and resets everything to the factory state, which might solve the problem. Tap Settings, tap General, tap Reset, and then tap Reset Network Settings. When your iPhone asks you to confirm, tap Reset Network Settings.

- **Reboot and power cycle devices.** Reset your hardware by performing the following tasks, in order: restart your iPhone, reboot your iPhone's hardware, power cycle the wireless access point, power cycle the broadband modem.

- **Look for interference.** Devices such as baby monitors and cordless phones that use the 2.4 GHz radio frequency (RF) band can play havoc with wireless signals. Try either moving or turning off such devices if they're near your iPhone or wireless access point.

- **Check your range.** If you're getting no signal or a weak signal, it could be that your iPhone is too far away from the access point. You usually can't get much farther than about 115 feet away from an access point before the signal begins to degrade. Either move closer to the access point, or turn on the access point's range booster feature, if it has one. You could also install a wireless range extender.

- **Update the wireless access point firmware.** The wireless access point firmware is the internal program that the access point uses to perform its various chores. Wireless access point manufacturers frequently update their firmware to fix bugs, so you should see if an updated version of the firmware is available. See your device documentation to learn how this works.

- **Reset the router.** As a last resort, reset the router to its default factory settings (see the device documentation to learn how to do this). Note that if you do this you need to set up your network from scratch.

Caution

You should keep your iPhone and wireless access point well away from a microwave oven; microwaves can jam wireless signals.

iTunes doesn't see your iPhone

When you connect your iPhone to your computer, iTunes should start and you should see the iPhone in the Devices list. If iTunes doesn't start when you connect your iPhone, or if iTunes is already running but the iPhone doesn't appear in the Devices list, it means that iTunes doesn't recognize your iPhone. Here are some possible fixes:

- **Check the connections.** Make sure the USB connector and the Dock connector are fully seated.

- **Try a different USB port.** The port you're using might not work, so try another one. If you're using a port on a USB hub, trying using one of the computer's built-in USB ports.

- **Restart your iPhone.** Press and hold the Sleep/Wake button for a few seconds until the iPhone shuts down, and then press and hold Sleep/Wake until you see the Apple logo.

- **Restart your computer.** This should reset the computer's USB ports, which might solve the problem.

- **Check your iTunes version.** You need at least iTunes version 9.2 to work with iOS 4.0.

- **Check your operating system version.** On a Mac, your iPhone requires OS X 10.5.8 or later; on a Windows PC, your iPhone requires Windows 7, Windows Vista, or Windows XP Service Pack 2 or later.

iTunes doesn't sync your iPhone

If iTunes sees your iPhone, but you can't get it to sync, you probably have to adjust some settings. See Chapter 6 for some troubleshooting ideas related to syncing. Another possibility is that your iPhone is currently locked. That's not usually a problem for iTunes, but it sometimes gets confused by a locked iPhone. The easy remedy is to unplug the iPhone, unlock it, and then plug it in again.

You have trouble syncing music or videos

You may run into a problem syncing your music or videos to your iPhone. The most likely culprit here is that your files are in a format that the iPhone can't read. WMA, MPEG-1, MPEG-2, and other formats aren't readable to the iPhone. First, convert them to a format that the iPhone does understand using converter software. Then put them back on iTunes and try to sync again. This should solve the problem.

iPhone-supported audio formats include Audible Formats 2, 3, and 4; Apple Lossless; AAC; AIFF; MP3; and WAV. iPhone-supported video formats include H.264 and MPEG-4.

Your iPhone doesn't recognize your SIM card

If your iPhone doesn't detect your SIM card, try this:

1. **Eject the SIM card tray from the top of your phone using the tool that came with your iPhone or a paper clip or pin.** Press the tool into the little hole on the tray and it should pop out.
2. **Make sure the SIM card is free of dirt and debris.**
3. **Reseat the SIM card in the tray and slide the tray back in.**

If this doesn't solve the problem, then your problem is a larger one and you need to contact Apple or your cellular provider.

You can't get your iPhone's serial number

There are times when you might need your iPhone's serial number. For example, if you contact Apple support, they'll ask you for your iPhone's serial number.

Under normal circumstances, you follow these steps to get the serial number:

1. **Connect your iPhone to your computer.**
2. **In iTunes, clicking the iPhone in the Devices list.**
3. **Click the Summary tab.**
4. **Read the Serial Number value, as shown in Figure 13.7.**

13.7 With your iPhone connected to your computer, use the Summary tab to get your serial number.

If iTunes doesn't recognize your iPhone, you may still be able to get the serial number by following these steps:

1. **Connect your iPhone to your computer.**

2. **In iTunes, choose iTunes ⇨ Preferences.** The iTunes preferences appear.

3. **Click the Devices tab.**

4. **Hover the mouse over a backup of your iPhone.** As you can see in Figure 13.8, iTunes displays a message that includes the phone's serial number.

13.8 Hover the mouse pointer over a backup of your iPhone to get your serial number.

If you can't boot your phone, if iTunes doesn't recognize your iPhone, or you don't have a backup of your iPhone, you can still get the serial number. In that case, shut down your iPhone, remove the SIM card tray, and then read the serial number that's printed on the side of the SIM tray.

Glossary

3G A third-generation cellular network that's faster than the old EDGE network, and enables you to make calls while also accessing the Internet.

802.11 See *Wi-Fi*.

accelerometer The component inside the iPhone that senses the phone's orientation in space and adjusts the display accordingly (such as switching Safari from portrait view to landscape view).

access point A networking device that enables two or more devices to connect over a Wi-Fi network and to access a shared Internet connection.

ad hoc wireless network A wireless network that doesn't use an access point.

Airplane mode An operational mode that turns off the transceivers for the iPhone's phone, Wi-Fi, and Bluetooth features, which puts the phone in compliance with federal aviation regulations.

app An application that is designed for and that runs on an iPhone.

authentication See *SMTP authentication*.

Bluetooth A wireless networking technology that enables you to exchange data between two devices using radio frequencies when the devices are within range of each other (usually within about 33 feet/10 meters).

bookmark An Internet site saved in Safari so that you can access the site quickly in future browsing sessions.

cloud The collection of me.com networked servers that store your MobileMe data and push any new data to your iPhone, Mac, or Windows PC.

cycling Letting the iPhone battery completely discharge, and then fully recharging it again.

data roaming A cell phone feature that enables you to make calls and perform other activities such as checking for e-mail when you're outside of your provider's normal coverage area.

discoverable Describes a device that has its Bluetooth feature turned on so that other Bluetooth devices can connect to it.

double-tap To use a fingertip to quickly press and release the iPhone screen twice.

EDGE (Enhanced Data rates for GSM [Global System for Mobile communication] Evolution) A cellular network that's older and slower than 3G, although still supported by the iPhone.

event An appointment or meeting that you've scheduled in your iPhone's Calendar.

flick To quickly and briefly drag a finger across the iPhone screen.

FM transmitter A device that sends the iPhone's output to an FM station, which you then play through your car stereo.

GPS (Global Positioning System) A satellite-based navigation system that uses wireless signals from a GPS receiver — such as the one in the iPhone — to accurately determine the receiver's current position.

group A collection of Address Book contacts. See also *smart group*.

headset A combination of headphones for listening and a microphone for talking.

Home screen The main screen on your iPhone, which you access by pressing the Home button.

IMAP (Internet Message Access Protocol) A type of e-mail account where incoming messages, as well as copies of messages you send, remain on the server.

Internet tethering Using your iPhone as a kind of Internet gateway device where you connect your iPhone to your notebook — either directly via a USB cable or wirelessly via Bluetooth — and your notebook can then use the iPhone's cellular Internet connection to get online.

keychain A list of saved passwords on a Mac.

magnetometer A device that measures the direction and intensity of a magnetic field.

memory effect The process where a battery loses capacity over time if you repeatedly recharge it without first fully discharging it.

MMS (Multimedia Messaging Service) A technology that enables a cell phone to accept and send a text message with an embedded media file, such as a photo, video, or map.

multitouch A touchscreen technology that can detect and interpret two or more simultaneous touches, such as two-finger taps, spreads, and pinches.

pair To connect one Bluetooth device with another by entering a passkey.

pan To slide a photo or other image up, down, left, or right.

passcode A four-digit code used to secure or lock an iPhone.

piconet An ad hoc wireless network created by two Bluetooth devices.

pinch To move two fingers closer together on the iPhone screen. See also *spread*.

playlist A collection of songs that you create using iTunes.

POP (Post Office Protocol) A type of e-mail account where incoming messages are only stored temporarily on the provider's mail server, and when you connect to the server, the messages are downloaded to iPhone and removed from the server. See also *IMAP*.

power cycle To turn a device off, wait a few seconds for its inner components to stop spinning, and then turn it back on again.

preferences The options and settings, and other data that you've configured for your Mac via System Preferences.

push To send data immediately without being prompted.

ringtone A sound that plays when an incoming call is received.

RSS feed A special file that contains the most recent information added to a Web site.

silent mode An operational state where the iPhone plays no sounds, except alerts set with the Clock application.

slide To drag a finger across the iPhone screen.

smart group A collection of Address Book contacts where each member has one or more things in common, and where Address Book adds or deletes members automatically as you add, edit, and delete contacts.

smartphone A cell phone that can also perform other tasks such as accessing the Internet and managing contacts and appointments.

SMS (Short Message Service) A wireless messaging service that enables the exchange of short text messages between mobile devices.

SMTP (Simple Mail Transport Protocol) The set of protocols that determines how e-mail messages are addressed and sent.

SMTP authentication The requirement that you must log on to a provider's SMTP server to confirm that you're the person sending the mail.

SMTP server The server that an Internet service provider uses to process outgoing e-mail messages.

spread To move two fingers apart on the iPhone 3G screen. See also *pinch*.

SSID (Service Set Identifier) The name that identifies a network to *Wi-Fi* devices.

synchronization A process that ensures that data such as contacts, e-mail accounts, and events on your computer is the same as the data on your iPhone.

tap To use a fingertip to quickly press and release the iPhone screen.

tethering See *Internet tethering*.

touchscreen A screen that responds to touches such as finger taps and finger slides.

transceiver A device that transmits and receives wireless signals.

trim To edit the start point and end point of a video recording or a voice memo.

two-fingered tap To use two fingertips to quickly press and release the iPhone screen.

vCard A file that contains a person's contact information.

.vcf The file extension used by a vCard.

wallpaper The background image you see when you unlock your iPhone.

Web Clip A Home screen icon that serves as a link to a Web page that preserves the page's scroll position and zoom level.

Wi-Fi (Wireless Fidelity) A wireless networking standard that enables wireless devices to transmit data and communicate with other devices using radio frequency signals that are beamed from one device to another.

Index

The Genius is in.

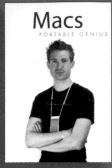

Macs
PORTABLE GENIUS

978-0-470-29052-1

Mac OS X Leopard
PORTABLE GENIUS

978-0-470-29050-7

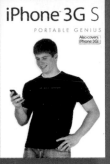

iPhone 3G S
PORTABLE GENIUS
Also covers iPhone 3G

978-0-470-52422-0

Final Cut Pro
PORTABLE GENIUS

978-0-470-38760-3

iMac
PORTABLE GENIUS

978-0-470-29061-3

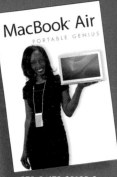

MacBook Air
PORTABLE GENIUS

978-0-470-38108-3

MacBook
PORTABLE GENIUS

978-0-470-29169-6

MacBook Pro
PORTABLE GENIUS

978-0-470-29170-2

Switching to a Mac
PORTABLE GENIUS

978-0-470-43677-6

iPod & iTunes
PORTABLE GENIUS

978-0-470-38259-2

iLife '09
PORTABLE GENIUS

978-0-470-41732-4

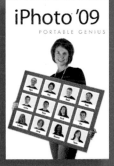

iPhoto '09
PORTABLE GENIUS

978-0-470-47569-0

The essentials for every forward-thinking Apple user are now available on the go. Designed for easy access to tools and shortcuts, the *Portable Genius* series has all the information you need to maximize your digital lifestyle. With a full-color interior and easy-to-navigate content, the *Portable Genius* series offers innovative tips and tricks as well as savvy advice that will save you time and increase your productivity.

Available wherever books are sold.

⊗ WILEY
Now you know.